To Mary, with love

ACKNOWLEDGEMENTS

Many people have helped me with this book. My thanks go to Mary Eames, Douglas Powell, Keith Runton, Brian Dale, John Hardy, Sergeant Golton at Ilkley Police Station, the staff at Ilkley Library, the staff at the Bradford District West Yorkshire Archive Service, and Evelyn Cowie of the *Ilkley Gazette*, who manhandled so many dusty volumes without a word of complaint. Finally my special thanks go to Andrew Sharpe, owner of the Grove Bookshop, for all the thought and kindness he has shown me on my many visits.

LIST OF ILLUSTRATIONS

Photographs on the jacket and in the text are from the following sources:

Ilkley Remembered, Olicana Museum and Historical Society (Ilkley, 1976);
Images of England: Ilkley, Mike Dixon (Tempus Publishing: Stroud, 1999);
Images of Ilkley, Eileen Mellor (City of Bradford Metropolitan Council Libraries Division: Bradford, 1982);
the *Ilkley Gazette*.

While every effort has been made to trace copyright holders for illustrations featured in this book, the publishers will be glad to make proper acknowledgements in future editions in the event that any regrettable omissions have occurred at the time of going to press.

On Ilkley Moor

takes its name from Llecan, the old British word for rock. Ptolomy the geographer called it Olecanon. It is Olicana in Richard of Cirencester, in the Doomsday book Illicleia. In 1220 they spelt it Illeclay touching nearly the modern sound. In the Bolton Compotus 1290 to 1325 it is Ilkley. In Kirby's Inquest AD 1285 Yelkeley; in Speed's Chronicle Heckeley, on the rustic tongue it is Heethlay.

— Robert Collyer, *Ilkley Ancient and Modern*

Call it Ilkley.

There are four directions from which to approach Ilkley. The first is the savage way, over Rombalds Moor, from where the marked stones emerge and the path rides bare (later, the holiday route the mill workers took). The second is the Roman and thence the paternal route (the way of overseers and owners), coming across over Blubberhouses on the north side of the valley and down past the studied elevation of Middleton Lodge looking out on its domain (the Mediterranean, the Catholic route, facing the sun). The third is water's way, via the Wharfe, running with the wave of the river as it gathers its great power, the mystery route of the ghostly Strid and the White Doe (the route of birth, the route of death). The fourth is money's flight, up from the mire of Bradford and Leeds, charging up the river the wrong way, like a salmon searching for its breeding ground, to lay its newly minted eggs in these bright clear waters.

ILKLEY (1)

Standing on the huge lettered rock, the clink of climbers' chains at the back of him, the breath of other untutored scramblings fading as they make their way back down the grassy, bee-infested footholds, he can see, lying in that open valley at the foot of Rombalds Moor, the town where he first learnt the art of forgetting. To the north hangs the first rise of the wild hill country, stretching up to the Scottish border, where sheep, strong enough to withstand the bitter winter chill, still graze. To the south, further down the valley, the haze of the once vast industrial complex, shaped like a heart, which pumped day and night for the body of the nation – Leeds, with its mills and great engineering works; Bradford, head of the wool industry; and beyond, in a ragged clump, the other working towns and their forgotten products, Huddersfield for worsteds, Halifax for rugs, Barnsley's linen, Morley's tweeds: Yorkshire's woollen right ventricle to Lancashire's cotton left. Caught in the middle, between the hills and the haze, stands the town itself, with its wide streets and avenues of trees, its tumbling wooden-bridged garden, and its regiment of imposing houses that snake up the hillside to touch the moor. Down there, to the right, is the open green of the Ben Rhydding Sports Club, where the journey that he must now follow and in which he recognizes he played no part, ended. Closer to the town on the other side, before the bend in the road, where the railings stopped, shines the meridian blue of the lido, which has hardly changed since he last played at its edge more than forty years ago. When he drove past earlier in the day and peeped through the fencing, though he could not be sure that the slide was still the same slide, there was no doubt that the pyramid fountain, with its concentric rings rising like a wedding cake out of the water into the air, layer on layer to the foaming, frothing top, was the same, the water cascading over the sides. It was as if he had never left, had never grown older, still six, the same water, the same laughter rising out of the splash.

The broad flat surface of the larger rock which is part of the entity known as the Cow and Calf is not a smooth rock, marked only by the weather and clambering hands. It is festooned with names, the graffiti of a hundred years and more, a diary, a census, a record of those who have come and those who have gone. Those of the previous century are more elaborately carved. Facing him as he pulled himself up was the mark of the hand of E. M. Lancaster of the XXIV Foot, 1882 (the same year that Sir Garnet Wolseley defeated Colonel Arabi Pasha at Tel-el-Kebir). There are messages from that time too, texts from scriptures chiselled out by zealous pilgrims in awe of the God who had created both them and this. Ranged in a half-moon like the message above a doorway, he finds the inscription S WILL FIND YOU OUT. Tracing the lost word he understands swiftly that the S forms the last letter in the word 'sins'. SINS WILL FIND YOU OUT, says the rock.

He walks back and forth, treading on their memory, speaking their names out loud. E. Douglas Hunsley 1895. Near to it, on the very lip of rock the precariously named J. Clarke, balancing his life out in 1814. Then

Basket DB
RS. SJ. AJ
1976

and underneath

1990
PERCY
CHARLES
FRANKS

Having come here for a purpose, to trace the fault line of his own history, he searches for the year that saw its inception. There are a number from that decade. KL, FS, 1953; a C. Moss from the USA in 1951; in 1952 J. W. RAY; in '57 a bald Fishbury. Yet he cannot find one for 1954. 1954 does not exist. He is disappointed. He had hoped for a mark.

The story of Ilkley, of modern Ilkley, began with the growth of the hydropathic establishments in the years between 1840 and 1870. Though the spirit of the Ilkley water was known beforehand, and the White Wells bathhouse perched between the town and the moor, with its steep climb, its crude plunging bath, had gained a reputation as an effective but brutal cure, it was the coming of hydropathy that advanced the town's prosperity and population beyond anything which it might have ordinarily hoped for. Hydropathy made it respectable. Hydropathy gave it dignity. Hydropathy for a brief time made it fashionable. Hydropathy, invented by a Silesian farmer, Vinzenz Priessnitz, and brought to Ilkley by a stuff merchant who had visited Priessnitz's Hydrosumanian Temple in Graefenberg and rushed back to build his own, here in Ilkley. Ben Rhydding.

Later there grew others in its shadow, but Ben Rhydding remained the most glorious. Though Hamer Stanfield founded it, it was a Scottish doctor William Macleod, editor of *The Water Cure Journal and Hygienic Magazine*, who had studied at Malvern under most famous of all the hydropathic doctors, Dr James Manby Gully (amongst whose patients were listed George Eliot, Dickens and Tennyson), who was to turn Ilkley's burgeoning hydropathic cure into an industry. Macleod started as an employee but by 1863 he had bought the premises outright, lavished money on them, extended them, turning rigour into splendour. Ben Rhydding, built in baronial style, accommodating eighty patients, with twelve private sitting rooms and bedrooms blessed with huge baths and unlimited water: below them a gymnasium, a bowling green, a library, a billiards room and above, thirty-five domestic servants freezing in the attic. In the morning a strict regime of bathing and drinking water: in the afternoon relaxation and long walks along the moor. The Ilkley Cure. Assault by water.

Other emporia opened. Wells House, Craiglands, Troutbeck, The Grove. But hydropathy's fortune fell as quickly as it had risen. Quicker. Macleod let go of the reins in 1873 in bad health, sick from the one condition he knew hydropathy could not contain: heart disease. He died two years later. Quacks eager to ride the cold current of success initiated its decline: hypothermic deaths abounded. A year after Dr Macleod's death came the murder which was to destroy its credibility completely: the poisoning of Charles Bravo in Balham, a handsome young barrister and sexually insistent drunk, whose wife, Florence, it was revealed, had once taken the famed Dr Gully as her lover. Hydropathy was finished. Ilkley was luckier. The disdain that stilled the waters might have silenced the town too, but by that time the railways had been built. Now Ilkley was connected with Leeds and Bradford and the men who owned those clanking mills. Ilkley became a rich man's town and though in the long years between money's settlement and his own childhood matters had evened out, there was still at that time a scattering of wealth, lying, like a factory's sweepings, on Ilkley's valley floor.

When he was taken on his tricycle (a red one with a boot which opened and shut) on to the main shopping area on a Saturday morning he would be always struck by how much room there seemed to be, not simply the width of the streets and pavements themselves, but the space to be found upon them; so few people to avoid, so much space to race up and down, space to bang and bash. He banged and bashed it so frequently that his mother had been told by the greengrocer that he had never seen a tricycle in such a state – though what could a greengrocer know of such things. It was so easy, head down, charging about, oblivious to what might lie ahead. He did not know then that the reason for this space, this emptiness, was not that it was a small town, or that its population was mean or had turned suddenly belly-up, but simply that while he banged and crashed below, the residential streets above were swarming with vans, green and blue and that deepening shade of shoe-polish brown which gave at once a sense of both independence and subservience, vans with their owners' names hand-painted on the sides, vans driven by men in aprons and caps, wielding baskets and order books and stubby pencils behind the ear; vans with back doors which swung open to reveal trays of bread and cake, a marble slab loaded with wet fish, a slatted wooden floor stained with the darkened blood of its hung meat and parcels of wrapped sausage. Boys there were too, boys on bikes, great cast-iron jobs with no gears for the steep roads, only a loaded wicker basket up front, a slice of metal from handlebar to saddle bearing their employer's name, a name that told the boy to mind his manners and no dawdling on the way back. Up and down they travelled all, to the houses where the matrons lived, waiting for their side-entrance knock. Those who lived in Ilkley had their goods delivered.

There must have been small houses in Ilkley, but in truth he cannot remember any. Even the ground-floor flat in which his family lived was part of large semi-detached building, one of a long row following the flow of the river. All he can recall are large houses that sat deep in dark and hidden gardens, or if not protected thus then guarded by a bleak set of steep steps after which one stood, an intruder, in a porch of almost feudal dimensions, with a sluice of a letter box out of which poured words of harsh dismissal. There had been something uncertain about these houses, every man jack of them now converted into residential homes for the old and sick or centres for such conspiratorial-sounding organizations as the World Mohair Centre. For in his childhood, though it was reputed that ordinary families lived in most of them, like the inverse of a lucky dip, an ungodly number contained the residue of a past age – crazed old men made mad with money, hiding somewhere between the front door and the neglected garden that ran riot behind their treacherously spiked walls. Somewhere up the hill lurked the man who had bought a grand piano back from Leeds and, having enough grand pianos in his mansion already, placed it under a chestnut tree, thumping out its warped notes whenever the fancy took him. Down the road, in another gloomy pile, sat the half-blind widow who every year gave a fireworks party of fabulous dimensions to which the only close witnesses (excluding the rockets) would be her terrified Pekinese and her profoundly deaf gardener. Money seemed to cascade out of these overflowing pockets, pointlessly and endlessly, like the wedding-caked fountain he so favoured at the lido. The Ilkley Cure. Drowning in money.

Looking down to the long stretch of the town he can see it all, or rather nearly all. One thing is hidden from his view, and yet he knows it is there. It is the thing he is seeking out; his eye can trace the line he knows it takes, following the clues of the bridges and the roads and the line of trees that mark its path. For it is not the Cow and Calf which dominates the town; it is that other thing – that wet tumbling thing, the thing that never ceases, which is always on the move, even when frozen, expanding, contracting, flowing ever forward – the river, the Wharfe, rising at its source some two and a half miles above Oughtershaw, falling six hundred feet to its junction with Skirfare and then through hills of rock to Burnsall, the woods of Barden, the old Priory and its graveyard and then Ilkley, Otley, Wetherby, Tadcaster and the Ouse.

In summers past there were boats to hire, and for the price of a pint you could push out from Mr Dell's stone landing stage, trail your hand, and glide under the overhanging branches along its quiet brown water, see the park, the sports club, the tennis club float beneath the New Bridge, watching the town at play. They play there still, leaving their satchels and shoes in the bridge footings halfway across to wade about in the water. Near his old garden gate lies the sandbank where families gather to bathe, with an overhanging branch from which the braver souls can drop in. Swimming, splashing, even a little dam-building. But in the winter and spring, in the flood months, when the snows have melted and the moors let slip their icy cover, the river becomes a rage, charging head down, furious, impatient, twisting and turning, thundering through the town, the colour no longer the clear brown of the soaked peat, no longer something which one might want to drink, but dirty yellow and sludgy white, like a rabid dog foaming with flecked spittle, snapping at the town's heels, making those who approach it wary, fearful lest it strike out in its all too predictable wrath. This too is the water of Ilkley. It is the same stuff, after all. But try a dip now. And what of the little dams you made? Here comes a great snagging branch and a dead sheep. Here comes the foam, here comes the thunder. Here comes Michael Airey on his tricycle, with his nanny and his brother Jonathan and sister Nicola in tow. It is Tuesday afternoon, March 30th 1954. Here comes the Ilkley Cure.

He is staying at Moorview Hotel, on the Skipton Road, built by Joseph Smith, adventurer, explorer, a very strange place indeed, not because of its decor or proprietors, far from it, they could not be kinder, but because of the fact that it is identical in shape and structure to the house four doors down in which he himself grew up. When he takes his breakfast it is in his parents' bedroom he cuts his bacon and slices his egg; when he steps into the high-ceilinged drawing room it is his parents' front room in which he is standing (under which bay window lay the entrance to his holly house), and when he knocks timidly on the back-room door to ask a wholly unnecessary question, it is the bedroom he shared with his elder brother into which he peers: the long window at the back overlooking the lawn, the little forest and the dip where the iron swing stood, and beyond that the nettles, the little gate, the towpath and the river.

It is stranger yet, for sitting in his room, preparing to go out and roam the town, he has discovered that it was in this very house where the event that he imagined had brought him here reached its dramatic climax, for up this very garden stumbled the stabbed boy, bleeding from the knife wound in his neck, banging on this back door, banging not simply from blind hope but because he knew that the doctor lived here. 'A man has stabbed me,' the boy said. 'Am I going to die?'

This was the story he had come for originally, the stabbing of a schoolboy on his way to the playing fields of Ghyll Royd School; this stabbing at the bottom of his own garden, with the police cutting down the nettles in search of the discarded knife; this stabbing by the ragged man who had sat on the bench waiting, a man from the dark town of Leeds, a man who lived an odd life with another odd man in an odd lodging, an intruder who had found Ilkley out and come to punish it for its sins – its wealth and privilege (had he read the rock's scriptures?) – who had gone out that day filled with an uncontainable rage, who found its echo bubbling alongside him on that winter path. He had written a note to his lodging companion, beginning in a curiously scriptured tone, one of dignity and composure, and ending in a throwaway fatalism that stretched far beyond his time: 'I write this with deep regret. This morning I smashed my bike up. I was trying to fix the rear light but I could not make it work and it seemed to get the devil in me. I could not help myself. I don't know what I am going to do and I don't care.'

So Peter Lawrence Hudson of Victoria Road, Hyde Park, Leeds possessed himself of a dagger-type knife known as a 'William Rogers knife' and came to Ilkley by train. 'I'd made up my mind to kill someone and I sat down on a seat for two or three minutes and two lads came past me on bicycles. I walked slowly along the river bank and heard something behind me. I saw a lone boy on a bicycle. I waited until he approached. When he saw me he stopped. I stabbed him. He dropped to the floor and I ran away, ran away to the Skipton Road, hid the knife and walked about Ilkley.' Later Hudson sent a postcard from Blackpool to the police wishing them well in their investigations, informing them that if they looked hard enough they might find the knife one mile south of the river (hidden, in fact, under a laurel bush in a small plantation in Queen's Road). 'I may give myself up but don't bank on it. Signed Potential Killer. PS. I have got a new knife.'

They caught him within a week. He showed no remorse for what he had done.

This was the tale he had gone to retrace, as a witness to times that had not changed, but when he presented himself at the offices of the *Ilkley Gazette* to find the record of this event, it was not this story which drew him close. It was the other, the one that taught him the art of forgetting, how to erase all foolish memory that might otherwise keep him awake, ticking in his head. He had been leafing through the years '52, '53, '54, unable to remember in which the stabbing took place, half expecting to see a photograph of himself in the infant percussion band, or perhaps his brother's name. Didn't he win some sort of writing competition then? Whatever, he could not find what he was looking for, though he became more and more mesmerized by the grainy pictures unfolding before him. First the wedding-cake fountain, a photograph of men cleaning it in preparation for the summer months to come, and though he did not immediately appreciate the significance of this, as he turned the pages slowly, photograph complementing photograph, ordinary photographs not of weddings or Rotary clubs but everyday pictures of the town's innocent, steadfast heart, townsfolk skating on the winter tarn, mending the wooden bridge crossing the tumble of Herbers Ghyll, he began to feel the warmth from the quiet municipal pride that such towns as Ilkley generate steal over him. But he could not find the story. The woman at the newspaper's office, eager to help, rang the retired editor. 'Look for the picture,' he advised, 'not the story.' Moments after she put down the phone, he turned another long page, and there, at the bottom, was the photograph he had not expected, not the towpath and his garden gate and a policeman standing in the tangle of the slippery bank, but another, of an empty road and a line of trees and an unexplained end to a wooden fence. Above he read:

'Considerable sympathy has been aroused in Ilkley this week by a tragedy which resulted in the drowning of Michael John, the six-year-old son of Mr and Mrs W. E. Airey, of Beckfoot House, Middleton, Ilkley.'

It was the first time he had seen the name in print even though he had carried the sound of it with him for more than forty years. Michael Airey, six years old, who lived in the white house halfway up the hill on the other side of the valley, opposite where he now stands. Michael Airey, who helped him push the nursery school summer house round on its circular rail, in imitation of the great marshalling device to be seen at York, the railway turntable. Michael Airey. His best friend. The boy had been out with his nurse, his sister and his brother, out for a walk along the Denton Road. It was Tuesday afternoon and he was riding his tricycle, given to him, like his very own, at Christmas. Jonathan was walking beside his nanny; Nicola was in her pushchair; Michael rode ahead. As the reached the spot known as Nell Bank, Johnny cried suddenly, 'Michael! Michael!' but though the nanny ran to the end of the fencing she could see nothing. The Wharfe was very close, very fast, swollen with the might of the moor. She ran for help.

He devoured the story, fingering the letters, tracing the words, speaking the name out loud. At first he was paralysed by the potency of the page, unable to move. It seemed to him that there was nothing, apart from the arbitrary date, to suggest that this event had not taken place that very week. Like the river forever passing, it seemed that Michael Airey was still here, still drowning, had never stopped drowning, still riding that last cold journey down to Ben Rhydding and the Sports Club and the stretching arm of Police Constable Smithson, the water cascading over him . . . turning, turning, turning. The Ilkley Cure.

He left with a photocopy of the story under his arm. He has been walking about the town ever since, first along the other side of the river, past the sewage works, making his way out towards the little island that lies near the spot, standing at the water's edge, looking down the slow bend where the branches hang and the water sings, thinking of all the quiet things of life this bend must have seen. Later he crosses the suspension bridge and walks back to the place itself, a place that seems hardly changed, though the river is a good deal lower than it would have been that late March afternoon. Now he is standing on the Cow and Calf. Halfway up on the opposite side stands the white of Beckfoot House, Michael Airey's home, suddenly glinting in the sun. He sees the slope of the garden and the expanse of French window directed south towards Leeds, and the little road that leads down. He sees it all so clearly from the vantage point of this rock. Here comes Michael Airey now, with his nanny, with Jonathan holding the kite, a toy thing on a simple string, and his sister in the pushchair. It is mid-afternoon. They have left the house no doubt after *Listen with Mother*, sung the nursery rhyme and heard Daphne Oxenford tell the story. There is a slight wind in the air, and they are wrapped up well. Michael pedals down the slope, the others follow. When they reach the Denton Road and the wide stretch of grass by the bank, the nanny unfurls the kite and together they watch it flutter over the raging water. The river thunders and roars only a few feet away, almost next to them. It is both terrifying and wonderful, but they are worried that the kite might snag a branch or dip too far into the water. They move on, a walk to the lido perhaps and then back to the house for tea. Michael Airey climbs back on his tricycle and pedals ahead. Suddenly his brother calls; the nanny does not know why but all of a sudden there is an empty space, nothing, no Michael, no tricycle, no cry, nothing. Michael Airey has gone, one moment gleeful and purposeful and pedalling like crazy; the next moment, gone, falling under, choking, cold, frightened, gasping, gulping, fading, dead. Now he has passed his nanny and his brother Jonathan and his sister Nicola; now he has left his tricycle, more battered now than his friend's will ever be; the boot is waterlogged and the bell no longer rings; now Michael Airey has released his grip, he is turning and twisting, floundering under the rage of the mad wet plunge, under the toll bridge, past the man now running alongside, trying to keep pace with him – he saw something floating down the river which looked like the back of a head, face downwards and absolutely limp – his nanny's calling voice fading, the water roaring. Who passes that spot now and thinks of him? Who remembers Michael Airey and what he might have been – Jonathan, Nicola, the nanny who flew the kite? What became of her? Did she marry, have children of her own? What coloured tricycles did they receive on their sixth birthday, and by what rivers did she let them ride? And when she peered round her children's bedroom door and looked at their sleeping heads, did she think of Michael Airey – so much Michael Airey one moment and then Michael Airey no more?

He has not forgotten the name, and looking out upon the scene, from Beckfoot House to the ground-floor flat on the Skipton Road, he is trying to understand why he has carried the name within himself for so long; what has driven him this close to the drowned boy? There is a part of him that believes that without Michael Airey's death he would not be himself; that Michael Airey made him, made him think of the mystery of Michael, of what he was and what he might have been, save for the simple trick of – what? A bump in the road? A flick of the eye? A look back to nanny?

Now, standing on the rock, he wants Michael Airey to be always here, for people to read his name and perhaps wonder.

He wants to carve out Michael Airey's name and hold it fast on this slab of rock, but he carries no hammer or knife and he knows that a smudge of stone would be washed away before the winter is out. He searches in his pockets for something sharp. A paper clip? A clinking sound distracts his attention. Below, a young man is teaching his girlfriend the art of seeking handholds, standing underneath her, holding her body a touch more than the immediate tuition demands. Next to them a boy is adjusting the saddle on his mountain bike. On the ground between them, beside a set of ropes and pulleys, there lies a small efficient hammer. He calls down to the couple and asks them if he might not borrow it for moment. The man looks warily at him, as if he fears he might snatch it up and hit them about the head with it, so he tells them what he wants it for. The man, looking disdainfully at his incompetent footwear, tells him that he is not sure, that he doesn't hold with that sort of thing, writing on the rock. He shrugs his shoulders and begins to search for a stone. It is better than nothing. The boy with the mountain bike calls up, 'You could try this,' and throws up a small spanner. He has never been very good at catching, and as it travels through the air he worries that it will hit his hand and bounce away down some impossible crevice. But it homes into his palm like a falcon coming to the glove. He walks over to where he can see the white of the Beckfoot House and the path and the tricycle pedalling down. He starts scraping out the letters. It is harder work than he imagined and he cannot fashion the letters as neatly as he would like. But he is still Michael Airey's best friend, the only best friend he ever had, the only best friend he will ever have. Perhaps Michael Airey is his only best friend as well, his constant companion, keeping his counsel all these years. And it comes to him, in the chipping and scraping, remembering those unhurried photographs in the local newspaper, that there is more to do here than this simple dig of rock, that looking out over Ilkley he wants to seek out other walks upon other Ilkley paths, to set his compass to Ilkley's field, to journey into its distant cries and soliloquies. Though no historian or archaeologist, there is spadework he could do here, lifting turf and rock, forgotten artefacts that he might wipe clean, a threshold he might cross. And though is is clear that his life too lies scratched somewhere upon Ilkley's surface, as far as possible he wants for the town to take the lead, for Ilkley to be the principal and Ilkley to be the chorus. So let it be Ilkley, then, and as many of its folk as the town can muster. And let it be your Ilkley as much as his. For we are made from the towns and counties of this land. Our bones lie here, on our doorstep and under our feet.

It is done. He smoothes the rock over, brushing the chipped dust free. The name is clean and fresh:

MICHAEL AIREY
ILKLEY 1954

THE MOOR (1)

Ilkley Moor is part of a larger moor that stretches from Guiseley in the east to Skipton in the west. Geologically it is of itself: further to the east, beyond Harewood, the rock found is of Permian limestone: to the west, up from Addingham, mountain limestone, but here the world is marked by millstone grit, that fierce black stone that lies scattered about the length and breadth of this lonely scope. It is cold hard stuff, this millstone grit, as its name suggests, and presses down upon the body of the moor like a string of abandoned baubles, lending a stern uncompromising quality to the moor's character, an immovable darkness to its roving light, bringing acid to its damp soil, abrupt edges to its soft heathered slopes, and chilling the waters that fall upon its purifying surface. Like Ilkley, the moor's calling card has been delivered under various guises; Rumbles, Rumles, Romelies, Rumeley, even Romell, but has settled finally upon Rombalds, the normally absent apostrophe denoting an ownership long since vacated.

In days when such figures stalked the imagination Rombald was the name of the giant who strode upon this wild tract of land. He could not live below. Below was the dragonflyed swamp, in which if he were ever so foolish as to venture he would sink up to his arms, while running down to it on the boulder clay slopes stood thick forests of oak and ash to flail at his waist, alder and bramble bush to snag at his calves and ankles. So he strode on high, from bare peak to bare peak, as a boy might spring from barnacled rock to barnacled rock or leap the banks of a silver stream, supremely confident in the space he can master and the innate skill of his nimble feet. It was Rombald's land to command, this northern wilderness, Rombald's weight which compressed the peat earth so firm, Rombald's tread which shook the piled boulders loose, made them roll and rumble and hang in precarious tumbled shapes, Rombald's hands which reached out to clutch and squeeze at the liquid clouds, as a boy might burst floating bubbles on the wind. A boy is a giant then, his jumps huge and sure, but here, one day when the giant had left those years, a boy no longer, but instead a proud young beau, eager to impress his young wife, to demonstrate his dexterity, his sureness of touch, his sense of pace and balance, to entice her perhaps into an outdoor embrace up on Cam Fell (the only place nearby that might safely contain such momentous couplings) – or if not to her, then to his giant self and the boyhood sway he imagined he held still over his old plaything. Whatever, his eyes firmly fixed upon his reflection rather than his feet, jumping across the valley, he slipped and as he slipped brought his foot hard up against the dark and belligerent rock that stood out upon its eastern edge, overlooking the treacherous dank below, kicked it flat in the middle and split the belly open, a gangling offspring falling out, Ilkley's firstborn, Caesarean breached, branded with the giant's errant footprint, stumbling in those first unexpected moments down the steep slope, coming to uncertain rest on the very lip of the moor itself. The Calf, born of the Cow. And when his wife saw his misfortune (and his folly) her hands flew to her mouth (laughing at his foolishness) and dropped what she was carrying in her apron-held skirt, namely a bundle of smaller rocks (for pummelling Rombald's dirty washing, no doubt), and these, rolling out from beneath her feet, pushed by her heels as she ran to help her sprawling, bawling man, came to rest all in a heap in what is called the Skirtful of Stones. A land, therefore, marked by giant strides.

For the bedroom which he shared with his brother his parents bought him an indoor swing. How it was to be anchored to the floor, whether the manufacturers expected his father to hammer in six-inch nails through the carpet into the wood or whether their design relied on weight, gravity and a certain timidity amongst the infant class he cannot remember, but a proper swing it was, of proper swing size, and, for a Christmas present, strangely unsettling. Nine foot in height and dressed in dull industrial red, it filled the space in the middle of the room with a frightening energy, a huge metallic skeleton with long metal-rod arms and intimidating feet of iron, a steel Rombald, born of a fiery furnace and hauled that celebrated night over the bare hills. He could imagine its silhouette towering against the sky, see the dark tiny men straining at the ropes as they hauled its steaming, hissing frame up over the moor. And now it was here, this reluctant gift, caged in a boy's room amongst milksop bedspreads and stuffed baby toys. No rocks in its arms, instead a metal seat for a boy to sit upon, to be held in a tight embrace. He had read the stories, he knew what giants did to boys, how they caught them and carried them off to their lair in the mountains, how they slept and snored all day waking for their supper of small-boy pie and a barrel full of beer. What might a mechanical one have in mind? He gripped the metal-rod arms cautiously and lifted himself on. The swing trembled, he could hear the creak of bolt and nut. Raising his arms, he stuck his legs out, and began to rock, forward and back, hearing the links clink above him, his hands gripping tighter, his outstretched feet taking command of the air. He began to rise into the upper reaches of the room, swinging in that space beneath the high ceiling which he had presumed to be uninhabitable. It was different up there. The room shrank before his very eyes. For the first time he became aware of the limits of the room's dimensions, how close his head was to the ceiling, how his back pushed almost against the wall, how cramped and crowded it seemed with his mother and his father and his brother standing below. How he wished they would move out of the way, that the room might grow bigger, that the walls might fall, that the ceiling might collapse, that he might swing higher and higher, caught in a great swoop of freedom. And as if it had heard his wish, the iron swing began to move across the carpet towards the long window, its long holed feet breaking into a shuffling gallop, like one of those tin horses he had that moved of their own accord when placed on a tilted table. It was making for the garden outside. The swing was going to crash through the glass, wade across the icy Wharfe and disappear up to the woods and the moors beyond, with him locked in his arms. He tried to jump free but he dared not. There was a part of him that did not want to, that craved to be captured by this giant, taken to his secret lair, where he would learn giant ways, run half naked under the moon, hide behind rocks watching his father and mother hurry by, scouring the moor for their lost son. The swing gathered momentum, drawing closer to the long plate glass, but in its haste caught the leg of something, his bed perhaps, and began to lose its balance, falling sideways, tipping him out of its clutches on to the safety of his knitted bedspread, while it rolled and clattered to the floor, ending up on its back, looking ridiculous, his father, his mother relieved, his brother laughing at their clumsy antics.

It stood there for four days, an outcast, forbidden to be touched, for fear, it was said, of prejudicing its return, but more likely, he thought, of re-awakening its reckless spirit. And in those housebound days, while he walked around and played under its dark shadows, he grew to feel pity for it, for what it was and how, like the rabbit in its cage outside in the yard, a swing in a room was not a fair equation.

They lie there to this day, those stones, the Skirtful ungathered, the watchful presence of the Cow lowering uneasily while below her great Calf for ever falters, torn from her mother's side, never to return. But despite the parting they have grown old together mother and daughter and from their vantage point have witnessed the many gatherings below; heard the river turn from trickle to flood, seen the woodland expand and shrink, watched family and farmstead take hold, heard sheep clattering about their feet, felt walkers and lovers and those steeped in folly and despair climb upon their backs, brand their black haunches, and stand, an immobile travelling rodeo, to be witnessed by the surrounding crowds, riding upon their tamed rock beasts.

Aye, stand on the lip of Ilkley Moor and be a giant too. It is not hard as the mist rises to lift the huge rock and hurl it into the hidden beyond. But it is not all giant's work. The rocks are marked by other forces, grooved and planed by nature's cold carpenter, the glacier, sanding down the jagged surface in its inexorable retreat. The returning water has imprinted its image too, frozen no longer, but free to move and fashion the stone to its own fluid requirements, stone to the west, stone to the south, stone in the heart of the moor itself: the one-time quarry of Hangingstone where men will come with chisel and hammer to carve the houses and halls which give the town its dark and airy gravity; further along Rocky Valley and Ilkley Crags, further still, looking out over the western reaches of the town, the jut of the Swastika Stone, while at their back, dropped perhaps as she rushed to her husband's aid, the great stone bracelet trodden into the flat earth into the circle now named the Twelve Apostles.

And these constructions, these places (and places they are, deliberate, as one might lay a path), become sources themselves, as the water that runs about them is a source. The nature of Ilkley's birth, can, like all such structures, be seen, touched, examined by foot and hand and eye: and curiously, in this travelling quarter, there are other signs that no giant, no glacier, no rush of water could make, marks bronze-aged, hammered right here, into this rock.

By the time the giant retired limped and bruised, men had started to make their way along the higher ridges, leaving the swamp to the fowl and the fish and the daily cast of his net. They sought flint, looked for a passage across the Pennines to the west. They found it in the Aire Gap, a break in the ridge near Skipton, a crossing two hundred feet lower than any other route between Scotland and the Peak District. And this formed a horizontal bar that touched that curved spine route that ran the length of Britain, the Icknield Way, that long strip of raised land stretching from Avebury to the Wash, dusted with a light soil unable to hold timber, and thus formed the wide grassy track of antiquity, extending northwards to these northern wilds by way of the Wolds of Lincolnshire. Here, giant-free, one could walk east to west or west to east as easily as one might travel north to south, south to north, marking tread along Britain's high-plained cross

and below them, the Wharfe.

THE WHARFE (1)

The source of the River Wharfe is on the slopes of the wild moorland of the Camm. This is where it begins, a wet land, high and
lonely, wrung with the sodden squeeze of it, the curve of space on
its breadth and in its birth (the spread of these broad lips as it
bubbles forth down the two haunches, wetting the shorn tufted
grass), a straggle of blasted trees sentinels of its genesis, their heads
bent to its passing, its lullaby wind-spoken and lark-harmonized, a
clear call muffled at times by rolling tides of cloud and mist, the suck
of land and the drench of rain: here it begins, this tiny thing, in this
huge and lonely cradle, in the dip of the final reaches of the moor,
the clouds taking colour from the life below, the grass ever wind-
shifting; no road, but a tract of water and beside it, marching high
across the moor, footpaths and tracks pitted like the skin of man,
rough, stretched close across the earthy skull.

> (There is a sound to it, as if it is the sea that lies beyond
> the final rise, rather than the earth, though scent and the
> bend of the denuded tree tell you different. But you can
> hear waves over the sand, hear the stir of grain and pebble
> as the water gathers its harvest

The Wharfe opens its beat to the world quietly, holding secrets in
its heart, in quiet recollection of all that has happened and all that
will happen, as if all history could be stored here, sunk deep into
the earth, stored in a vast cold cavern, to bubble up again to start the
pilgrimage once more, washed through the sponge of grass and

beaten, like bundles of clothes, over the smooth pumice of rock. It is a broad cup, a basin, a bowl, the place where the great game is born, where the bowler spins his ball, where he throws his loop, where the world spins and hits you a glance. See the ball spin and start its journey. You run after it, looking up, hoping not to drop the catch.

Follow it now!

THE MOOR (2)

Of hard stone, flint is the fifth and exposed to the air changes with age, milk blue, chalky white, ivory, yellow and brown; the sequence of patination. When flint was scarce and the east coast inaccessible, chert was used, dull black, dull brown or green in colour, with a softer edge and thus more difficult to work.

The flint was worked to a sharp edge, struck with a glancing blow, leaving a flat striking platform: sharper blows broke off flat flakes, leaving shaped on an anvil the working core, to be trimmed to particular requirements with hammerstone. It was hard bent work, dressing skin, working bone, fashioning tools to mark the rock, to realign it to their spiritual intent.

They began to clear this land, this small dark people, moving with the seasons fashioning pastures for their flock; wild grain the hoped-for harvest for their roaming world. A brief land of uncertain pasture, soft underfoot; goats for bracken, pigs to grub the roots, sheep to eat the grass. The flock, of which they were a part, moving on as the soil grew exhausted, to be reoccupied in later, convalesced years.

Now we see the signs, not of their coming and going but their dwelling, the mark of their holding driven in high up on Rombalds Moor. Here custom and ritual took hold. They took stock of this place, and indented it not by the stamp of their feet but by the clench of their hand and the beam in their eye, burrows for their dead, buried with the tools of their trade, flakes of history hidden amongst the bracken and rock, and on the rock itself, more than this, markings, which are named Cups and Rings for the indentations and circles around them. To the untutored eye they appear as the land must have been below, swampy, amoebic; they swirl like primeval soup, cloudy now in intention. Priest the father hands on to priest the son, the reading of their written message, like all professions, clear only to those who have been taught the signs. Praise to the Mother with her swirling breasts; praise to the Sun who gives life too, praise to the unseen Eye who must note it all. Though fixed upon the rock they are strangely fluid, wriggling organisms placed on a Gritstone Petri dish. In Spain these marks whirl unattached on the rock, likewise in Orkney and Ireland and the bare reaches of Scotland. But here on the moor there are chiselled ladders linking one cup to another other; breast to sun, sun to eye, eye to breast, an unfathomable bridge, connecting what to what, unless it be a celebration for the art of pollination that they have learnt, the need for links in man's life, to build himself over space, joining one age to another.

And new people walk on Rombald, the Beaker Folk, taller, fairer than their predecessors, come from warmer forest lands, looking for trade and new routes to carry it, daggers, axes, amulets and earrings. In their former glades they had built circular shrines fashioned from the trunks of trees, so here, above the treeline, with this gritstone scattered about, they kept their architecture and transferred the design to stone: it is found where the moor stretches out, before it starts the descent down to the next valley and the River Aire, before it allows the intrusion of a landscape other than itself, twelve stones laid out in a fifty-foot circle, the Twelve Apostles. Its erection marks the spot where Rombalds Way is crossed by the track from the Aire (Bingley) to the Wharfe (Ilkley). Twelve stones laid out and erected to mark the ground where tribal chiefs met, where announcements were made, celebrations and marriages conducted, where disputes might be resolved without force, in short where business and treaties could be enacted, the stone circle a witness to their peaceful intent, a sign demoting that the area was described under the protection of the Sun and the Mother and the Eye and thus neutral for all. None carried arms within its sphere and speech was privileged and free.

It is not true now, the moor is no longer alone. Across the moor, some fifteen miles away, sit the spiked puffballs of RAF Menwith Hill, the listening posts of our intrusive age, cabled to Virginia, eavesdropping on our grumblings and seditious thoughts. Unlike the Twelve Apostles they are impossible to count. He has tried to tie them down from various vantage points, but he has arrived at a different number on every occasion. They multiply, they subtract. From here he can count twelve, a number most likely influenced by the presence of the stones surrounding him. From the road into Harrogate he uncovered twenty-three, while up on the Weston Moor Road out of Askwith the number shrank back to fifteen. Their elusive quality, their ability to shift and merge, is as appropriate to their time as these solid citizens are to theirs. Here they are squat and dark, and though some have fallen they are part of the earth and the weather surrounding them. Across the way their colour is white, they look soft, as light as air. You could wake up one morning and find them gone, floated away to spring up in some other moorland outpost. They are fenced off, sign-protected, as closed as the Apostles are open. They cannot be touched, for to touch them would be to anchor them, to render them as of us. But we would not want to touch them, there is no cause for it.

So they built their ring, to listen and celebrate their time, built it here, to work the connections of man to the hard world he had inherited, planted it and their markings high, not through the necessity of remoteness, but because they were the closest to what they knew to be above them. This is where life starts, on the barren reaches of the world, to hold a bloody infant to the stars, to hear its squeal amidst the lashing of the wind. It is important to understand this distinction, to regard the moor as closest to their heaven, as opposed to its taller cousin, the mountain, where there is nothing but rock and ice. Here, on the moor, there is heather and grass and the sound of water. It is where a people might live unaided, where they might perish, surely, but where lurks the first possibility of survival, of men and women and the mastery of what they stand upon. It is the closest living man and his living earth might approach the sun, the moon, and the hidden eye, the first place to suck on heaven's milk, or burn from heaven's fire, where a man might heft the burden too, and feel the potency of the earth's parentage. Here the spark of life cracks through the gloom, where the mist unveils.

ILKLEY (2)

The Romans came to Ilkley and called it Olicana, and in their long time built three forts, first of wood, then of stone, on the natural hillock commanding the crossing of the Wharfe. In this district lived the tribe of the Brigantes, of their own, but with the tide of logic running, willing to be allied to the new power, as long as pride and a sense of opportunity did not flood the gate. The northern areas were sure and the roads give testament to that, roads from Ribchester to the great settlement at York, where the myth of the lost Ninth Legion took base, and crossing it here another link of keeper and kept, the route from Manchester to the Brigantian capital, Aldborough. The first fort founded by Agricola was dismantled by Hadrian and transported with its troops to his wall of subjugation and protection. The Brigantes saw their chance, and took it, the province turning uneasy, disturbed, not under yoke. So the Romans returned and built a stronger fort, ramparts wider and built of clay rather than turf, and stayed in Ilkley and along its roads marched to their centres of control. Thirty years later it was aflame, the garrison withdrawn along with most of the Roman army, as Roman Britain's governor, Clodius Albinus, set his sights on Rome, and wanting the Empire whole, for his keeping, took his troops to Gaul to take Rome.

Hadrian's Wall abandoned, the forts they left behind torched with flaming throats, a dark defiance rising. Ilkley burnt, as did they all. But Clodius lost, and the victor of the struggle, Septimius Severus, sent Virius Lupus to govern. Three hundred years they stayed this time, and knowing their time and the unquestioned solidity of their Empire built their forts of stone. A mixed cohort lived in Ilkley, the 2nd Cohort of the Ligones, five hundred men, one hundred and twenty cavalry, the rest infantry. The men who served, sentries, patrols, living their full twenty-five years' service under the shadow of the great rocks, guarding arms and water stores, riding out on escort duty, protecting the tax collector on his Roman round, all the while watching out for outbreaks of disaffection, their cure at belted hand. But a domestic living mostly, clerks working out on wooden tablets rosters and notes of pay, assigning duties: ditches to clean, water to collect, fuel to gather, roads to repair, carpenters, masons, medical orderlies, while outside, the local traders, farmers with sheep and cattle, pigs prodded to market, butter and cheese sacked, a black-smith for the farm, a potter for the shelf, an inn lying in the wake of business, while on a the market stall a soldier buys a bracelet for an Olicana queen. Roman soldiers could marry now, local girls with Celtic tongue learning the Latin for love and duty

(In 1844 was found a gravestone, a Cornovian girl from Shropshire, an army wife who died at thirty, with long plaited hair and, thus married to the application of state, given Roman citizenship with her husband and their children

In this manner did Rome spread.

And when Rome left, the fort dismantled, institution and reason gone, these things remained, the roads, the crossing, Rombald's great mark, and below it, Agricola's footprint placed astride the Wharfe.

THE WHARFE (2)

Like the beginning of this river, the track that runs alongside it (as a father might his young child on those first unaided pedals) seems to emerge too unasked from this high bowl of offered earth. Today there is a light rain falling, light but constant, as if it hangs in the air, a permanent feature. Water on the ground, water in the air, water touching water, water turning sky and earth into itself, running down the long and silent slopes. Now for the first time you can see river's liquid shape, the direction of its movement, gauge its sense of lonely purpose. But though this is the Wharfe's beginnings, it is not the Wharfe yet, for it has not taken its fill of moorland waters, nor rushed over the mothering rocks. Curlews call, and out of sight the distant plea of sheep, while here the simple slip of water trickles over the black squid-ink press of land.

The dark sponge quality of the land invites him. Leaning forward he dips his hand, not only to feel the freshly born water running alive over his fingers but to savour the peat itself, to tear a wet clump of it from the bed, to press it to his face, to squeeze it, and see his palms stained dark brown, the colour of an American poem. There is no reason for him to move from this spot, for in his hand he has grasped the enormity of loss, that illusion of liberation and freedom that only landscape can perform. He is reminded of something, something concerning skin and a buried longing, but he knows not what: something distant.

The river is a stripling now, young planted, and like the drain-protected saplings that have been set on the hill nearby is in need of gentle guidance and protection. It has passed the small clump of trees that came to be witnesses to its birth, and now flows past a small stone bridge, though not under it, for it is not yet river enough for such a thing. The bridge stands across from a stone barn which itself is some fifty feet down from the river's first dwelling (which looks like a school, though it would be a long way for children to walk, though good perhaps for the placing of history, the long silence of what has gone before, and how you might fit in that). It serves the Wharfe's first visible tributary, which runs down steeply to the right of the barn, over an organized paved gully into a bevelled channel under the bridge: on the other side, four stone steps before a small pool and the slow descent to the young river. The barn is covered in scaffolding, and two men in woollen hats are poised on the wet and shiny planks, hoisting buckets of cement. To their left, a few yards up the daffodil-clustered slope, stands another bridge, smaller, barely visible, a little grass-covered affair, built for sheep, and under it, tucked quietly out of the rain, sits a black dog, alert and watchful, intent upon the signs of an intruder, the rain falling in front of his quick and thoughtful face.

However, it is not the dog as such that strikes him (though like many dogs there is that peculiar quality to his expression, as if there is a part of a dog which would like to be human in order to converse), but the manner of his sitting, up on his haunches, in that verdant hollow, as if looking out from a small and well-protected cave. Ah, now he has it, Nelson, who lived above him in Farleigh, and who for a time became his trusted companion in the green holly house under the drawing-room window in which he took up residence whenever the weather and his mother permitted. It was Nelson's mineral blackness, the gleaming shine to his radiant coat, that and his willingness to follow him patiently at all times, which prompted him first to pack the boot of his tricycle with tricky lumps of coal and pile them up in the corner of his holly house and which led him, a full year later, to the magical pile of soot at the top of the drive. Like the silver container on top of the mantelpiece (where banknotes were sometimes stored), the soot pile was forbidden territory. There was an invisible six-foot exclusion zone which his mother had laid around its island perimeter. But, like the indoor swing, the more he looked at it the stronger its magnetic power became, and one day sheltering in his holly house from a sudden rainstorm, streams of water falling across the entrance, Nelson sitting with him staring out, the soot pile plainly in view, the thought came to him. He would give himself a soot bath.

Knowing the unspeakable wickedness of the intent he bided his time, waiting for many mornings and afternoons, before his mother, for reasons he cannot now recall, left him alone. Perhaps she had forgotten some groceries and had to hurry down the Skipton road to Fletcher's; perhaps she was busy in the back garden; perhaps she had been drawn to the Wharfe, was walking along the footpath, watching it carry her thoughts far away. Whatever, all he can remember is that he began in the knowledge that he had the time, walking towards the pile in sober contemplation, bucket in hand. Digging in however, with his sandpit spade, was like taking his first alcoholic drink, instantly intoxicating. Reeling back gloriously light-headed, he marched into the bathroom, turned on the taps and poured in the soot. The water thundered, swirling vapour clouds rose in the air, enveloping the room. He sneezed. He took off his clothes and stepped in, stirring the compound with invisible feet. It was of the same consistency as the powder paints he was allowed to use at his infant school, Miss Thorpe's; while some dissolved instantly, much floated on the surface in large indigestible lumps (reminiscent too of his mother's mashed potato). There, however, the similarity ended. At school, in the basement classroom (where he first taught himself the art of hanging upside down on the climbing frames attached to the walls), he was cosseted in a large apron with the table wrapped in newspapers, and Mrs Galloway walking down the rows watching out for mess. Here he was naked and alone, about to ascend into the animal kingdom. He bent down and swirled the water with his hands. Dark streaks leapt up the sides of the white porcelain, indelible tears splashed upon the wall. The water rose up past his ankles to an inch below his knees. He turned off the taps. He scooped a handful of wet soot and wiped it on his arms and stomach. He shivered with excitement. It was time for him to baptize himself.

When taken to the lido he had always been afraid of jumping off the diving board or edge, for he did not like to go completely under – a fear greatly increased by Michael Airey's death – but here there was no such hesitation. Quickly he slipped under, lying on the bottom of the bath, holding his nose for as long as he dared before bursting up again, gasping. He began to rub the mixture over his body, on his arms and legs, over his chest and his bony back and the infant bump of his genitals. He looked down upon himself and saw that he was different now, transformed, in love with the animal inside that had spoken to him. How wonderful it was, to smear his body with this outrageous paste, to defy all civilized law and become a heathen. And so easily done! Suddenly lying there was not enough. He needed to move, to feel this liberation on his limbs, to be nothing but a painted and primitive boy, running amidst all encumbrances, and so he levered himself out of the bath (no attempt to pull the plug) and began to run through the flat, rolling like a dog on his counterpane, marvelling at the footprints he made upon the carpets, the handprints on the walls, markings a savage might make or a tramp might leave, messages to another world pressed on stone, stamping the stain of his life on that seemingly motionless age. He achieved a certain immortal savagery that day. He doubts if he ever achieved it again.

And the water drops: captured by the fall of rock and directed by ravine, smothered in boulders, strewn across dip and valley by giant's angry arm. From Oughtershaw, after passing under an iron-tooth comb hanging from a hank of wire, after a wedge of sunken farmhouses and one raised church, standing lonely on a plinth of stone, it drops, hard and fast. You cannot see it, only imagine its breathless cry as its plunges past the steep tangle of trees that mask its headlong rush. This is where the Wharfe gains its first confidence, a young river flapping its wings, taking its early flight, its faltering nursery steps a thing of the past. It moves with sudden speed now, emerging at the other end of the valley rude and confident, leaping sure-footed rock over rock, too fast perhaps, too confident, tumbling now, somersaulting stone upon stone in overeager haste; but Beckonsmond breaks its fall and emerges out of the wood, boisterous and knee-grazed, to join hands with another, less precipitous, infant, raised on the other side of the wood and, as if pausing to catch its breath after its brash exertions, or in consideration for its less adventurous companion, slows down before descending, as if on a slide, to Deepdale, where it skips to Yockenthwaite, over sheets of flat rock, indulging in a watery hopscotch. It is very close here and playful to touch; there seems no distinction between river and bank, between man and child, between the water and the grass that comes down to its very edge, which, unlike its tough and wiry predecessor, is soft and green, like an untutored lawn.

(On the opposite hill a farmer with a quad bike races up the steep escarpment, his collie keeping a nervous mother sheep at bay, working her with fierce intelligence. The farmer jumps down and grabs the sheep by the horns and bundles her into a little cart; and then her offspring too, chased and scooped up, stuffed alongside. The dog, work accomplished, stands apart.

The bike turns and in motion the dog leaps up, balancing on a narrow platform at the rear. Raised on scrambled moorland, the sheep has no sense for this, the wheel, and how equilibrium is different when described by the machinery of man. Her feet paddle uselessly as she bangs to and fro against the sides, squashing her bleating infant in horrible rhythm. The bus-conductor dog sways from side to side, looking down upon her with contempt.

Down to Hubberholme, of Hubba, of the Viking race, who plundered along this river, and Pastor Thomas Lindley, who lived at Halton Gill, six miles over the moor, and holding the living both here and there never missed passing over the wild of Horse's Head on his pony, winter or summer, 1,900 feet above sea level and six miles to walk, answering the charge his worried landlady used to make, that there were days when he should not attempt the journey, with the reply, 'Duty, missus, must be attended to.'

(At a baptism at Hubberholme church, mishearing the name Ambrose, he baptized the child Amorous instead. The child's father, a Stanley, called on the clergyman the next day to have the name altered but Lindley would not, saying that the register could not be altered and the child must be Amorous to the end of his days, adding that with such a burden there was much vigilance required in the matter of temptation. And the child grew and stuck with his name, and became known throughout the dales as Amorous Stanley, licensed hawker, a title which he strove to justify all his life.

Down towards the guardian gates of Kettlewell, the waters of the Wharfe flow through a long stretch of valley, the river sunk into green pasture bordered by woodland, above a land of hidden caves and shake holes and old mineshafts, the mist of Yockenthwaite Moor at the river's back. Springs and waterfalls pepper this holed surface, drains and gutters and ravines the means of sluicing it, the Wharfe gathering in strength as it reaches the neck of Kettlewell, passes under the bridge, Kettlewell, the base station for the hills of Wensleydale, Kettlewell the last entrance for retreating Celts where, out along the high fork leading up over to Coverdale, another final stand might be made against invasion, Roman or Scot, depending on age, a stubborn land aloft then, which spirit trickles down to these reaches, nourishment in the miles to come.

From Kettlewell, by narrow fields striped by low stone walls, it meets the Skirfare coming in from Foxup Moor, running through Litton and Arncliffe. From its source to here, some twelve miles, the Wharfe has fallen something of six hundred feet, the motor for its sudden surges lower down.

[September 1673] On the eleventh of this month a wonderful inundation of waters, in the Northern parts. The river Wharf was never known within memory of man to be so big by a full yard in height running up in a direct line to Halhillwell. It overturned Kettlewell Bridge, Burnsey Bridge, Barden Bridge, Bolton Bridge, Ilkley Bridge and Otley, and the greatest part of the water mills and carried them down the water whole, like to a ship.

The base broader, the river wider, flatter, moving in those long slow curves that grace so much of its later passage, its rhythm established, moving along as if in a procession and on either side a garland of admirers as it approaches the gates of its inheritance, where the guardian sentinel hangs, the huge escarpment of Kilnsey Crag, an inland cliff overlooking an inland sea. It leans watchful and inquisitive, questioning the river's credentials, its age, its ability to administer the lower reaches of the dale. It stands firm, seeking the Wharfe's pass and its mark of authority, and there is need to climb this rock, to view what has happened to the Wharfe and what the future might hold.

On the summit of the Crag, looking north, he sees the themes and notes of the Wharfe running over the rhythmic page; he sees the opening stanzas flowing into broader motifs; he sees movement divided, pace changed; he sees construction and proposition coming together, as the Wharfe approaches. Then, raising his head, looking south towards Grassington and Bolton Abbey and Ilkley, he sees the gathering clans of the symphony, sees the swell of string and the rise of horn and the march of drum, sees them sailing by as the Wharfe sweeps forward, turning magnificently in the brilliant light

The river has come of age.

ILKLEY (3)

A silence, a weight of the unknown, falls over Britain, rarely revealed. The Dark Ages they are called for the black hole of silence that has sucked their life and their artefacts in, the vacant veil slipped over Britain's face never lifted, the abandonment of that order seen as dissolution, a return to 'barbarity' (realigning the judicial crosses marking the Roman way). Descent? Maybe they had had their fill of civilization, of Rome's money economy and its necessary structure, and shunning the scroll and the tablet abandoned the writ (and thus posterity) for words given form only by their proudly savage breath, the mouth reflecting too the shout of a people returning to the collectivity of the tribe, and who began, unwittingly in this seeming barren time, to lay the foundation of the look of known Britain, clearing, draining, preparing the forsaken land for sowing and swine, while at the same time returning it to the mysteries of Rombald's age, naming forest or fen or wherever with regard to the spirits therein; this the last true heathen time, with regard to nothing but itself, before Christianity rowed ashore, to impose chartered time once more. And Ilkley was in on this, as were all our new-sprung towns, idle, half desolate, and yet, though with nothing much to boast of, it would not have been lost, this Ilkley; it had the meet of its roads still and its favoured river crossing for whatever meagre passage remained (there would not be much; the needs of trade, the strings of administration, for the most part disappeared). Safer to stay put, not to venture on the broken highway, to keep one's head down, cultivate the land, raise pig and sheep and family.

THE MOOR (3)

A wild place of great reach, and covering its folds, from the rim of its bald head to where the Wharfe runs at its feet, uninhabited swathes of forest and deep paths running as embedded veins to risk the ride upon. So great was the profusion of trees it was said that a squirrel could run from Skipton to Knaresborough without touching the ground.

ILKLEY (4)

Land of William de Percy. In Ilkley, Gamel had three carucates of land to be taxed where there may be two ploughs. William now has it and it is a waste. Time of King Edward it was valued at twenty shillings. There is a Church and a priest. Wood pastures, one mile long and four quarentens or furlongs broad. The whole manor is one mile long and eight quarentens broad

– Domesday Book

This is how it will remain for centuries to come. A rutted path, a few farm dwellings, a church, a manor house, in time a blacksmith for the farmsteads, small huddles where men must live to work the pasture land, women to bear the children, children, should they survive, to carry the same yoke. There is no reason for this Ilkley to grow, those ancient capitals vanished, the crossing of the Wharfe here not as important now, Aire's gap too in industrial decline. In the slow length of time, though, events surround the village, swoop down from the hill, spring out of the forest, or are brought to its foundations courtesy of the river, from where they seep up lintel, plaster and thatch, into the bones of those who dwell within. They absorb the Wharfe's potions, inhale the moor's air and such medicines and such oxygen bring change.

THE WHARFE (3)

Above Ilkley some six or seven miles lies Bolton Priory, that great ruin which through its empty window and fallen stone looks out upon the long curving sweep of the Wharfe, the buildings and this accompanying water a flowing mixture of sorrow and beauty, of tranquillity and turmoil. A mile above it, in the depths of the ancient oak wood, lies the initial source of this eternal and perpetuating grief, a narrow channel of rock through which the river must pass.

Before the ruin, before the Priory, under the Saxon Lord of Skipton, there was a hall built here, Bodel-tun, and a wooden church. This is the verdant age, where in its fertile complexity the land overwhelmed man in its munificent capacity. There are meadows now along the river bank (Ilkley too), for grazing cattle and sheep, while stretching out lies the forest thick and lush, brimming with deer and boar, prowled by wolf and bear, eagle on the wing above, fish leaping from the silvery current, fleeting figures of game darting through the trees to escape the cry of the horn, the rip of the hound's tooth. A hunting time.

To this came the Normans, and the lands granted to Robert de Romille, a favourite of the Norman king. A marriage of William de Machines, a descendant of the Saxon earl, to Cecilia, heiress of the Norman, sealed the gift. They had a daughter Alicia. In the twelfth century William Fitz Duncan, a Scottish chieftain, descended upon the valleys of Craven with an army at fire and sword, butchered and raped, taking bloody possession of what he saw. Another hunting time. And for his own he took this Saxon daughter, made legal the possession of Skipton by marrying her. A son was born, named Romilly, known as the Boy of Egremond, who grew to be a hunts-man, and hunted at his pleasure throughout all the wood, knew its dips and paths, its hidden ravines, as only intimacy can, and thus grew familiar and careless with its ways. And a daily delight was to do that Rombald thing, and mark his dexterity and his possession by a leap, not as a giant might, on high, but down in the wood's deep embrace, where the widened river is forced quickly through a tight rocky pass. Though fearful in its voice and frantic in its boiling, the gauge of it can be leapt with ease, hence its name, the Strid.

Returning from a chase one day with greyhound on leash, Romille did as was his habit and leapt the fissure, but the animal, less sanguine as to his or his master's ability, hung back, and the Boy of Egremond and his charge were pulled back over the divide and fell in. The Boy, swiftly sucked under, was carried away and drowned. The hound, treading the same water, scrambled ashore further down. That night, the Boy's body yet undiscovered, storm water flooded the upper reaches of the Wharfe and stole his body away for ever. The forester took himself home, announcing the dread news to Lady Alicia with a question.

'What is good for a bootless bean?' he asked.

The mother, recognizing immediately that some catastrophe had overtaken her son, replied 'Endless sorrow.'

She gave the monks of Embsay the grounds, so that they might move their priory there, and build it alongside the place where his body has passed, a place where they might sing and pray to life's eternal beauty and life's eternal sorrow.

It does not look that deep or dangerous (ten foot of bare rock this August): the approach of the water appears flat, a slight disturbance in the distance between two projecting rocks before flattening out to meet the first gully. But here, hidden in the narrow depths, is where the Wharfe gains its immense strength. It has gained authority by now, its heady descent and long sweeping passage through village and country has seen to that, and if left in this state its grace would not be diminished, but here, in this sunken place, it is driven, like a ribbon of steel through foundry rollers, between these merciless boulders to be hammered and squeezed into something precious and hard, its boil frightening, its drive deafening, a portent of the terror and compulsion of the mechanical age, emerging at the other end utterly transformed, its constituent atoms compressed, charged with a new electricity, and thus shaped it is fused into water of an implacable strength, which, from this moment, it never loses.

And so in history as in legend, on both water and land, the Wharfe and the moor, we have this simple fact, the fall of man, the slip of his foot and the mark it makes on the landscape's soul from Rombald to the Boy Egremond, from him to Michael Airey, and beyond, borne away from this country by the waters of the Wharfe. This is a river of bones. Though there are other places where the Wharfe has carried men and women away, it is this stretch from the beginning of the Strid to the falling away of the coming town that commands those with lives to lose. There should be a monument to those who have been lost to the Wharfe, to those who have slipped, jumped or been pushed, to those who have felt for their own dead reasons impelled to topple in and take the Ilkley Cure.

FATAL ICE ACCIDENT

[January 30th 1897]   A most lamentable accident, when two boys whose intrepidity led them on Sunday afternoon to venture on to the frozen portion of the river near the bottom of Stourton Road and to the south east of the tennis courts. The water at this point lies very deep and still and a day or two's frost is sufficient to give it an angular covering of ice. Arthur Berridge and Stanley Waugh, two of St Margaret's choristers, ventured on to the icy portion and meeting with no mishap communicated the fact with their friends with the result that several of their number set off in high glee once school was over. Berridge and Waterhouse got pretty well mid-stream before the ice gave way (Waterhouse added to his weight by dancing upon it). Seeing his companion fall Berridge went to his aid but the ice gave way again and Berridge fell in. Waterhouse was able to swim but his coat rendered him helpless to keep himself

45

afloat. Mr Steinthal, whose house Wharfemead overlooked the event, went to the rescue, and got within a few feet of the place and laid a stick for Berridge and told him to hold on. The poor lad clung desperately in earnest, with pleading eyes, and Mr Steinthal did his best to pull the lad towards him, but the weight of his wet clothing made it impossible. To get a grip he put a foot a little more forward but he too fell in, in water more than eight feet deep. It was only with the greatest difficulty that he managed to get his shoulders on the ice and heave himself up. Mr Spencer Tetley came with a rope but by this time the water at the hole was calm and placid, with scarce a ruffle on its surface. Arthur Berridge, 13 years old. Son of George Berridge, Oak Royd Terrace, Ilkley, coachman to Mrs Haigh. Leopold Waterhouse, 13, eldest son of Robert Waterhouse master painter 4 North View.

[30th April 1828] Miss Poole, the daughter of a London solicitor went to Bolton. On looking at the Strid she approached to near the rock, became giddy and exclaimed, 'I am going, Oh I am going,' and at once sunk into the boiling surge. Some days elapsed ere even her remains could be discovered.

In 1894 a Keighley man Mr Christopher Bailey who had the advantage of being a very powerful swimmer decided to see for himself what things were like in the hidden whirlpools and chasms under the rocks. He used a ladder and remained at a depth of 25 feet for nearly three minutes. He found tree trunks almost bleached white in ledges of rock, and projecting in some cases four or five feet, grim reminders of what would happen to a human being if the waters sucked him under. The surface gives no clue to the perils beneath. The surface water flows quickly it is true but with a smooth surface. Deep down the waters are aboil, and indication of the hidden fury may be seen in the occasional air bubbles which come to the surface.

[September 1897] Edward Hudson of 6 Chapel Lane was proceeding along the footpath when he heard a woman cry 'Oh Paradise! I'm going!' followed by splashes and a sound of someone struggling in the water. He searched along the bank but could observe nothing, nor hear any further sound. A boat was procured and at daylight at 5.30 they came across the body of a woman, Henrietta Diblah, a domestic servant employed by Mrs Carr of Easby Lodge. Of strong religious convictions at one time she had been engaged but the man jilted her about three years ago. She had no friends in Ilkley and on her day of rest went up to her room. Monday was a normal washing day. She made the customary preparations such as paring extra potatoes and in every respect carried out her daily life.

Mr G. Hodgson saw his sister Miss Winifred May Hodgson of Ilkley throw herself into the Wharfe at the Strid, following a depression caused by a broken engagement. Her brother was on a visit with his wife and on Thursday afternoon went to the Strid where the river was in fine spate. Just as they were about to leave they saw Miss Hodgson leap into the Strid and disappear.

Coroner: I understand you had been there some time.

Mr Hodgson: Yes I saw a notice on a tree and I was going towards the notice to read it really.

Coroner: Did you call her by her name?

Mr Hodgson: Yes, I called Freda. My sister was known by the name of Freda.

Coroner: She was then standing close to the river?

Mr Hodgson: Yes, within a few feet of the rock.

Coroner: But she did not answer?

Mr Hodgson: No. I thought she did not hear me owing to the sound of the rushing of the water. My wife turned round to go back to her, and I also followed. My wife spoke to her and was about to take hold of her arm when my sister gave a leap into the water.

47

Coroner: Did she sink or float down?

Mr Hodgson: I ran to the edge of the water immediately and I could not see anything at all. Then I ran for one of the long poles that are kept there. When I got back I caught sight of the body about 100 yards down the river. I ran down the bank as fast as I could but I never caught sight of it again.

The body was recovered on Friday, washed against the one of the islands in the middle of the stream at the spot known as the Meeting of the Waters. The same day a letter was found in Mrs Hodgson's desk. She wrote it about three o'clock before they started out.

Inquest on Allan Aingill Wood 26 farm labourer whose body was recovered from the Wharfe. Colin Wood said he last saw his son alive on Wed afternoon May 18th.

"I was delivering milk opposite Mr Hudson's, out on the Skipton Road."

"And there were no suspicions that anything was the matter?"

"No. In fact he said he was coming down to see me on the Sunday."

"Had he ever suggested that he would do away with himself?"

"He had not. He talked of going to his brother in Canada and that is where I thought he had gone."

A somewhat singular incident has occurred in the connection with the drowning of the two lads at Ilkley last week. A fox terrier belonging to Mr Steinthal accompanied that gentleman down to the river on Sunday week, and was witness to his efforts to save the lads and much that followed. Previously it had shown no disposition to visit the locality, but every day since it has visited the scene of the accident and continued to do so up to Monday, on which day the ice had become so rotten that it gave way beneath the dog's weight, light as it was, and the sagacious little animal was precipitated into the river. It was a strong swimmer but getting under the ice it shared the same fate as the lads whose deaths it seemed to be lamenting. On each occasion the dog went down to the river it was observed to scratch about the place where the two lads went in; though for what purpose is not quite clear unless it be that the dog was under the impression that the bodies had not been recovered, although it is said to have been present when one lad was taken out. The dog was evidently guided by some sort of instinct in which there was much reason, and its pitiable fate is somewhat remarkable in face of the existing circumstances. A number of people made efforts to rescue the animal, but the current was too strong and took it under the ice, the scene being one in many respects resembling the awful tragic affair of the previous week.

It is an old ragged country, rotten logs and dark moss, over-hanging trees with a thin mist lingering in the branches. Surprisingly, he is alone, though he can hear departing voices through the trees. He walks to the edge where the river thunders, and sits. The notebook he is carrying slips from his fingers and falls from his lap on to one of the lower ledges of rock where half of it hangs over the edge, enough to make it dangerous for him to try and pick it up from the near end. He will have to go down and retrieve it. He is conscious of the Egremond story, and how his own balance is not what it was, jumping over seaside rocks or cycling down the road arms at his sides both unpractised pastimes. Should he climb down where the rock is wet he could disappear into the folds of the water in the clutching of his hand, to carry what he has written to Michael Airey and the Boy of Egremond and all the others kidnapped by the Wharfe, but how tempted he is to draw the Strid close, to confront its raw power. (He is reminded by the noise of it of how foundry workers would run across the hard skin of beds of setting molten metal in order to save time, and how, one time, legend had it, a novice, taking cue from his betters, ran across one that had not solidified sufficiently to carry his weight and who fell through, his body bobbing up out of the liquid, as a body does through buoyancy, his pain not yet registering, as his father – for son followed father then, it was expected and needed by them both – took hold of his head and pushed him back under.) He steps up to the brink of the rock, below the foam bubbling up from the deep, looking at the pool swirling, and he wonders why those who wish to end their story don't do that any more, take their lives through water. A bridge, a cliff, a handful of pills, but rarely a river now. Is it because we no longer appreciate a river's power, no longer live in thrall to the mystery of water, that the river as poem, or religious highway, no longer exists, or is it simply that most of us can swim now and do not imagine that such a stretch could take our life (as it can with ease), or is it that other aspect of our lives, that warm and enclosed even in our travelling we do not relish getting wet, choosing even in death an end without such obvious cold discomfort.

He climbs down, drawing closer to the magnet of the Strid, balancing awkwardly on one of its slippery lips, looking across to another ledge directly opposite. It would be good to jump, foolhardy too, with no one here, and a notebook and a fountain pen to worry about. A honeymoon couple drowned here only last year, one falling in, the other jumping down to rescue no doubt, or perhaps pulled in by a desperate, disappearing, outstretched hand. They had woken from their honeymoon bed and carried their honeymoon kisses to the heart of the river, where the Strid embraced their life and took their happiness and their hopes for its own. You could kiss a lover here, or see them drown, hold a child back or see it drown, smoke a cigarette, lie across the knotty rocks, picnic with friends, dream alone, the choice is yours; you could wait for kingfishers, sit until the sun sets, watch the dark take hold. Or you could jump down, pick up your notebook, take one step back and with one leap think of Michael.

THE MOOR (4)

The moor and uplands were given to sheep, the ground moving from forest and bracken to bog and heath. So sheep determined the aspect of this land, its fortune riding on their woolly backs, their incessant nibbles and clambering giving view and the responsibilities of space, giving the water that final unaffected run, and in the end, giving it the means by which the men would return in flocks, build the roads and the houses and the heart of the village, to make it a centre.

THE NEW LEICESTER. The head should be hornless, long, small, tapering towards the muzzle, and projecting horizontally forwards. The eyes prominent, but with a quiet expression. The ears thin, rather long and directed backwards.

THE SOUTH DOWN. The head is small and hornless, the face speckled or grey, and neither too long nor too short. The lips thin, and the space between the nose and eyes narrow. The underjaw of chap, fine and thin; the ears tolerably wide, and well covered with wool, and the forehead also, and the whole space between the ears well protected by it, as a defence against the fly. The belly is as straight as the back. The belly well defended with wool, coming down before and behind to the knee and to the hock, the wool short, close, curled and fine, and free from any projecting fibres.

THE CHEVIOTS. The inhabitant suited to a still more elevated region and colder clime. The head polled, bare, and clean, with jaw bone of good length. Ears not too short. Countenance of not too dark a colour. Neck full, round, not too long, covered with wool, and without beard or coarse wool beneath. Fleece fine, close, short and thick set; of a medium length of pile, without hairs at the bottom and not curled on the shoulders and with as little coarse wool as possible on the hips, tail, and belly. A sheep possessing these properties in an eminent degree may be considered as the most perfect model of the Cheviot breed.

– From Bischoff, *Woollen and Worsted Manufacturers*

ILKLEY (5)

The Catholic Middletons owned it now, the Manor of Ilkley and Stockeld Park, the family pacing their days in recusant time, in the manor overlooking the town, their purse emptied by the state, their lives suffering under the law. In the days of Elizabeth and beyond, during the Civil War aye and for long after, they had a burden to bear, which was their own witness, and which their kind bore as best they could, without shaking the weight from their shoulders, rather parcelling it amongst themselves equally, so that they all might carry the weight, and none fall completely. No matter their skill or inclination, no matter the heart or the head, these were the rules such families were enjoined to obey.

No Catholic may send their child abroad No Catholic may practise law No Catholic may practise medicine No Catholic may hold office at court No Catholic may possess Catholic books No Catholic may posses objects of Catholic devotion No Catholic may possess arms No Catholic Peer may sit in the House of Lords No Catholic gentlemen in the House of Commons No Catholic above sixteen may travel more than five miles No Catholic may Marry through a Catholic priest No Catholic may be buried by a Catholic priest. Fine £20. Catholics who did not attend the Established Church fined £20 a month

Travelling beyond the Strid, seeking out the ruin of Barden, it is clear how fiercely they must have regarded this land, not simply because of its remote beauty, but the allegiance it demanded in the way they lived. The country is both enclosed and rapturously open, thus those who dwell upon it are simultaneously locked in and set free. It is this, as much as history that explains their fettered ties, the deep pockets of stubborn resistance that exist still. It is their world and no other's, and that loyalty, when called upon, is more than a Crown's inheritance, or Parliamentary diktat. Their allegiance is rooted to these paths and those who tread upon them.

And the cloth connection was taking hold now, twenty thousand men and women working the stuff down in Bradford and Halifax, and scattered homesteads up and down the vales spinning wool, weaving cloth, wattle fences for Ilkley's annual sheep fair stuck down along the river, and up the road the mills of Addingham. But no great love of Bradford would the Middletons have. It was a Calvinist town, entrenched in its dislike of Rome and the Crown's Popish officials come to bleed it dry: Bradford besieged by Civil War Royalists and butchered by them too. Small wonder that the Middletons kept their counsel, small wonder that they took hold of Ilkley and gripped it tight to their chest, not simply proprietorial but guarded in the same manner as they held their religious services in hidden chapel above the porch, wary of strangers and those who rode in with inquisitive eye.

(the Middleton women, their men standing with the King, fearing the outcome and their own domestic vulnerability, wrote letters to their neighbour Parliamentary Thomas Fairfax, begging his indulgence.

A wife wishing in 1645

> 'as to blot out the memory of my husband's trespass. But esteem him as he really deserves – one that truly honors your lordship, though his great cares of fears and jealousies might cause him for the present to forfeit your lordship's good opinion'

a sister hoping in the same breath

> 'not to suffer through my brother who has broken his

promises with your lordship; which I vow my lord I was altogether ignorant'

Fairfax recognizes the pleadings of his class. The Middletons keep their manor, to live and die inside their stone walls and wood-stacked fireplaces, their feathered beds and tapestried walls, while in the village below there are hard livings to make, for every seed sown another withered

[1780]   William Nelson of the parish of Ripon and Sarah Rigg of this parish by licence. Witness William Cunliffe and Hugh Barret 22nd March

[1782]   Mary ye daughter of Wm Nelson of Ilkley, labourer and Sarah his wife, born ye 2nd of March, baptised ye 11th of April

[1791]   Mary, daughter of William Nelson of Ilkley, pauper and Sarah his wife died May 8th buried May the 9th . . . aged 9 yrs

[1792]   Hannah daughter of William Nelson, pauper and Sarah his wife born July baptised ye 15th Sept.

[in 1801]   John son of William and Sarah his wife of Ilkley, miller, born Oct. 18th, baptised 21st

[1802]   John son of William died Sept. 10th bur'd 12th

So Ilkley, a damp and dismal place, despite the graceful setting of the river and the dark bloom of the moor. From its height, coming from solitude, as it has always done, the water flows, gushing from the unknown, clear and cold. And thus it begins again, this village, this mean straggle of houses and manorial suspicion, begins again with the moor and the thing in which it is soaked, Water. It has clung to the moor, cleaned it, made it heavy. It is the moor in liquid form, liquid rock, liquid peat. It takes its taste, its acidity and its clarity from the moor's rock and the moor's height, takes its temperature from the moor's hidden heart and comes, in a torrent, as a cold spring. But as in religion wine in the sipping can turn to blood, here, under the shadow of the Cow and Calf Water is turned to Medicine – the Ilkley Cure. They take note of it. The message is sent abroad, to neighbouring manor and village, packed off on horse and carriage to be handed out in Leeds and Bradford and the streets of York, urging those in need to abandon physic and comfort, and head out into this bare wilderness, in the name of self-improvement.

> Ichley-Spaw springs out of a mountain, a mile high, and consists chiefly of limestone and free stone. The water is very clear, brisk and sparkling; has no taste, colour nor smell different from common water, is of the same weight. Its bason and course are of no other dye than that of a common spring. About thirty-five years ago, there were a house and a bath built, about a furlong below the original spring, which spring was brought down in stone pipes. The first spring, near the top of the hill, was very weak and small; this, very large and strong; whereby there appears to be a larger mixture of other springs with this
>
>   – 1734 Thomas Short: *Natural, Experimental and Medicinal History of the Mineral Waters of Derbyshire, Lincolnshire and Yorkshire &c.*

the getting there improving but slowly

> In the year 1751 Metcalfe commenced a new employ: a stage waggon between York and Knaresborough, being

first on that road, and conducted it constantly himself, twice a week in the summer, and once in the winter

During his leisure hours he studied measurement in a way of his own; and when certain of the girt and length of any piece of timber, he was able to reduce its true contents to feet and inches; and would bring the dimensions of any building into yards or feet . . .

between the Forest Lane head and the Knaresborough Bridge, there was a bog, in a low piece of ground, over which to have passed was the nearest way; and the surveyor thought it impossible to make a road over it: but Metcalfe assured him that he could readily accomplish it. The other told him, that if so, he should be paid for the same length as if he had gone round. Jack set about it, cast the road up, and covered it with whin and ling, and made it as good, or better, than any part he had undertaken . . .

He then agreed two miles of road which lay through Broughton to Marin; and two miles more which lay through Addingham, and over part of Romell's Moor. The same trustees acted for those roads, as that of Colne. These he completed, and received one thousand three hundred and fifty pounds from Mr Ingham of Burnleigh and Mr Alcock of Skipton.

– From: *The Life of John Metcalfe, commonly called Blind Jack of Knaresborough*

and with the increase of custom:

[26 April 1791] Robert Dale takes the opportunity to inform the public that he is now fitting up two commodious baths, with sitting rooms adjoining thereto, for the

accommodation of such persons as may wish to visit this Spaw for the benefit of their health.

his advertisment paying off, for a year later,

An essay to elucidate the Nature, Origin, and Connexion of Scrophular and Glandular Consumption, including a brief history of the Effects of

ILKLEY SPAW

Scrophula In the stages of obstruction and ulceration, I have for many years witnessed its efficacy; more especially if persisted in for a number of weeks or months; – and here I beg leave to call the attention of medical men to the powers of

ILKLEY SPAW

which has maintained its credit almost since the commencement of the present century, on account of the virtues which is has displayed in the cure of Scrophula. By what means it first excited the public attention I know not; but without the sanction of any medical writer, it has uniformly forced itself upon the notice of all descriptions of people in its vicinity who labour under the influence of Scrophula. A respectable clergyman, long resident, informed me "that he never knew a scrophulous patient give the waters of that place a fair trial, without either experiencing benefit approximating to a cure, or being materially relieved."

That spring, which has given celebrity to the place, issues from the side of a hill about half a mile from the village, and flows not less than thirty gallons in the minute. It was first enclosed by the late Mr Middleton Esq. and it has since been accommodated with baths, dressing rooms &c, by the present lord of the manor. The prospect from the spring has ever excited the admiration of strangers. – I visited the spring, and I examined it by all the tests used in the analysis of water; – the results of my experiments convinced me that it contained the least

58

extraneous matter, of any water hitherto described; and that its salutary qualities reside exclusively, in the remarkable coldness, softness and purity of the element . . . when poured into a glass it is remarkably clear, bright and sparkling; from its extreme purity and softness, it is perhaps calculated to enter, those minute vessels of the animal frame, which are impervious to other fluids – A very large quantity of the water may be drunk, even immediately before dinner, without seeming to distend the stomach, and without in the smallest degree, impairing the appetite.

– Dr Mossman. 1792

They called it White Wells, built halfway up the Moor, leaning out of the slope like an old signpost, and a long journey getting there, a halfway house between civilization and wilderness, an exit and an entrance, the motif to the town's intent. It is rudely built, rough baths of stone surrounded by stone walls, but not roofed, just of sufficient height to preserve modesty and protect a body from the Rombald wind; cold water and the cold air. Two baths, two dressing rooms to each, and from them a door into the open-aired chamber, and steps down, into the bath. Two can bathe there, if bathing is the right word, if steps are the appropriate means of submersion. Overhead reads the inscription, *This holds 1150 gallons and fills in 13 minutes*, and by God it is fast, and by God it takes your breath away. After the gasps and the breaking of your heart, a swift shivering followed by a numbness, as on a hilltop, stranded on the moorland snow, the cold subsiding and to your surprise, a pleasant drowsy feeling swimming over, as if there is nothing more to be done in this world except to take one's time. It would be easy to float, to drowse, to idly bathe in safety. This is no Strid to suffer you away. Then the attendant comes, to urge you out, to rise up from those steps and feel the blood rush back, the head awake, and a glow stealing over you that you have never felt before. You step into the air refreshed, invigorated, a body reborn. You look down. It has been raining in Ilkley. Now you have to get down, without sliding down on your rear, or worse, slipping on the rough-cut path and breaking your leg.

Yes, how to get there, from the seat of the town to the cold-water bath? You could walk, climb up the slippery slopes in your many layers, strip and plunge and dress again, and pray that you may survive the journey down, or else you could avail yourself of the town's braying water transport, Ilkley's scuffed donkeys, trotting along Ilkley's muddy streets, tied up outside the proprietors' thatched cottages, nibbling buttercups and grass, hee-hawing their jokes up and down the moor. As Ilkley's fame grew and its visitors increased there grew convoys of them, William Riggs' along Brook Street, Mr Butterfield's business looking out on Church Street, and later, his great rival, the man who took over from Riggs, Donkey Jack, a wool-comber by trade but who bought Riggs' business and made it his own, Donkey Jack with his buttoned waistcoat, black and taut, his long loose jacket with drooping pockets (filled with sugar-lump bribes for his beasts no doubt), and atop his head a battered top hat, music-hall comical, a master of ceremony of sorts, goading his audience to the chill waters, their petticoats and long skirts damp-ened, their trousers mud-spattered, hats firmly held and shoes and boots trailing from the placid beasts as they plodded to the perched house on the hill. Donkey Jack the Ilkley gondolier, his donkeys aping the Venetian lion, hoofs astride both land and water, Don-key Jack sailing across the wide streets on his fleet of donkeys, a philosopher king ferrying his betters to their redemption: Donkey Jack with the beast of saviours, Donkey Jack on the mud-slipped steps. Donkey Jack don't take the waters, Donkey Jack don't step ashore, Donkey Jack he tops his pipe, and chuckles at the cries that make even his beasts' ears twitch (for they have sensitive souls like all their ilk, their hide masks their predicament and pain); two donkeys and a carriage carrying four, 1s. 4d. per hour or 8s. per day; asses 3d. per hour, 4d. to the Wells, 5s. per week. A week? Yes, a week. You could stay for as long as your body and spirit could take and while you were here, (when they had one) they put your name in the paper, like they did the dead and the married and the new-born. Seeing the commerce of it, houses were lent over to rooms or tailor-made for the purpose. Trade was coming.

This is the constant drip of it, the way it spouts out of the ground and runs down to the mud-packed street. The first true settlers pulling along their meagre baggage and apprehensive family, attracted by the scent of water, seeing the profit of this water, names that would spread through the town like the heather on the hill, Thomas Beanlands and his son Joseph manning the baths, and down below, shopkeepers.

496 inhabitants in 1821. 254 males, 242 females, and ninety-nine houses between them: a vicar, a squire, a solicitor, a grocer, a wheelwright, two butchers, a corn miller, a master of the free grammar school. Strange ways for the old farms and farmers these new folk brought too, the composure and colour of the village changed almost overnight: the dun glow of thatch, the soft weight of it sinking into the landscape replaced by something harder, related if not belonging to the rock.

When Ickringill added a lean-to to his shop he roofed it with the first blue slates that ever came to Ilkley. Some of the old farmers from the other side of the river, seeing the piles of slate stacked up, asked him what he was going to do with them and when he told them they shook their heads at the ignorance of the man. 'They'll never turn water,' they said. 'You can't nail them together and you can't glue them. It's a mammy.'

Visitors they had, in regular flows, the first reachings of recognized commerce, of supply and demand, of delivery:

[1825] THE DEFIANCE, Leeds, via Otley, Monday and Tuesday at 7am, Thursday and Saturday at 8. Inside 5s., Outside 3s., stopping at the Lister Arms

[1829] Boarding Houses Mr R. Batty Wells Road; Mrs Beanlands, ditto; Mr J. Beanland, Bridge Land; Mrs Bolling, Hangingstone Road. Lodging houses at the Messrs W. Bell, a grocer, Paul Bottomley, butcher, John Birch, blacksmith, J. Showsmith, confectioner and shoemaker,

John Parrott, Kirkgate, John Vicars, Kirkgate, S. Watkinson, ladies' boot and shoe maker.

Ilkley getting used to strangers.

[1833]   William Brown elected Dogwhipper and Sexton:

To be decently attired on the Sabbath day and to be ready to hand company to their seats.

To preserve decency and order during Divine Service, in the Churchyard and Street adjoining.

To have 2s. for making a grave four feet deep, 3s. for five, 4s. 6d. for six feet. To preserve decency and order for funerals.

To use his best endeavour to persuade relatives to bury the corpse on the North side of the church.

To toll the bell fifteen minutes on the death of a parishioner
> 6 strokes for the death of a child
> 8 strokes for a woman
> 10 strokes for a man
> After fifteen minutes the age of the deceased rung out in scores.

It takes on the appearance of a frontier town, out on the Klondike or the Oklahoma fields, an outpost of sudden failure, gold-fevered or some early cattle outpost, where markets and mountebanks thrive, twelve saloons, a one room jail and a lone sheriff with a tin star pinned to his jerkin. You can tell by the look of the men, as if they are prospectors all, searching for the riches buried deep somewhere in this earth, see it hang in the folds of their clothing and leggings, feel it weigh upon the bones of their weary wives, see it in the tight grip of all their hands and on their suspicious but unrepentant faces, how they wish to make their stamp upon this earth, fashion it under their feet. You can tell what an outpost it is by the photographs of the travelling circus that appears down the main street, the crazy man on stilts placing top hats on first-storey windows, on the tasselled cowboy doffing his Buffalo Bill hat, by the dancing bear sitting with his keeper, a young boy inquisitively near while behind a mother bites her anxious fingers: a frontier town and yes, there is oil here too: it is dug for in the hills, it bubbles up through gritstone pores like the slick-black Oklahoma fields. In its pure, quickly harnessed gush, it becomes Ilkley's potency, its seminal fluid, determining the town's shape and character. This water is not only a substance which one can bathe in, help a scaly skin, but is now transformed into a balm that can serve the complete body, a newly harnessed medicant to replace the cup and the leech and the phials of mercury: and thus did this running water become not simply the lubricant to Ilkley's gathering machine, but a source of salvation: now came the time to stamp Ilkley's water mark on the map; to build temples to this water on the edge of the moor, where water priests would administer water rites, where penitents would be converted into believers, be plunged under and come up baptized, where they would worship water day and night, pray to its infinite properties: Ilkley a water Lourdes, a refuge of trial and hope and incarceration.

And the first of these, built outside Ilkley, under the eyes of the Cow and Calf, up from the village of Wheatley (its name soon drowned under water's thunderous roar), was Ben Rhydding.

It has the same multitudinous aspect as those great railway stations that lie in the hearts of our cities, but whose tentacles have yet to reach this valley; here, with its myriad gaze, is built a watery Kings Cross, a sluiced St Pancras, while inside, wandering like a lost dream, are gathered the wounded and shell-shocked, those who have succumbed to life's exhausting war. Ben Rhydding then, not only a temple but also many buildings, a terminal, a dressing station, and like those other steam buildings, an exhibition hall too, glass-casing its own wares, those weary travellers who have made their reservations before undertaking their long and arduous journey.

BEN RHYDDING

A Series of Observations on the power of the
Human Organism to cure itself of Diseases by the just
application of the natural stimuli only.
By Dr William Macleod

of all branches of knowledge, that of physic is the most unsatisfactory and the least advanced. Physiology, organic chemistry, pathology, the knowledge of diseased structures, and the diagnosis of disease have made great advances during recent times; but our knowledge of the power of drugs to cure diseases has not so progressed (we refer to the drug art as taught in our colleges and medical schools). Medicines are as lame as their benefits, and as inconsistent in their cures as they were in the days of Hippocrates who when dying consoled those who stood by and lamented his decease saying he had left three excellent physicians behind him, Air, Water, and Diet,

Priessnitz was born on 4 October 1799 in the hamlet of Graefenberg in Austrian Silesia. At the age of eight, his elder brother dead, his father blind with grief, he was set to work on the family farm. Sitting dreaming one day he saw a young roe which had been shot through the thigh drag itself with some difficulty to the source of the local spring, manoeuvring itself so that its wounded thigh was entirely covered by the running water. Priessnitz watched with breathless interest. He saw it return to bathe at intervals throughout the day, (and returning to that same spot) observed the animal's improvement from day to day; experimented on injuries to farm animals – and at the age of fifteen was already a medical adviser to his neighbourhood.

An accident at eighteen, driving a large cart loaded with oats, Priessnitz was thrown, had his front teeth knocked out, the heavy waggon passing over his body. 'Having broken two of my ribs and a surgeon having told me that I never could be cured so as to be fit for work again I resolved to endeavour to cure myself. My first care was to replace my ribs, and this I did by leaning with my abdomen with all my might against a chair and holding my breath so as to swell out my chest. The painful operation was attended with the success I expected. The ribs being replaced I applied wet bandages to the part affected, drank plentifully of water, ate sparingly and remained in perfect repose. In ten days I was able to get out.'

He wore a wet compress for a year. If he heard of anyone having bruises, external injuries, he lost no time in recommending cold water as the means of obtaining a thorough and speedy cure. His reputation spread. Invited to Bohemia and Moravia with his sponge (as yet his only implement). He lost his mother in 1826, having been tossed by a bull. In 1829, an accusation was brought against him charging him with being a quack doctor, who in opposition to laws of his country undertook to treat patients without being authorized. The magistrates sentenced him to several days' imprisonment with an additional punishment of fasting, but on appeal the ruling was overturned and in 1831 he obtained official permission to conduct his hydropathic establishment. Renewed complaints determined the Imperial Office to send Baron Turkenheim to Graefenberg, where he was welcomed by several ladies of Viennese society. 'He is no impostor, but is filled with the purest zeal. This new cure and this extraordinary man therefore deserve the full attention of the Government.'

The biography owes much to Colonel Ripper of the Austrian Army, Priessnitz's son-in-law. Chief promoter of the excellent railway system to Graefenberg, extending the network of forest paths, and at his instigation hundreds of hammocks were placed near these paths in every direction, enabling visitors to inhale the health-giving air of the

pine forests. Founder of the Mutual Aid Society of Bath
Attendants.

The erection of Ben Rhydding was due to the beneficence of Mr
Hamer Stansfield, formerly Mayor of Leeds (a stuff merchant), a man
of wide reading and thought, who on returning from Graefenberg in
1843, cured of a long-standing illness, conceived the idea of insti-
tuting an establishment to give people the benefit of the new system.
As a result a private company was started, a site selected on Rombald's Moor and the building put up at a cost of £30,000. It stands
on its commanding site, with a flag floating gaily from its topmost
turret, and with the adjuncts of foliage and bold hills it presents a
most imposing appearance. In commemoration of the event, and in
honour of the founder, a marble fountain was unveiled, bearing the
description,

In memory of
Vincent Priessnitz,
the Silesian Peasant, to whom the world
Is indebted for the blessing of the
System, of Cure by Water,
This fountain
Is gratefully erected and inscribed by
Hamer Stansfield.
Ben Rhydding, May 29, 1844

Priessnitz's only son Vincent showed a special predilection for
cold water. Whenever he felt unwell he was quite ready to
become his own physician, prescribing either a cold compress,
a dripping sheet, or some other application. He was able to dis-
tinguish the efficacy of each of these with accuracy and used to
say to his nurse when the occasion occurred, "I want a dripping
sheet. I must have another compress. That does me good."

The edifice is in the old Scottish baronial style suited to the rocky and moorland scenery. Built in the shape of a capital E, the house is so planned that the windows on three sides command wide prospects – above the stony stretches of Rombald's Moor, marked by the Cow and Calf. From the hills above flow the springs which supply the place with an abundance of the purest water. Built on a sandy soil, rain never lies on its gravel walks. The estate consists of about two hundred acres of ground, a great part of which is laid out with a view to the advantage and pleasure of the patients, affording them opportunities for varied exercise. Should the sun beat down too strongly on the lower levels he can enjoy the breeze of the uplands, and when cold and storm are raging on the height, the grounds by which this establishment is surrounded will be found to command a more sheltered climate than even the banks of the silvery Wharfe.

C. Darwin to J. D. Hooker: Down, Sept. 11th 1859

My Dear Hooker

I corrected the last proof yesterday and have now my revises, index, &c., which will take me to the end of the month. So that the neck of my work, thank God, is broken . . . As soon as I have fairly finished I shall be off to Ilkley, or some other Hydropathic establishment . . . Oh good heavens, the relief to my head and body to banish the whole subject from my mind!

Do the temples throb? Is the eye full and confused, because of over-determination of the blood towards the brain? Hesitate, I pray you, before thinking of the lancet, for other expedients are in store! A footbath for instance affords unfailing relief to headaches arising in tumefaction of the cranial vessels; and still more energetically the *sitting bath*. Or – do you wish to allay general irritation, and produce sleep? Then away, to an infinite distance, with all opiates. The *wet sheet*, or envelope possesses an efficacy, which belongs to no drug in the "Metria Medica".

1870 early morn of Good Friday arrived at the Kings Cross station, armed with luggage, meerschaum and morning paper – an open window in the smoking carriage, (a genial breeze sweeping through) arriving at Leeds at half four. Leeds alive with excitement evoked by a grand teetotal procession and fete. I took the six o'clock for Ilkley – no longer a dull hamlet but a lively little town, with a show of bright freestone and light blue slate, of tower and spire and belfry

LEEDS, OTLEY, AND ILKLEY

The Public are respectfully informed that the

WELLINGTON AND RAGLAN
COACHES

Run from the Old George Hotel, Bottom of Briggate, and the Wheat Sheaf Hotel, Upperhead Row, Leeds.

The Wellington will leave Leeds every morning at 10.30; Sundays at 8.30; by way of Headingly and Otley; leaving the Queen's Head, Otley, for Ilkley at 12 a.m.; Sundays at 10. Returning from the Lister Arms Hotel, Ilkley, for Leeds, at 4 p.m. Sundays at 5; leaving Otley at 4.45 p.m. Sundays at 5.45.

WILLIAM WEBSTER, Proprietor

Charges Hydropathic Department

Introductory consultation fee £1 1s. 0d.
Board, lodging, medical attendance and baths for one patient per week £3 6s. 0d.

Or with use of bowling green and gymnasium, with teacher £3 10s. 0d.

Charges Hotel Department

Board and lodging per week £2 9s. 0d.
A child above eight and under 12 years £2 0s. 0d.
Under eight years £1 0s. 0d.
Private servants – men £1 4s. 0d.
Women £1 1s. 0d.
A private sitting room, per day 3s. to 4s. 6d.
per week from £1 1s. to £1 10s.
Bed for single night 3s.
Dinner at the hydropathic hotel, two o'clock, for the friends of patients 2s. 6d.
Serving meals in private rooms, for family, per week £1 1s. 0d.
For single visitors 10s. 6d.
The use of the gymnasium and bowling green per week 6s.
Bath attendants, waiters, chambermaids, porters, and boots, are included in the above charges.
NO GRATUITIES ALLOWED

The following articles are kept for sale in the office by the clerk

Writing and Blotting Paper	Liver Oil
Envelopes	Tar Pustules
Sealing Wax Quills and Steel Pens	Wax Candles
Postage Stamps	Tapers
Tincture of Arnica	Night Lights
Arnica Ointment	Wax Vestas
Arnica Plaister	Marking Ink

The first physician placed over the new establishment was Dr Rischanek, who he brought from Graefenberg. Being German he did not adapt easily to the ways and habits of English people and did not get on with them very well. After three years the proprietors engaged Dr William Macleod of Edinburgh, one of the most successful hydropathists, Fellow of the Royal College of Physicians, Edinburgh; member of the Edinburgh Medico-Chirurgical Society; Lecturer of Physiology and joint editor of *The Water Cure Journal*.

Sir, –

I have consulted about as many doctors as there are letters in the alphabet. One tells me that my liver is affected; another, that my stomach is inflammatory, another that I am dyspeptic; and so on – all which things may be synonymous, for aught I know; but not one of the said doctors has yet been able to remove my unpleasant symptoms. I have perpetual pain in my right shoulder blade; frequently considerable uneasiness in my chest; and almost continually a great weight on the bridge of my nose; together with headache, dry throat, &c. Now, as I have, I think, pretty nearly exhausted the Metria Medica, without receiving benefit, allow me to ask if you think the water treatment in any way applicable in my case; and if so, under whose care would you recommend me to place myself?

I am, &c

A Great Sufferer

[August 13 1847]   It is against our principles to recommend any one hydropathic establishment more than another. We would nevertheless take this opportunity of saying that we cannot in sufficiently strong terms advise every one who wishes well to hydropathy not to put himself under the care of any individual who has not received a regular medical education.

It may perhaps appear to some that this resolve of ours is inconsistent, since the discoverer of the system we advocate and practise was not brought up to the medical of any other profession, but that, on the contrary, he was an illiterate and uneducated individual. Priessnitz is one whose great genius, sterling talents, and subtle powers of thinking are capable of over-turning every rule and of dissolving the most reasonable and most warrantable objections into nothingness. In a word, Priessnitz is the natural medical genius of the age.

Entering by the principal door, which is the centre of the building, we are admitted to the outer and inner porch. At the end stretches a corridor to right and left, traversing the main part of the building, and from this, in corresponding with the eternal plan, two shorter corridors start at right angles, and traverse the wings. Almost the whole of the ground floor in the central portion of the house is occupied by public rooms or apartments. Here there is the Dining Room, a very handsome apartment, looking towards the West 46 feet by 26 feet and affords comfortable accommodation for eighty patients, with their friends; the latter, as well as general visitors, having apartments in the hotel which forms the centre of the building. On this floor also are the Reading Room, the Billiard Room, the Stewards' and House-keeper's apartments, the Clerk's Office while the wings on this floor are occupied with Bedrooms and Private Sitting Rooms, varying in size but all commanding exquisite views.

The patients' bed rooms are 15 feet by 12, and 10 feet high; they are each fitted with its separate bath, and an unlimited supply of water; besides which there is a large bath-room on each of the three floors, containing a plunge bath and a douche. On the ground floor of each wing are hot water, hot air, and vapour baths and in the adjoining room steam apparatus for the local application of stiffened joints from gout or rheumatism, affections of the nerves, different states of acute and chronic sciatica, &c.

Heat is effected by steam pipes which run along on either side of the corridors, the effect being aided by the numerous pipes which permeate the house, conveying hot water to the Taps. Ventilation is effected on Watson's principles. Several large Ventilators in the roof give free egress to foul and free admission to pure air.

The beds are in the Elizabethan form, their white curtains scrupulously clean; counterpane, sheets and curtains as white as snow, the light colour of the furniture and dimensions enhanced by the plate glass of the windows.

Every apartment has its own special Ventilator, placed above the doors and so effectual that when the patient leaves his bed in the morning he finds the atmosphere of his apartment as pure and pleasant as it would have been had the apartment remained unoccupied.

In the adjoining woods are two very powerful douches, one for ladies and another for gentlemen, with dressing rooms attached. On a large terrace, levelled for the purpose, an extensive gymnasium has been lately erected, and furnished with apparatus suited to all degrees of strength . . . and in a room within the building, means are provided for exercise in those therapeutic movements, the theory of which has been so skilfully elucidated by Ling of Sweden.

Charles Darwin to J. D. Hooker Oct. 15th 1859.

My Dear Hooker,

I have been here nearly a fortnight, and it has done me very much good, though I sprained my ankle last Sunday, which has stopped me walking. All my family come here on Monday to stop three or four weeks, and then I shall go back to the great establishment, and stay a fortnight; so that if I can keep my spirits, I shall stay eight weeks here, and thus give hydropathy a fair chance. Before starting here I was in an awful state of stomach, strength, temper and spirits. My book has been completely finished some little time.

Our motives are to be made known the laws which regulate health; the modes by which diseases are cured; and the conditions by which they are to be prevented. Our aim is to enlighten society generally on these points, so that they may clearly see and fully comprehend the uncertainty, the complexity, and the dangerousness of the drug art, as now practised in our cities, towns and villages – an art at once destructive to the patients and demoralising to the practitioner – no holiday task. The water cure is a *fact*, which no misrepresentations, no virulence, and no assertions, however unscrupulous, can annul. – In spite of the calumnies of the profession, and the deep-rooted prejudices of the public, we have no less than fifteen hydropathic establishments in Great Britain. What in 1841 was called "a nine days' wonder", "a passing quackery", "an ephemeral humbug", is now pronounced to be a system founded on laws acknowledged to be true by the greatest minds labouring the sciences of physiology and organic chemistry.

By the by supper was announced and a pleasant chat with new arrivals

Indian generals colonels administrators London and Edinburgh lawyers Liverpool and Glasgow merchants Manchester and Leeds manufacturers American consuls travellers Australian squatters gold miners Town and country rectors Heads of colleges medical men Artists authors literati old English gentlemen Wives mothers sisters daughters cousins and fair friends.

Under the term, Water Cure – a term unhappily chosen, but one which custom now requires us to employ – we shall explain how it is that natural stimuli remove diseased actions. *The effective curative agent in diseases is emphatically the energy which we term the VITAL FORCES – that Energy of Life, which assimilates external matter with our organism, and sustains its complex functions. The principle, be it observed, involves no theory regarding the ultimate nature of the VITAL FORCE – it* assumes that there *is such* a power; and that an agency which, within the realm of nature, plays so distinguished a part, must be, and actually *is*, endowed with the strength enough to carry out its proper purpose, to sweep away obstacles which menace and withstand these, and to repair the wrongs and injuries occasioned by the accidental interference of any conflicting energy. This capacity to repair, has been termed the *vis medicatrix*, or the curative power of Nature. This *vis medicatrix* is not any separate or substantive power, whose especial duty it is to watch over and amend; it is, on the contrary, merely an expression for the persistency of the vital force itself. By the speciality of his being man is elevated into the guardian of himself; but for that very reason, he may do wrong, thwart the laws of his existence, and insure disarrangement and misery. Not over the character of the VITAL FORCE, but over the circumstances essential to its free action. To prevent the occurrence of such faults our only resource is a *healing art*, varied in its appliances, though simple and direct in its aims.

Half past six – that indefatigable immerser of humanity John arrived armed with a pail of hot water and a sheet huge and white which he unfolded as if meaning business. He quickly turned the tap, dashed the pail of hot water into the bath stirred the mingling current and refilled his pail with the tempered fluid.

All preparations made I was into the water in a trice, John saluting my neck and shoulders with the contents of his pail.

Every morning he came in unannounced, carrying two tin buckets, with his shirt sleeves turned up and an immense linen sheet flung over his shoulders. He emptied the water in a slipper bath, brought in like a coffin on his head, and then without the smallest ceremony, pulled all the clothes off me, until I was obliged in self defence to jump out of bed.

No sooner had I than this rascal spread a large blanket on the mattress, threw his rascally wet sheet over it, adjusting it with as much nicety and care as if he was preparing me for a delicious bed of roses. The moment he gave the signal I bounced on the bed with a shout, raised the house and flinging myself down was immediately enveloped.

It was so odd, to have a great fellow with hands as hard as horn, rubbing away at your back, whilst you were occupied in the same manner in front – rubbing I say as if human backs were made of Babylon brick . . . a wet bandage was then folded tight around my body, from the pit of my stomach to the pelvic bones, and dressing quickly I went up to the hills to the well, where I swallowed two or three tumblers of water; and after an hour's walk returned to breakfast with the appetite of a wolf.

At a quarter to eight a bell sounds through the corridors and another more powerful is rung on the outside of the house and these are rung as warning bells to quicken the lazy who are still in their bed-rooms, and to gather the stragglers who may be scattered through the grounds. A second bell at eight intimates that breakfast is on the table; the stairs, corridors and entrance hall are crowded with streams of hungry inmates.

The fare at breakfast is plain, nutritious, and abundant. Tea, Cocoa, and Coffee are the beverages, while Eggs, Bread and Cold Meat are the more solid, and substantial viands. The breakfast occupies nearly three quarters of an hour. At a quarter to nine another bell is rung. It intimates the gathering to a feast of a very different kind. At that hour the Doctor assumes the character of Chaplain of his household, and his patients and visitors belonging to different denominations and secular professions assemble to hear a portion of the scriptures read and kneel before the Shrine of their common Heavenly Father.

The religious service being over, the consultation begins. This is held in a small room adjacent to the Drawing Room. Male and female patients have precedence on alternate days and are summoned from the Drawing Room, in rotation ruled by the length of time they have spent in the Establishment. The consultation takes place between the hours of 9 a.m. and noon, except Monday, when Dr Macleod will visit the gentlemen in their bed-rooms, between the hours of 5 and 6 a.m., and consult with the ladies at his usual time in his consulting room. On his first arrival each patient is furnished with a blank book. This he takes with him, to the Consulting Room, and on this the Doctor records the baths for the current day and the one required the following morning.

A. E. aged 43 married; vasculo-nervous temperament. Had when young a good constitution. Took high honours at Oxford. Had been a severe student while there, and for two years after he left it used to study fifteen hours a day. At length he became nervous and his bowels very much constipated. For this latter complaint he took a compound colocynth pill, – at first once a week, then twice a week, then every other night, then at length every night. His stomach became deranged, and his physician prescribed for him tonics, and blue pill with a purgative in the morning.

"My memory now became very bad, my head confused; a misty veil seemed to extend over the front of my brain. I went and travelled East but with no benefit. I then tried several baths on the Continent, but with just as little advantage. In Naples I was recommended by an English lady to take some patent pills, which she stated had done her much good. I took them, and at first I derived benefit from their use. Indeed, I fancied I was to be well in no time. My head felt clearer, my strength was better, and my spirits lighter. I continued taking these pills every night for about two months, when they began to lose their effect. I increased the dose and once more I felt myself improving. I continued to increase the dose, until I took thirty every night. At last it became so troublesome to swallow the pills, that I had them dissolved in about the fourth part of a breakfast cup-full of water, and in this way I took my dose every night. I persevered in this treatment for fully two years during which time I took fifteen thousand pills. I gradually became worse, and now I am miserable and useless. I dare not read my Bible, or hear it read, my thoughts are so bad. I dare not tell them to you. I do not sleep over two hours at night, and then my sleep is restless, and my dreams frightful. My life is a misery to me. All good seems to have left my soul. My thoughts pour through my brain like water through a hole in a barrel – I have no power over them."

Tongue pale, soft, swelled, and covered with a thickish white fur. He had a bad taste in his mouth in the morning. Appetite variable; sometimes voracious, and at other times he had none at all. Had great flatulency and acidity of stomach. Bowels never opened without medicine. Enemas had no effect upon them.

This gentleman underwent a course of hydro-therapeutic treatment for a lengthened period. During the first three months he scarcely improved at all. But at the end of them he had a severe diarrhoea for four days. It commenced suddenly and stopped as suddenly. The odour from the matter evacuated was horribly offensive. After the diarrhoea he felt a great deal better in his bowels and stomach; but the head symptoms in were no way improved. Four weeks afterwards, an eruption came out under his abdominal compress. The odour from this eruption was exactly similar to that of the vapour of aloes and scammony; and his compress became filled with a substance having a similar smell. So great was the quantity of matter eliminated, and so strong the odour, that the patient was obliged to rinse out his compress every hour; and every time he did so, a dark brown substance, like lightish coloured finely ground clay, remained at the bottom of the basin. At the end of the fourth day the secretion had very much diminished; and on the seventh day, it had entirely disappeared. This foetid matter was extracted by the abdominal compress about every five weeks, for several months. After that time, large boils began to break out on different parts of the body, and they continued to appear for about three months. The pus of these boils had an offensive odour, was thick, and of a darkish green colour. The patient now felt himself well. His appetite was good. The dyspeptic symptoms had disappeared; the bowels operated of themselves daily. The head symptoms were greatly improved. He could now read his Bible with comfort. This gentleman, fearful of a relapse, remained under my care for months after he was apparently cured. Before he left Ben Rhydding, the head symptoms, and the uncomfortable ideas had entirely disappeared. His memory became gradually stronger and stronger. At present he holds a living in the Church of England, and performs his duties vigorously, and with comfort to himself.

1. THE AFFUSION – The Patient sits in an empty bath or tub, and water is poured on his neck and shoulders from a hand basin, or he is laved with soaked towels.

2. THE DRIPPING SHEET – The Patient stands in an empty bath, or with the feet in two or three inches of warm water, while the attendant, lifting from his pail a sheet dripping with water, covers him with it, and rubs vigorously behind, while the patient rubs with what vigour he has in front. The sheet is speedily warmed when it is thrown aside, and the patient enveloped in a dry sheet, when the rubbing process is renewed. Of great value in colds, fatigues and languor and debility. A great favourite of Priessnitz *who used it almost in every case.*

3. THE SHALLOW BATH – which the Patient is given in an ordinary slipper bath, five feet long, the depth of water varying from two to six inches. The patient sits in the bath with legs extended, while the attendant throws one or two pails of water over the head and shoulders. Body and limbs having thereafter been well splashed and rubbed for perhaps two minutes, the patient steps out to be dried and rubbed as usual.

After every bath, patients should dress themselves as speedily as possible, and take active exercise in the open air for a considerable time. Gentlemen should defer shaving till their return from their early morning walk. Ladies are especially requested to attend to these remarks.

After breakfast prayers and after the doctor's levee, which I attended for advice, I began to ramble. The houses of the village are mostly boarding houses; and one may lodge here for any sum between 8s. and £3 per week. July and August are the most fashionable months of the place although no people of fashion go to it. It is the spa of the middle and working classes without the excitements which usually belong to such resorts. For so far as amusements are concerned, Ilkley is dull enough, neither social parties, balls, nor concerts. Everyone amuses himself in his own way and no one is particularly anxious to become acquainted with the other.

A broad and shallow brook flows through the village, down the Main Street from the Moorlands. In this street are two temporary Bazaars, where children buy drums and penny whistles to split the ears of the sick men lying in chambers of the houses where these little Joshuas also reside. One of these Marts, close to the bridge at the end of the street is kept by an Italian, who sold me, I remember, some English cabbage leaves rolled together, for foreign Havana cigars. This man is an Italian, you see him all day long, when he is not busy with his customers, making artificial flies, mending tackle – standing in his shirt sleeves smoking a huge Turkey pipe, with one hand thrust deep into his breeches pocket and a great hairy cap on his head. When he first came to England he used to travel with French baskets; and as his fortune increased he bought a stock of fancy goods and attended fairs. Of late he has adopted Ilkley as his own market town, and resides there all the season.

The visitors wander up and down the streets draped in all varieties of male and female costume, taking no notice of each other. Troops of donkeys, with children in panniers, stout buxom girls, old men, and invalids mounted upon them – who solemnly pass you, like a procession through some May fair in the March of Death: that is to say unless one of the asses should happen to prove refractory and refuses to go, or bending his stubborn neck throw his rider with a triumphant He-haw, and then a loud burst of laughter dissolves the solemnity of the scene, and renders it a little more human

C. Darwin to L. Jenyns Ilkley Nov 13th 1859

My Dear Jenyns,

I have been much out of health this summer, and have been hydropathising here for the last six weeks with very little good as yet. I shall stay here for another fortnight at least.

Please remember that my book is only an abstract and very much condensed, and to be at all intelligible, must be carefully read . . . I know perfectly well that you will not at all agree with the lengths which I go. It took long years to convert me.

I fear this note will be almost illegible; but I am poorly, and can hardly sit up. Farewell; with thanks for your kind note, and pleasant remembrance of good old days.

The Compressed-Air Bath is a chamber constructed of iron plates riveted together like those of the boiler of a steam engine, so as to be perfectly air-tight. It is provided with a close-fitting door, and several small windows, each of a single piece of plate glass, strong enough to resist a much greater pressure than that of the compressed-air. A steam engine, of power proportioned to the size of the chamber, works a pair of force-pumps, which communicates indirectly with the chamber by a pipe opening under its floor, which is pierced with numerous small apertures, so that the air may enter with as little noise as possible. As a general rule, the pressure is raised about the ½ of an atmosphere, that is, about 7½ lbs per square inch above the ordinary pressure of the air. This is done at the rate of one pound in four minutes, the rarefication taking place at the same rate. The duration of the bath and the amount of pressure, however, require to be regulated by a regard to the character of the disease, the organ in which it is situated, the vital force of the patient, and the condition of the nervous system.

The interior, which is lined with wood, is furnished with seats, a couch for the weak patients, means of communication with the attendant by a bell or whistle, and a contrivance for passing in and out small articles, such as letters, without disturbing the pressure of air inside. Though they get more than the usual supply of air, they are required to be quiet and grave when under its influence, for the direction runs: – 'Parties not to laugh or discuss in the Air-bath!'

My Dear Sir,

(I have got a bad finger, which makes me write extra badly.) If you are so inclined, I should very much like to hear your general impression. Remember it is only an abstract, and very much condensed. God knows what the public will think.

I have not seen one naturalist for six or nine months, owing to the state of my health, and therefore I really have no news to tell you, I am writing this at Ilkley Wells, where I have been with my family for the last six weeks and shall stay for some few weeks longer. As yet I have profited very little. God knows when I shall have strength for my bigger book.

The animal frame is a vast chemical workshop – decomposition and composition going on within incessantly, so that, at the close of a certain cycle or period, every organised body . . . literally becomes new. The time required for molecular renovation depends . . . with regard to the individual with the energy of activity of his vitality. The body of a man in fullest vigour, for instance, will be decomposed or consumed, and of course replaced, in one half the time necessary for the corresponding process in a languid, low pulsed individual . . . Whatever increases vital action and sustains that novel vigour, must, therefore, be regarded as *therapeutic*, or hostile to the permanence of specific derangements. Little matter it, in such a case, what may be the disease. Let him have a liver, old and flabby and present the appearance rather of a mummy than of Man; no matter, the wheels of the machine are busy and unless for some unforeseen check, the rage he is groaning over shall be transformed into their elements, dispersed and replaced. I refer, in evidence, to what is called a CRISIS in hydropathy.

A. B., aged forty, of slim make and nervous temperament. When a young man, went out to India as a cadet. Soon after his landing there he had a very severe attack of dysentery. To stop the progress of the disease, large doses of mercury were prescribed in rapid succession. He recovered; but in a few months afterwards had an attack of yellow fever. Again mercury was prescribed frequently, and in large doses.

(Nothing can be more pitiable than the condition of a man who has become victim of reckless and improper mercurial treatment. The slightest variation in the weather affects him. Cold or damp weather brings upon him pain of body and distress of mind. If he stirs abroad, he must be wrapped up, and sheltered from every wind that blows. At home equal precautions must be taken; for often, unless a hot-house temperature is taken up, he is absolutely miserable.)

I placed him under a mild course of hydro-therapeutic treatment; he became stronger; his appetite returned, and his bowels were moving naturally. On the evening of the seventh week I was called to see him, as he did not feel well at all: his spirits became much depressed; he wept like a child, and all hope of cure seemed to be extinguished within. On the evening of the second day of this attack, a slight odour was perceived to come from his person. On the following morning the odour had become offensive. It was unmistakably the odour of salivation, and as offensive as I had ever perceived in any patient. Saliva began to pour from his mouth, and jug after jug was filled with it. He continued in this state for three days, when the salivation began gradually to decrease; and in a week it entirely disappeared. After the termination of the attack, he had for a while those joyous spirits which belong more to childhood than mature age. Such unalloyed sensations he had not felt since his return from India.

C. Darwin to W. D. Fox Ilkley Nov. 16th 1859

. . . I like the place very much, and the children have enjoyed it very much, and it has done my wife good. It did H good at first, but she has gone back again. I have had a series of calamities; first a sprained ankle, then a badly swollen whole leg and face, much rash, and a frightful succession of boils – four or five at once. I have felt quite ill, and have little faith in this "unique crisis" as the doctor calls it doing me much good.

Merchants, Agriculturists, Soldiers, Sheriffs, Edinburgh writers to the *Signet*, London Barristers, Solicitors, Episcopalian Clergy, English and Scotch Dissenters, Ministers of the National and Free Churches of Scotland, East Indian Nabobs, and lively, laughing, tricky sons of Erin go bragh are all mingled together, in the amusement of the Drawing Room, or the more serious employment of the Dining Table.

Two tables are required to accommodate all running parallel with each other. The person who has arrived last is placed at the bottom of the second table. As parties depart he gradually ascends towards the head of this table, which having reached he is transferred to the other table and ascends there according to the same rules. Fare is abundant. Soup and fish two, three days a week. While on other days joints and saddles of mutton, roasts of beef varied by fowls, cutlets, beefsteaks. Abundance of veg and puddings of every kind. Patients should not eat to excess, should rest a quarter of an hour before each meal and should undergo no hydropathic treatment for at least an hour and a half after a meal.

The company is again dispersed. The ladies retire to the drawing room or their own apartments. The gentlemen desport, some of them to the Library, others to the Billiard Room, while the more languid seek repose on the couch or large chair in the bed-room. In the patients' case the afternoon bath looms in the distance. To prepare for this, whether the Sitz, Rain or Roman Bath be prescribed, exercise is again demanded, and accordingly we see patients walking as if for a wager, and they do tell us, to use a Ben Rhydding expression, that they are "getting up the steam" for the afternoon manipulation.

4. THE DOUCHE is a column of water two or three inches in diameter, descending from a height of twelve or fifteen feet, and made to fall aslant on the shoulders and along

the spine. It is an appliance of such power and peril that it is not used at all at Ben Rhydding. The 'Wave' and 'Spouting' Douches are, however in constant requisition. The Wave douche is a horizontal 'gush' of water like a small cascade before which the patient places himself and turns as he pleases. The spouting douche is a horizontal jet from a flexible tube and can be directed on any part of the body. The back, chest and throat are frequently subjected to this douche: the patient merely taking off his upper garments, and with a waterproof sheet to protect the nether – great use in chest and throat complaints, stiff joints, sprains.

5. THE SITZ BATH – An ordinary tub will do for this bath, but in the more convenient form the patient sits down in water of sufficient depth to cover the abdomen, having his shoulder covered by a blanket. The sitting is prolonged ten, twenty, thirty minutes, according as the bath is intended for a tonic, an aperient, or a derivative. The effect is manifest in the redness of the parts immersed after the patient rises and the tone imparted by a shorter one, the relief to the bowels by a longer one, and to the head by a still longer one. A short running sitz, with its constant ingress of fresh cold water by one aperture and an egress of the heated water by another is an incomparable tonic to stomach, bowels, liver, womb, spine and all parts subjected to its action.

6. THE WET SHEET ENVELOPE – On the patient's bed, covered by a single blanket, is smoothly spread a coarse linen sheet which has been soaked and wrung out. On this sheet the patient lies down on his back, and the attendant wraps it firmly round his body. Over this the blanket is firmly tucked in in like manner, great care being taken to prevent evaporation. A down or feather bed is then placed on the whole and tucked well under to effectually retain warmth. The body creates its own warmth. A gentle moisture next shows itself and at the expiration of three quarters of an hour the patient is taken out to undergo the prescribed

form of ablution, which will be more or less powerful according to the condition of his body. It relieves internal congestion, and thus is of first rate importance in chronic diseases. Its poultice like properties serve to eliminate foreign and effete elements from the system, as the slimy condition of the sheet when taken off, and its offensive odour of aloes, scammony, or whatever other drug the patient has been in habit of saturating his system with, bears witness.

C. Darwin to J. D. Hooker Ilkley Sunday Nov. 1859

My Dear Hooker,

I have just read a review of my book in the *Athenaeum*, and it excites my curiosity much who is the author. I fear from the tone of the review that I have written in a conceited and cock-sure style. There is another review in the *Gardeners Chronicle*. Some of the remarks are like yours, and he does deserve punishment, but surely the review is too severe. Don't you think so?

I shall stay here one fortnight more, and then go to Down. I have been very unfortunate; out of seven weeks I have been confined for five to the house. This has been bad for me, as I have not been able to help thinking to a foolish extent about my book. I long to hear what Huxley thinks . . . I am very bothersome, farewell.

About five o'clock the afternoon treatment is over and the mail arrives, bringing letters and the London papers of the morning, duplicate copies of the *Times, Telegraph*, besides private supplies, British and Colonial, to enliven the waning hours.

From T. H. Huxley Nov 23rd

My Dear Darwin,

I finished your book yesterday, a lucky examination having furnished me with a few hours of continuous leisure. Since I read von Bar's essays nine years ago, no work on Natural History or Science I have met with has made so great an impression upon me . . . Nothing, I think, can better the tone of the book, it impresses those who know nothing about the subject. As for your doctrine I am prepared to go to the stake, if requisite, in support of Chapter IX., and most parts of Chapters X., XI., XII.

I trust you will not allow yourself to be in any way disgusted or annoyed by the considerable abuse and misrepresentation which, unless I greatly mistake, is in store for you. Depend upon it you have earned the lasting gratitude of all thoughtful men. And as to the curs which will bark and yelp, you must recollect that some of your friends, at any rate, are endowed with an amount of combativeness which (though you have often and justly rebuked it) may well stand you in good stead.

I am sharpening up my claws in readiness.

Ever yours faithfully T. H. Huxley

November 24th 1859. First edition published, and all copies sold first day.

C. Darwin to T. H. Huxley Nov. 25th

My Dear Huxley,

Your letter has been forwarded to me from Down. Like a good Catholic who has received extreme unction I can now sing 'nunc dimittis'. I should have been more than contented with one quarter of what you have said. Exactly fifteen months ago, when I put pen to paper for this volume, I had awful misgivings, and thought perhaps I had deluded myself . . . and then I fixed in my mind three judges on whose decision I determined mentally to abide . . . Lyell, Hooker, and yourself.

At length seven o'clock arrives. The bell is heard once more, and thus intimation given, that Tea, Cocoa and Toast are on the table. At this meal we may observe, that evening dress, though not enjoined, is expected, at least in the case of those who intend to join the party in the Drawing Room. In this room every kind of in-door amusement, with the exception of cards, is afforded – Draughts and Backgammon, Chess and Squails are at hand. Instrumental and Vocal music and the merry reel and country dance, gratify the ear, cheer the heart, and while the time away. At nine p.m. a waiter introduces the Ben Rhydding supper. It is in keeping with the character of the place, consisting of a glass of cool and clear water. By ten the Butler enters with stately and dignified air and extinguishing five out of the six gaslights, which had previously illuminated the apartment, gives a broad hint that the hour for separation is nigh. The gentlemen either descend to the Reading Room or gather in small committees to laugh or argue another hour away. 'Tis only another hour that they have. By eleven the gas is turned off. Bedrooms, Public Rooms and passages are plunged into darkness and thus ends a week day's routine at Ben Rhydding.

CURIOUS PHENOMENON

A patient at Ben Rhydding, looking out from his bed-room window soon after ten o'clock at night, has on more than one occasion been surprised to see certain luminous spots moving about at an uncertain rate, and in various directions, at a distance of from five to six feet above the ground. Their general direction was to and fro along the terrace, but they sometimes extended to the bowling green and gymnasium. They vanished when on one occasion the patient endeavoured to approach them, leaving a disagreeable odour behind. It has been suggested that both luminous spots and the odour are attributable to lighted Cigars; but this is impossible, as all Smoking is strictly forbidden in Dr Macleod's Establishment.

In 1859 the *Origin of Species* was published and my father got terribly overdone and ill. When the book was finally off his hands he went to the water-cure establishment at Ilkley and we followed on Oct. 17th. It was a miserable time, bitterly cold, he was extremely ill and suffering, and I also was ill, the lodgings were wretched. I look back upon it as a time of frozen horror.

Mr Priessnitz went after breakfast to visit his patients at Freiwadau, and while there perceived a numbness and loss of his right arm; but made light of the warning, for on his return home he took the cold bath, and went to dinner. Immediately after, he was found in a state of insensibility at the door of his secretary's room. His breast and feet were immediately chaffed with hands wetted in cold water, and, in a few minutes, a shallow tepid bath having been prepared, he was placed therein by his secretary, Herr Bohm.

In this bath Mr Priessnitz was rubbed for half an hour by eight men, and cold effusion was also repeatedly applied to the head. Having shown signs of returning consciousness, he was taken out of the bath, and placed upon the bed, where he had a relapse, but not of so long duration as the first attack. He was again rubbed in the shallow tepid bath as before, and when taken out of it and replaced in bed, fell asleep, and slept for twelve hours, at the end of which time he returned to consciousness.

For a week afterwards he took thrice daily, three successive wet sheet packings, followed each time by the shallow tepid bath. For another week he took every morning the shallow tepid bath and the cold bath in combination, – that is, going repeatedly from one to the other, beginning and ending with the tepid bath.

The next day he went to Johannesburg on business. The day was cold and foggy. He returned late, chilled. He got up several times and in order to get warm after a cold bath went to saw some wood. His wife and daughters were worried. 'Do not fret, my beloved ones. I shall get well again. Is there not a God in heaven and cold water to help me?' Growing weaker his wife, fearing the worst, asked if he wanted to see a doctor. 'No,' he answered, clear and determined. On Nov 28th he again wanted to go downstairs to saw some wood after a cold bath but yielding to his wife's entreaties allowed the wood and the sawing material to be brought into his sitting room. At about nine o'clock he went once more into the sawing room to warm himself but soon pushed it aside saying, 'Take that away I shall not require it anymore.' These pathetic words made a painful impression on the assembled family. At two o'clock again the wife asked if he wanted a doctor. Again no. A few minutes to four he got up from the couch, dressed himself in a long warm gown and sitting upright looked out on the beautiful hillside woods which he loved his whole life. A little later he shivered and asked to be rubbed with a wet sheet, and went back to his bed. Scarcely had he been placed in the horizontal position when his face and hands convulsed. Priessnitz was dead.

ILKLEY (6)

Bite into the hard rock of Ilkley; water lies at its sweet centre. In the spring of '52 they round up the water, the men of trade, and form a company, Ilkley Waterworks, directors William Bolling (property), Edward Usher (parish overseer), Francis Dobson (carrier), Edward Hudson (lodging house keeper), George Brumfit (coach proprietor), other members including Dr Rischanek, Ben Rhydding's embittered first physician long since ousted, who still wants to dip his hands into the stuff one way or another and build a covered reservoir on the moor. Four years later, directly below it, the first of the other hydros throws up its head, the dominant square splendour of Wells House, where Darwin first stayed, with its bowling alleys and skating rink, its badminton and croquet lawns; in '59 comes Craiglands, built by the first Dobson, Michael, and run by his sons Jabez and Henry; four years later, in between the two, their poorer relative, the Troutbeck; all of them, like the distant palace of Ben Rhydding, built on the out-skirts of the town, on the edge of the moor, as if, despite hydropathy's growing success, there is still the breath of the heathen about them, as if their covered arcades, their gymnasiums and frigidariums, their marble floors, their assistants with their wooden sandals and flowing white togas are altogether too Roman, too idolatrous for plain folk; but then, as their wealth trickled down, their outlook more familiar, their grip strengthened and they moved in closer, to consolidate their hold, Stoney Lea on Cowpasture Road, Marlborough House on Clifton Road to the east, and most insidious of all, the Spa Hydro, sitting with its French château turrets on the very lap of Ilkley's most respectable skirt, the Grove, and from which, in recognition of this matronly honour, it took its first name, the Grove Hydropathic.

Water is enclosed now, ruled and regulated. Brook Street's little stream running down the middle, with its wild flowers, its primroses, its columbines growing on its mossy banks, is covered over, the little footbridge dismantled, the stepping stones at the bottom, running like a dotted line before the tear of Church Street, dug up. The barns and cottages go too, a line of domestics on one side (where soon commerce would come knocking), a terrace on the other; John Wilde draper and next door Ilkley's own newspaper proprietor and picture-taker, John Shuttleworth, taking money from his first customers. They build it wide, Brook Street, wider than a street of such a town as this should be, its gaze across enormous, as if it is trying to mirror the long space it has at either end, at the top, ending where the steeper slopes to the moor begin, at the bottom, the slide down to the Wharfe.

Now the Middletons begin to loosen their ties, Peter Middleton, fierce guardian of what was his, dying and his eldest son William Joseph setting out with the first parcel of land to sell. '65 he inherits, the same year as the railway reaches in, and '67 the first sale; the land freed for building. And it needs building now, for though the hydro has brought the town visitors, people to amble up the street and buy their pennyworth of goods and who are accredited in Shuttleworth's paper as Court guests are in the *Times*, this water, fluid substance that it is, cannot set its guests into town permanence, and provide residence. That comes with the railway. That comes with the warp and the woof of wool. That comes with dirty Bradford.

Bradford

ERASMUS DARWIN

From *The Botanic Garden*

CANTO II

Inventress of the Woof, fair LINA flings
The flying shuttle through the dancing strings;
Inlays the broider'd weft with flowery dyes,
Quick beats the reeds, the pedals fall and rise;
Slow from the beam, the lengths of warp unwind,
And dance and nod the massy weights behind. –

Taught by her labours, from the fertile soil
Immortal Isis clothed the banks of Nile;
And fair Arachne with her rival loom
Found undeserved a melancholy doom –
Five Sister-nymphs with dewy fingers twine
The beany flax and stretch the fibre line.

So now, where Derwent rolls his dusky floods
Through vaulted mountains, and a night of woods,
The Nymph Gossypia treads a velvet sod,
And warms with rosy smiles the watery God;
His ponderous oars to slender spindles turns,
And pours o'er massy wheels his foamy urns;
With playful charms his hoary lover wins,
And wields his trident, – while the Monarch spins.
– First with nice eye emerging Naiads cull
From leathery pods the vegetable wool;
With wiry teeth *revolving cards* release
The tangled knots, and smooth the ravell'd fleece;
Next moves the *iron hand* with fingers fine,
Combs the wide card, and forms the eternal line,
Slow, with soft lips, the *whirling Can* acquires
The tender skeins and wraps its rising spires;
With quicken'd pace *successive rollers* move,
And these retain, and those extend the *rove*;
Then fly the spooles, the rapid axles glow,
And slowly circumvolves the labouring wheel below.

They had seemed so benign then, those machines, flowing silver
thread like the river below, to help the crofter and his wife, to make
their life easier; the poet could see that, see the stuff they made, as
fine as nature's silks, the fair Jenny at her lathe, spinning patiently,
her hair cascading down her back, her children playing at her feet.
He did not see the child dragged into the machine's arms, the mother
too, the family carried away whole into its dark domain.

Sept 13th. Rode through a most beautiful country to Otley. The roads in many places for a mile or two scarcely passable, the first four miles from Rochdale excessively bad, two miles in the middle between Halifax and Bradford excessively bad, a mile down to the bridge over the Aire, between Bradford and Otley, these parts are the worse, but it is a matter of great surprise that the whole of the road should be in such indifferent repair and some execrably bad through the whole of this manufacturing district, that the whole and sole cause where the road is not pitched is the not letting the water off or breaking the stones and that the whole distance from Congleton to Otley there were not twenty persons employed in either of these occupations, notwithstanding they tell you half the people are out of employ and every three miles at furthest there is a shilling turnpike for a chaise and pair. The environs of Rochdale, Ripponden, Halifax, Bradford, the bridge over the Aire and Otley are beautiful in the extreme were it not for the reflection that the greatness of Great Britain depended I may say principally on the defacing of the hand of nature in these parts by the hand of man, which produces not only riches in every way from exportation and taxation at home and raises in time of war an innumerable population which is seen over the whole district for the armies. One could not help regretting that scenes so romantic and lovely should be impaired and destroyed by the black steam engines, by the yarn, the cloth, the cotton, the morals of the people destroyed by being crowded together and the hammer of the water engine perpetually affrighting quiet and comfort from valleys which at first view one would imagine were placed by nature in the most remote and sequestered regions for the peculiar residence of innocence and peace. The seats or rather the villas of the manufacturers like the citizens in the neighbourhood of London have neatness to recommend them, but scarcely any character through the whole district that distinguishes one very much from another.

A need to move then.

Before Beeching's hired vandalism (compare his promissory notes of national destruction with the small change of smashed telephone kiosks and ripped cinema seats that were the new arrivals in those deserted stations) only the moors of Smilesworth and Spainton and high table land from which the Wharfe, the Nidd and the Ure spring were immune from steam's approach (yet they could hear its call, see its mouth whisper below). 1834 Leeds to Selby, and from then on an outbreak of rail fever, the north as infected as the rest of the country, delirious in their dreaming, waving schemes, issuing bonds, enticing money into its feckless embrace.

November 30th 1845 was fixed by the Board of Trade as the final day for receiving proposals for new railways. Notice was given that all plans lodged before midnight would be attended to. From early light they came, prospectors all, a thousand madcap schemes in their bulging pockets and imploring hands; blocked the corridors and stairways, pushing their way in the great sanctity of office thrusting their papers upon whatever desk or bewildered clerk they could find, all day without relief until the last gasp of midnight rang. But still they came, those who had missed the deadline, demented in their determination, forcing their proposals through whatever gaps they could find, under closed doors, through keyholes, tossed through an unguarded window, only to see them thrown back at them into the open street.

It took three tries to toe this line, three tries and twice as many companies, Leeds & Thirsk, Leeds & Bradford, Lancashire & Yorkshire North Eastern, Wharfdale Mark I, Wharfedale Mark II, before the Midland and the North Eastern hung up their differences and joined forces and built the cumbersome triangle that connected Ilkley with Leeds and Bradford. Men died in its construction, as men died on most constructions (as if the blood of them is the sacrificial ingredient needed to fix the mortar on these cakes), two in the deep Milnerwood cutting where the line climbs 1 in 197, Michael McBay buried by earth, Richard Holt struck by rock, the third man Thomas Scott run over by a tip wagon out of Otley; five hundred men blasting and digging in the ferocious wet weather, the land unwieldy and treacherous, covering a week's work in sudden landslides. 1865. The first train arrives and under its steamy spell the first lamppost is lit too, shining on the rough of the town, illuminating the sumps, the drains, the unholy meanness of the place.

Leeds had the better of it to start with, six North Eastern trains per day, through Arthington Pool and Otley (the wooden shack at Ben Rhydding still being hammered at), with the Midland pulling up five trains from Leeds and Bradford via Guiseley, but it was Bradford that lay closer to Ilkley's heart, the Aire that ran on the other side of Rombalds, the public house Dick Hudson's that lay at the foot of that moor where working men would sink great draughts of fuel as a train might drink its fill, before setting out across the moor to this distant relative, Bingley that could be seen, Bradford that could be heard, great growing Bradford flexing its muscle (1780, pop. 4,506; 1835, pop. 52,493), Bradford with its press of merchants, its close Germanic streets, Bradford, like Ilkley, with a temple to its own god, the Wool Exchange built one year before this railway line, adorned with biblical pillars and idolatrous statues, its congregation moving amongst themselves in their uniform moustaches and top hats, their language unintelligible save to the initiate, deals done with the shake of a bargaining hand. While Ilkley has been purifying its visitors, removing the bile that silted up whole lives, Bradford has been beating another lesson on its penitents' backs. Ilkley pours out water, Bradford pours out cloth. There was a new thundering now seemingly ceaseless like the water bursting from the Strid, clanking and clattering the day and the night, and like the water both cruel and wonderful, drawing one close to the soul of its spindle heart as if life could not be lived without it. The machine walked upon the land now, not singly but in regiments, as a conquering army, a new Rome, a new authority, with governors and proud generals to command, which demanded your tribe's allegiance, which carried you away from all you had known, transported you to a galley ship you could have never imagined, its oars blades of iron and overseers to whip you along, and you the slave, chained fifteen hours at a stretch to its deadening rhythm, reshaping your limbs, deafening your ears, trampling upon fingers, arms and legs, where you fell asleep exhausted at its side and where in the deperate hours of your rest, thrown down one and all into hold awash with your own filth, knowing that your world was gone, that there was no peace, no salvation, you fell upon one another in drink and despair, coupling as you might upon the same sodden bed, these children dropped and thrown into the beast's embrace, to be raised as offspring of its own. Bradford the steam, Bradford the engine, Bradford the iron, the coal and the cloth: Bradford the colliery, Bradford the foundry, Bradford the land of mills: Bradford the smallpox, Bradford the typhus, Bradford the canal thick with cholera: Bradford the deaf, Bradford the orphaned, Bradford father to the maimed and the crippled: Bradford where as Titus Salt observed 'iniquity runneth down the street, like water'. This is what the mullahs of industry came down to teach, that land was to be held in contempt and demonstrated as of no worth. And thus those brought in to settle upon it, to grow on Bradford's soil and teach this Bradford scripture were costed in like value (until others came riding in, the Donkey Jacks of religion and hope).

Sanitary Report of the Woolcombers 1845

Case 57. Family 11; rooms 2; beds 4; workers 5; females 5; coal; size 17ft by 15ft 4in. The extreme of filth and wretchedness; stagnant water near the dwelling: four persons work and sleep in a horrible hole seven feet below the surface. This case is beyond description.

William Pickles, fifteen years old, three foot nine inches in height, standing on legs bent both inwards and forwards. Got my knees bent with standing so long. Remember when my knees began to fail me; I had been at the mill not two years; it was at Anderson's; my knees hurt me very bad then; when we tired, you know, there was naught to sit on, was obliged to lay hold of someat to keep me up. It used to be very bad towards night; sometimes very sleepy; we used to get thumped sometimes by the overlooker, who was a woman; it was ten o'clock of the forenoon we used to get most thumped.

Alpaca and mohair, both grown in tropical or sub-tropical regions, high above sea level, with a dry and dusty soil: fallen fleeces (fleeces clipped from animals found dead and decomposing quickly) are slipped into the closely packed bales: unskilful clipping of the fleece also includes skin and blood of the animal:

on returning from his usual work complains that he does not feel very well. In such a case he may say at home that he has "opened a bad bag" whose offensive smell he noticed at the time. His wife observes he is perspiring freely. After a night characterised by profuse sweating, he gets up and goes to his work. He does not feel well but still, beyond the sweating, he is not conscious that there is anything much the matter with him. His mates notice that at work his breathing is rather hurried and the profuse sweating continues. After a few hours he feels that he can no longer work, "knocks off" and goes home. He changes his cold wet shirt, let us suppose for a dry one, and goes to bed, thinking that he will soon be all right. He is mistaken, however for soon he begins to suffer from a feeling of tightness across the chest, and now notices himself that his breathing is quick and difficult. He allows a mustard plaster to be applied to his chest, but finds that its weight is so distressing that it is speedily removed. He is at last persuaded to send for a doctor who finds him hopelessly ill. The man is in a state of collapse; his hands, feet, and forehead are cold and clammy with continuing sweat; his pulse is irregular. The surface heat of the body is lowered, although internally it is often increased; the breathing is very quick and laboured, the expression anxious, but the mind clear. There is no pain, nor shivering, nor thirst, nor vomiting, nor purging; nevertheless the man who was at his work a few hours ago is evidently dying.

– Dr Rabagliati M.A., M.D.
Honorary Surgeon to the Bradford Infirmary.

But there was money to be made here, but where to house it, where to give it a polish, put it on show, take it out for an afternoon's ride, where to build one's cloth castle? There were suburbs aplenty in Leeds, suburbs fit for this new wealth, far removed from the squalor below (or perhaps, with a distant view of it, in the haze of sunlight, and a taste in the wind too, to remind them what it was that gave them their wealth, their power, to see slavery's smoke). But there were no leafy shades in Bradford to wash their hands free of the smell of greasy wool, and fashion their own solidity. Not there, in the heart of the market place, besieged by the disease of the labouring classes.

They looked out over their newly planted forests of chimneys and from their cheap coal smoke saw the name of Ilkley writ black upon the sky. Back to the source from whence it came, back to the water and the land cleared by the sheep. Back to Ilkley.

So from Bradford, not Leeds, they came, these entrepreneurs, these owners, the managers, this new counting class, with their wives and their families and their ordinary pretensions, and in their luggage sack after sack of money, baggage cars filled to the very brim. Now, with the land freed up, the big houses are built, on wide residential streets, on the north side, up the west side from the Skipton Road, to the east and Ben Rhydding, on the upper Grove and all the roads leading up.

"We lived in a very big house in Wheatley Road called Burnside. The house had been built in 1876 by a Bradford mill owner and it was the most remarkably advanced in every way, ten bedrooms, two staircases, four stories. The basement was the same area as the house itself, it was huge. This was where the seven lavatories came in, 'cause the kitchen staff, just across the passage, went down steps to their lavatory, and the gardener had steps both on the east side and the west side down into the cellar, to save him walking all the way round. The heating apparatus was sunk into a pit so that if there was a burst it would not flood the whole area. My father told me it used a ton of coal a week, and outside every bathroom there was a shoot straight into the cellar for the laundry. There was a receptacle waiting on rubber tyred wheels which when full was led across into the copper boiler and from the copper boiler there were four basins with rubber squeegees in between them and then on the far side a drying chamber on the wall and all the washing was strung straight on to the drying chamber and then in another part of the laundry was where all the ironing went on."

laundry: not a word in Ilkley's earlier vocabulary

THE MOOR (5)

JOB SENIOR

His mother lived in Beckfoot and as a younger man he had worked in the fields ploughing and mowing and reaping. More importantly he was reckoned of his strength and his eye for stone, could lift rocks of great size, measure their momentum and the shape they might contain, and so built walls for farm and field that rose and fell with the lie of the land, stood against the weathers of the moor, kept their boundaries firm and the lie of them true: a man of stone then, who walked, like the giant before him, with rocks in his arms, a solitary man

(Ilkley is built for solitary folk. The idea of community, as opposed to civic regard, does not pertain. There is something solitudinous about the place, emphasized by the structure of those larger houses, the influence of those guarded stone porches and turret windows, above and below them the moor and the river, where one is borne away by thought; desolation, joy, resolve, it matters not which, nor in what company it occurs. And thus magnetized, some are drawn with terrible speed and complexity into their enveloping mass. Thus August 1914 Nurse Fletcher found in an isolated part of the moor above Highfield Hotel. Missing from July 31st, she was thought gone to Dewsbury but after her book and luggage were found a search was made of the moor. A shepherd found her lying in an old cart track exhausted and very ill. She had been on the moor for ten days and had managed to keep alive by drinking rainwater which she had caught in her shoe. Ten days unable to escape this open prison, ten days locked in the mind of the moor, moving day upon day, from light to dark, from human to beast, wandering across the burnt and soaking heather, crawling amongst jagged ruts, crouched against the shelter of stone, the savage shapes of her ancestors blind to her fingers, the town below, lit to be seen and heard too, and she in her own no-man's land, capable of only one descent, recognizing the simple need for water and the means by which a human may obtain it.

Job Senior came to Burley Woodhead and there grew dissolute as the length of his drinking and his years grew. He lived poor, employed scantily by farmers, his strength beginning to fail him, the waning of his years. When sixty he spied himself a wife. She was older than he by twenty years, and her name was Mary Barrett, a woman of means with a smallholding she had inherited from her first husband; and Job could see the shape of his future mapped by the lie of this land, by the deep walls of her stone cottage, by the productivity of her garden and the future bounty of the plot of land surrounding it, see how he might fit them together about him, the up and down of it and the boundary around, as he might, even in his faltering, walk on the moor by the light of his good fortune. So they married and she took him in, against the liking of her kinsmen, who saw what she possessed and what they would inherit pass into these unwashed hands.

But he was company, no doubt of that, could tell tales and sing miraculously in four sweet voices, alto, treble, tenor and bass, and to keep his throat just so he always took his water and his buttermilk warm and never washed, not even in marriage. When Mary died, for die she did, before him, as he had assumed, her relatives took the field, but Job managed to stave off the assault on the cottage. So here he lived, harassed by her kinsmen, growing potatoes in the small garden, his appearance, his wealth, his capability greatly diminished, a diet of starch and hops for sustenance. One evening, he returned late to find the dwelling lying broken in a heap of stones and her possessions, which he had thought his, gone. Too poor to summon the law he fell back on his old skill, no rafter of roofs or bundler of straw, but turned his back on his tormentors and built a cave out of the rubble, recognizing that which had been the parlour and pantry, that the stone above their bed, turning them inside out, to make rude protection against the wind and the rain and flurries of moor snow, but made it all the same, a shelter more than a dwelling.

And this they could not tear down, it was as a shrine or an altar, sacred and of the moor, its markings and its shape as mysterious and as powerful as the Swastika Stone, or any mark that finds itself upon this land, and when it was built he placed a meal bag over his shoulders and tied a belt about his waist and walked the moor, leaning on two crooked staves, one in each hand, each as crooked as his leaning legs, a pair of clogs on his feet with tops reaching to his knees and stuffed down with straw (as road tramps do with newspaper) and his coat so patched and mended it was as Lincoln's axe, no knowing where the coat began or where it ended or whether it was the shape alone that was true, walked the moor seeking alms, and in the getting of them took a practical view of his own discomfort, made play of it, sang boisterous songs and drank copiously, and became an entertainer, turning his life and his misfortune into a trade of sorts, the commodity his four voices and his bag of stories, and men would ride the moor to hear him, fill up barn and ale house, pay him his liquid price, and catch him when he fell, and place him on the straw on which he might sleep away the night and old memory.

But tricks are played on old befuddled men, what better sport than to make fun of a fool, and one evening they mixed his drink, spirits and beer and whatever other concoctions they dug out of the cupboard, stirred it up and poured it down, and though he wiped his front and smacked his lips, and sang his birdsongs, the lark and the plover and the cluck of the grouse, he quickly fell ill, and growing weaker was put up for a time in a barn at the back of the Wheatsheaf, before the parish sent him on to Otley, where he died aged seventy-seven.

They stopped the quarrying some years after, and Job Senior's cave was taken down by those same relatives, and the space where he lived rolled over. It stood only in his lifetime, and yet there is more thought for him now than many others who made the town. He kept its spirit, like Donkey Jack and other men of solitude, those who live on the edge of towns, its closest keepers. Their history is of itself, and lingers with the moving time. It is not simply in their defiance or the picture we hold of them, irascible and old, not the vanished romanticism of their discomfort, nor the attraction of their deliberate ignorance, the style of their dress and the manner of their coming and going, it is that there is no choice in the matter, to live in a huddle of stones, and to eat potatoes and to wander and be put upon a bed of straw. There are worse beds to be put upon and worse ways of passing your later years than walking across the moor, poor and miserable and three-quarters drunk. Half the houses in Ilkley are full of them, stuffed in the comfort of their single room, looking out.

Job Senior Died 1857

He would have seen Ilkley reach out, fearful and wary of its touch, like any other creature living there, heard the hammer blow breaking rocks, seen the men come up the moor to break the rock and carry it down for house and hotel, black smoke from blacker chimneys. Ilkley was changing, no time for songs from old crazy men. Let them roam the moor a few more years. But Ilkley needs pavements and drains, shops and shoppers. Ilkley needs regulations.

ILKLEY (7)

Yes, the town is growing now, growing fast, and there are men on its streets who want to further things, not simply their own lives and their own pockets, but in their conversations and the expressions of intent they regard Ilkley as lawless, that it needs to be governed, that it is time for the municipal sheriff to ride into town. In the year of the Bradford Wool Exchange, as men dig the cuttings and lay the lines that will connect them to that city, they form their first council, Brumfit, proprietor of the Crescent Hotel, Batty, a chemist, mason Hainsworth, farmer Ellis, farmer Lister, Thomas Robinson, cabinet maker, Macleod too among them, but they are ignorant of the ways of elections and electioneering, thinking, rude men that they are, that it could be done like that, as one decides to form a club, full of other agreeable like-minded fellows; tried to raise a levy, lobbed it into the Ilkley court only to have it snatched up and declared that they could not have it back, so disgruntled they left the game alone.

They are building without order, rock taken from the Hanging-stones Quarry, and the Skirtful, even, according to Ikringrill the Cow and Calf's lost companion, the Bull, rounded up, slaughtered and parcelled out to become the great face of the Crescent, Ilkley's first hotel; rocks levered and hacked out of context, the procession of wagons breaking the soft surface of the road below, back down past Cowpastures to the clear spaces of the village – for they called it a village then, and kept that name beyond the close of this century and halfway into the next, but it is losing its village look fast (if not its feel). The idea of Ilkley as trading post, as a centre, is taking hold, for the first time since the days of Rome, the trade in water starting it, and with it, Ilkley beginning to understand its attractions, a place not of health alone, but also pleasure, some wild and unattended up on the moor, but others with a guarded serenity, organized, a dingly dell running up from the Grove with its own little stream and elfish bridges, promenades down by the river, boats to be hired from the long-bearded Septimus Wray, rowing out to where his penny-paid boys have made their summer dam and kept the waters high, and later a turn taken in the pleasure gardens nearby. Hotels and boarding houses stand on their new street corners, advertise themselves in Shuttleworth's paper, the Crescent quickly followed by the Victoria overlooking the Wharfe out on Skipton Road (soon renamed the Middleton) 1867, the Royal a few years later, the Wells promenade to walk along, a pretty horse-spouting fountain to admire and a brewery company with their own Olicana beer and health-promoting stout. It is beginning to see itself as a resort, Ilkley town, a place where people come and people go, but within that frame those who know better, who live within it and its pretensions still call Ilkley a village, it remaining in their eyes always a place of broken smallness.

Macleod has opened up an office for the poor somewhere in the town, but it does not last the course. Perhaps the poor have had enough of cold water, they prefer a coal fire going. Ben Rhydding had its own station now, first not much more than a wooden hut, with carriages waiting apologetically outside to take them up through the magisterial gates, but Macleod tears it down and builds a station as befits his patients with his own money. Invalids and pale men besiege the town, the lodgings are full of the sick and infirm. Up from Ilkley station and down from the Hangingstones where he first worked out of his home, Robinson in '68 has built his invalid carriage factory with in '93 sawmills and showrooms from which emerge a line of improbable vehicles, invalid carriages and wheelchairs and most famous of all the Ilkley Couch, rolling on casters, with wheels and levers to raise the hopes of the afflicted.

They held their next attempt at legality four years later, 1869, in the vestry of the church, as if to pass blessing on the enterprise, and, an unnoticed slight, to hold it there too, to mark the passing of the Catholic hold, to solidify the presence of parliament's doctrine

John Ellis Jr 209,
Dr Scott 202,

John Dobson Snr 184,
John Lister, John Kendall, William Hartley 153
Dr Macleod 176

Clubs are springing up all over Ilkley for mutual benefit of one sort
or another. Clubs with rules and protocols, with agendas and aspirations. The Constitutional Club, the Liberal Club. On 23 April 1885
a cycle club. A good meeting with good attendance. Mr P. Lund was
appointed secretary, subscription five shillings per annum. Clubs for
politics, clubs for socials, clubs for those with more pressing matters.
Whatever their purpose, they all had their regulations to enforce.

Amalgamated Society of Carpenters and Joiners. Ilkley Branch.

May 3rd 1877

Committee met to consider the violation of rules by
Brother Charles Thomas while receiving sickness benefit.
It was decided to make enquiries of the Branch Officers at
the Branch Meeting following the reason why they had
paid Br Thomas for three days sick pay without receiving
due notice of his sickness also that Br Thomas be ques-
tioned with regards to being out of doors after the time
allowed according to rule and that he be fined his days
pay for so doing.

May 14th 1877

It was passed by a majority of the Members present that
Br Thomas be fined for being out of doors after time while
receiving sickness benefit, for one days pay and that he
send his notices of throwing on and off which he had
neglected to do so before according to rule. The reason
why he neglected to send them in before was ignorance
of the rules (thus supporting the decision of the previous
Comm. meeting)

July 20th 1877

Proposed by Br Edwin Brown that the best wishes of this Branch be sent with Br Wm Martingdale who is removing to Australia for the benefit of his health, and that he may have a safe and prosperous voyage to the distant land he is about to adopt as his future home.

They are not educated men. 'Auditors' are written 'Auditions'; Brother Hudson is 'Presedend'. Money comes in and money is paid out; jobs are scarce. They keep their tools oiled and ready, the chisel honed, the saw teeth sharp, hooded like some bird of prey stirring in its darkened shed, waiting for the hour when it is taken out and set free to do its bright work.

On 31 May 1897 comes the first financial entry other than a few sums scratched out on some faded margin.

Amalgamated Society of Carpenters and Joiners. Ilkley Branch.

In the Bank £64 4 3. In Treasurers Hand £5 19 4. Total £70 3 7.

ILKLEY LIBERAL CLUB

(Patrons G. J. Muff Esq.) President H. J. Johnston.
General Committee Messrs W. Mennel, G. Mennel, A. Thompson.

Annual General Meeting held in the Assembly Room. Dr Little is unanimously voted Chairman. He gets down quickly to the business of the hour.

"I am sorry to find that the '86 club balance sheet shows a falling off. The revenue from billiards has increased but the totals showed a balance against the club of £7 13s. 6d."

Mutterings. Mr Jabez Dobson, a large figure on the town's horizon, nods his head in agreement.

"Regarding the accounts I am afraid we have all got ourselves into a very indifferent way. A few years ago it was entirely different. Gentlemen who gave a pound were advised not to give so large a sum, as the club did not need it! That's why we lowered the subscriptions to 10/-."

The Chair: "Mr Naylor?"

Mr Naylor: "It's quite apparent to me that the club is going to the bad. At one time we had an Assembly Room Committee who attempted to let the room on a proper basis. It's a very serious thing to have a drop of income of £34 6s. 9d. We must try and improve on these matters."

The Chair: "Your Reverend wishes to speak?"

The Rev Clarkson: "May I suggest that officers of the Club take every opportunity of keeping the members up. Remind those whose membership has lapsed or is in danger of doing so. Of course some members are quite beyond such exhortations. Death had been very busy amongst us."

Amalgamated Society of Carpenters and Joiners, Ilkley Branch

Feb. 21st 1898, In Bank £93 19 3 Treasurers Hand £8 8 7 Total £102 7 10

C. Calvert 3d fine for owing 6/- Dec. 97
C, Calvert 3d fine for owing 6/- Feb. 98
E. Kelly 3d fine for arrears Sept. 98

ILKLEY LIBERAL CLUB

Payments already incurred

Dinsdale and Co. £26:14:2   Orme and Sons £2:14:8
Ilkley Brewery £24:13:8   J. Croft £7:6:5

"I would like to pass the resolution that the Secretary get a machine for drawing corks and the Reading Room Fireplace prepared."

"I will second that, Mr Hornby."

"I would like to pass the resolution that the Secretary obtain estimates for covering the seats in Billiard Room."

"I will second that, Mr Mennel."

"I would like to pass a resolution that billiard players should be charged 3d for twenty minutes and 6d for forty and that Secretary get two clocks with striking apparatus for every twenty minutes."

"Two clocks, Mr Gowling?"

'Two clocks.'

"I think one clock would suffice, Mr Gowling, for the best table."

"I will second that."

They buy their clock and install it. They pay their coins and watched by a portrait of the Grand Old Man play to the ticking of it, while their fellow combatants sit on their newly upholstered chairs. There is a fire in the fireplace and in the magazine rack copies of *Cassels, Strand, Pearson's Windsor, Harmsworth and Liberal: Illustrated London News, Ilkley Free Press* and *Ilkley Gazette, Leeds Mercury Supplement, Reynolds Newspaper,* the *Builder,* the *Yorkshire Daily Observer, Yorkshire Post, Yorkshire Evening Post* and *London Daily News.* They select their cue and rub their chalk, but as they bend their figures towards the felt, there is an intrusion in the room. A question arises in the minds of the members.

On a motion of Mr Green,

"I would like to pass a resolution that a sub-committee should be formed consisting of Messrs Peacock and Hornby to report at the next Committee Meeting if in their opinion the

clock in the Billiard room tended to benefit the club or otherwise."

"I will second that."

"Thank you Mr Stoddard."

And lastly, June 6th,

On the motion of Mr Johnston, seconded by Mr Hornby, the
following resolution was passed: in view of certain dissatis-
faction being expressed the clock in the Billiard Room is withdrawn.

The Secty was instructed to get some tobacco where he
thought fit.

(And in that month

Amalgamated Society of Carpenters and Joiners. Ilkley Branch.

In the Bank £45 4s 6d In Treasurers Hand £7 0s 5d
Total £52 4s 11d

He holds in his hand the Carpenters and Joiners book, oblong
with splodged writing, dark and difficult. Out of curiosity he skips
pages, decades, to see the life they led in later years, as they passed
out of the eighteen hundreds and moved towards the centre of his
own century, 1930. Brother W. Geddes of 5 Kimberly Street signs
the Vacant Book, on Saturday, Monday, Tuesday, Wednesday,
Thursday, Friday on, Sept 6th, 13th, 20th, 27th, Oct 11th, 14th,

18th, 25th, Nov 1st, Nov 8th, 15th, 22nd, Dec 8th; Brother E. H. Clarke on Sept 6th, 13th, Oct 14th, 18th, Nov 1st. He gives his address as 3 North Parade, but on Nov 15th he moves to 30 Alexandra Crescent, where he spends an unemployed Christmas. February, March, April, May 1931 he has work, but by June his name and initials EHC are ranged again from Saturday through to Friday, as is W. Geddes who had a leaner spring than him. Brother Hudson, Brother Wilde, Brother Hardwick, Brother Thackray, lean springs them all, Brother Geddes of Leeds Road, Brother Thackray of Tivoli Place, Brother Hardwick, Lister Street. W. Hudson though puts no address, just Ilkley in a large hasty scrawl, as if his address is not worth the mark, his W.H.s impatient, his name written once in August and then, unlike most who describe their names with care every time (a list perhaps of their skill, the hand that moves and works and feeds them reduced to this degraded mark on the page), a series of contemptuous ditto marks August 6th, 13th, 20th, 27th, Sept 5th and 12th with no other name in between.

My father was the foreman, he used to get a half-penny an hour more than the other men and that was all he got as foreman. It was my uncle's business Dean and Mennell, but Mr Dean he died. George was on the council. He was a neat worker my father, everything had to be just right. He used to walk about with his handcart, he enjoyed his work; my father was the better of the two, he did all the plans and kept the business going for him, when my uncle joined the forces, but we never reaped any benefit, he was not that type. He was quiet my father, the youngest of the three, he didn't resent it, never joined the union he wouldn't

He leaps years, ignoring their long hardship. Feb. 3rd 1940 W. Geddes is still there, still on Leeds Road, as is J. Hardwick. Others have taken the stage, new names, Fred Storey, Charles

Smith: by '42 Geddes' name is fading and others more prominently unemployed including T. H. Grange who hogs the book to himself from Feb. 1st '44 to April 25th a whole page devoted to no other name but his. 1954 he is there again and in '57 another Grange monopoly, reverting once again to sign his name every time required, an Andy Warhol collection of signatures repeated without deviation or change, except for the shades of ink, mostly light blue but at the bottom of the page, like the pull of a cold-water current a bather might feel suddenly, run two rows of a darker hue, where the life of T. H. Grange is struggling to swim ashore.

The years are hurrying by now, the book fading. He senses that its time has gone. '51 one entry: a pause, in '63, nine entries, two names, and on the next page comes the last, B. Harrison of East Parade. Not quite the last. In the back of the book he finds a note from 3 Middleton Villas, dated 18th January 1960. This is the address of the doctor who saved the stabbed boy. The note was once folded (carried maybe in a top pocket to be given to the sick steward), but has been flattened out to show the four folds.

In my opinion Mr A. Black of The Crescent Ilkley is still incapable of work by reason of a crushed finger.
— J. Smith

It was an election day when my father lost his fingers. He was in the workshop on the circular saw. I'd be in my teens, I wasn't working at the time. He wrapped his hand in a towel and walked on to the doctor's, that was in the Grove, near the little park, and when the doctor answered the door he nearly fainted when he saw him, and took him to the hospital. He was left with one finger and a thumb but he used to manage to fasten his boots up. He got about £400 then, that was how we paid for the house here, but he wasn't working the Christmas after, so we'd no money. The workmen clubbed up and bought us a chicken or we wouldn't have had any Christmas dinner. His brother never gave him anything. They don't, it's what they are, around here.

13 June 1884

Recommended that the Surveyor caution the gardener at the Spa Hydropathic Establishment against the waste of water in the grounds of that establishment.

Application from Mr E. Wade for the supply of water for two cows. Recommended that the application be granted on the condition that the extra charge be paid when more than two cows use the supply.

2 September 1884

Application from the Ben Rhydding Hydropathic Company

Recommended that the Ben Rhydding Hydropathic Company be supplied with water to their Establishment on the condition that they pay 10% upon the outlay of laying down the mains and the usual charge for every 1,000 gallons of water registered by meter.

11 June 1884

Surveyor reported difficulties in the connection with the supply to Ben Rhydding H. Estate. That same meeting recommended that a letter be written to Mr Butterfield informing him that complaints have been received about the conditions of the Baths at White Wells.

8 October 1884

Committee decided to visit the Old Reservoir to arrange re-roofing of same.

Recommended that application be made to the Justices at Otley for warrants to commit to prison the following Rate Defaulters who have all been certified by the police as having no goods upon which Distraint can be levied – on Alfred Smallwood, William William, Andrew Thornton,

Elizabeth Wood, Jacob Haywood, Robert Hardisty, Henry Caudle, John Brown, Dorothy Lambert, George Thompson and George Hobson.

In 1888 the railway line is taken further, the laid track first to Bolton Abbey, then in a six month to Skipton, shored up with viaducts and bridges, one black bridge in particular that cuts through the town, sent out across the centre of Brook Street, a bowstring girder 85 feet across, (iron replacing stone bridge on the ground, water in the form of steam, hot and airborne now traversing the former stream, cold and buried), a heavy weight carrying the clank of wheel and carriage, the butcher Hampshire's hanging poultry trembling at every piston turn. Next to his shop sits the squat hut of coal merchant Inghams, who erects a sign along the bridge's black length, with a huge hand pointing down.

INGHAM'S
COAL & ESTATE AGENTS

(In Ilkley the estate agents were coal merchants; they sold the coal in the winter and the houses in summer, cause houses didn't sell in winter and coal didn't sell in summer

The Ilkley Wells Hydropathic Company Ltd

Directors: Mr Alfred Harris Chairman, Mr Edward Birchall, James Smallwood, Charles Stanfield, Mr E. P. Thompson

[1889] Report reports a large increase in the number of Visitors and the balance of profit on house keeping shows an excess of about £100 over the previous year. Expenditure of

Capital has been £3,064 0s. 4d. includes New Billiard Room, Smoking Room, and Lavatories together with furnishing of the same. Important additions to the Stables and Dwelling Houses and new Summer Houses in the Grounds.

Ominously for the visitor the report continues: The cost has been greater than was at first anticipated, arising chiefly from a large extension of Lavatory accommodation.

Net Balance of Revenue as shewn by the Profit and Loss Account amounts to £2,988 7s. 3d. Directors recommend that a dividend of 7%, free of income tax, be declared which will amount to £1,864 and leave a balance of £1,124 7s. 3d. to carry forward.

Yes the water has its pull still, but in the courtship it is Bradford that is gaining ascendancy, Bradford to whom Ilkley will become pledged. Middelton sees the men besotted by Bradford, raising their hats to their tainted mistress, the source of their potency, enticed by the secrets of her trade, seduced by the flow of her language and her insatiable appetite. Bradford never tires, Bradford never stops, Bradford keeps them young day and night. They talk of Bradford in their clubs, they hurry to Bradford's clamouring presence; they cannot keep away from this Protestant seductress, spreading herself before them.

1890 and Middelton wants out. There is no place for him here. His first intention is to batten down the hatches, to sanctify what is his, to enclose the moor, and then do with it as he will, preserve it for his own, or, if income is the drive, to sell parcels of it up, mineral, peat, water; there is an abundance of material lying on this ground for him to be a stuff merchant of his own. It is easy enough for him to get his hands on it; apply for an enclosure. An inquiry will follow and if two-thirds of the owners are in agreement (and he being a two-thirds owner) the fence follows.

Hearing this Thomas Horsman, Ilkley's nurseryman and councillor, goes to see Middelton, takes him to the window, invites him to consider the view, the fact of what he sees, the blue-slate town, sombre in its dark-cut cloth, the ceaseless wash of the train and what it may bring on its tides, houses hammered up, paths laid, schools and sewers, churches and reservoirs, the town scratching like a dog, but needing those wild running spaces, the Wharfe and the Moor, the Moor and the Wharfe. We have the Wharfe, he says. Now give us the Moor.

Jabez Dobson comes down from Craiglands and calls a special meeting of the Board: 21 October 1892. Eli Ibberson, John Brown, Henry Ellis, John Foster, J. A. Middlebrook, John Beanlands, J. C. Barker, Wm Critchley, Thomas Horsman and John Illingworth, the names are there to read. And the decision. That the sum of £13,500 should be paid to Middelton's agents, plus £200 for fees.

On 1 February 1893 they make an application to the Local Government Board to borrow £17,000 to stump up and buy Ilkley Moor and all the other unruly bits of land, Herbers Ghyll, Hollin Hall Moor, the Allotments, Silver Well, Panorama Rocks, together with the mineral rights, and all powers and privileges owned by Middelton. In April '93 they hold an inquiry, hold it for two hours, with a strong attendance (this is their own town now) not one body stepping forward to give voice to opposition.

The deal is done, the moor is bought, and with it, Ilkley's soul. But no Faustian pact this. This is drawn out on a contract of generosity and understanding, knowing the town and its needs. The Middeltons pack their bags, take their leave. Horsman and Dobson pat their pockets and turn to other business. But this is their monument. Better than plaques and foundation stone which will grow dull, washed by rain and the dirty sweep of cars, the names on which, in fewer years than they would like to think, no one will read. Better this rock to make your unseen mark, your portly squiggles. Better this, Thomas Horsman, the moor.

And below the moor, before White Wells, lies the town's introduction to water, a small sip of it, like you might offer a child a taste of wine, water at its most tame, the tarn, a crude scoop of land at first, gathering whatever the moor might run down to it, like the town rough and ready. Once the councillors paced its circumference, they desired to beautify its barren precincts, to lay out a pleasant path around its kidney shape, build a shelter in case of bothersome rain, with a fountain at the centre. William Middelton gave consent, and the thing was built, but not without disquiet. Craiglands did not want it on its grander doorstep. They placed a dug-out stage above the tarn, from where the Pierrots, dressed in spotted costumes and pointed hats, entertained the crowd three times a day; humorists, vocalists, pianists. They look force-fed, this jolly team, perched up upon a rock, stuffed with good humour till it bursts out of their gills. How some must have longed to rise above the hide, hoped they had the feathers fit for flight, how others have known they had been winged, unable to do nothing more than give a feeble flutter before the breeze-ruffled water.

WATERWORKS COMMITTEE

18 January 1892

Tenders for the re-roofing of the Old Reservoir opened from the following persons

Armstrong Addison, Joiner – 31. 5. 0. (his tender to be requested to state whether the use of creosoted timber in the roof of the old reservoir would be likely to pollute the water in the Reservoir by the vapour condensing on the timber in the roof and ultimately finding its way into the stored water below. His tender to be accepted conditionally that their reply to the above query is satisfactory)

B. Gummerssall tenders rejected: 30. 0. 0. – Joiner; – 5. 0. 0. – Plumber; Slate – 29. 0. 0. Rejected

R. Nelson, Slater – 29. 7. 0. Accepted.

15 September 1892

The owner of the Wheatsheaf Hotel be noticed to convert the privies at the rear end of the Hotel into water closets, to erect an ashpit at the rear of the hotel and removed the urinal to a more suitable position adjoining the coal place in the yard in question.

Midland Railway Co. served notice to cease pollution of the

stream near Woods Place by the drainage from their Engine Sheds (black oil pouring into Ilkley Water). Mr Rev. Galli recommended that tenders be taken for the repairing of the scavenging cart and that an additional horse and cart be purchased by the sanitary department and a driver engaged.

20 October 1893

Samples of milk.

1.   G. Burton – Fair.
2.   R. Park – Fair.
2   (A). R. Park – Superior.
3.   Thackery – Suspiciously poor quality but not sufficiently bad to justify its positive condemnation as adulterated.
5.   A. Priestly – somewhat poor.
8.   J. Lawson – Genuine.
9.   Binns – Fine Milk, superior quality.
10. T. Duell – Genuine Milk. Very superior quality.

31 October 1893

Tenders for Four Cottages and Fire Station at Golden Butts
Mason: Messrs Ives and Co. – £664.
Fire Station: Mr John Brown – £523.
Plumber: Mr H. Garside – £59. 6. 0.
Slater: Mr R. Nelson – £84.
Plasterer: Mr R. Richardson – £84.
Painter: Mr J. G. Boden – £23. 18. 10.

My uncle George, he was superintendent, my other uncle Billy was a Sergeant, my father was fireman, and my cousin drove it, four of them on the engine. They called it the George Mennel after my uncle, all lovely brass, like the helmets; they used to have fire practice on the Tuesday night and when he went to funerals I used to polish his silk hat for him. I've the brush yet but the bristles are coming out.

10 January 1894

The quarry known as Hangingstone Quarry to be closed in March next in consequence of the defacement of the Moor in the immediate neighbourhood of the Cow and Calf Rocks.

and the moor itself humanized

10 January 1894

Trees to be planted

25,000 trees planted on the Moor: 14,000 Austrian Pines; 8,000 Scotch firs; 2,000 Silver Birches; 1,000 Larch

the cost of planting and fencing estimated £110 6s 8d. and would cover 20 acres.

Sites were visited by J. Dobson, J. A. Middlebrook and Horsman
12 acres at Hangingstone
3 acres south of the Tarn
2 south of White Wells
3 South Willey's Halls Shout

19 January 1894

Mr F. B. Muff's gardener be allowed to move a load of peat from the peat bog on Ilkley Moor at the usual charge.

16 February 1894

The Chairman of the Building and General Purposes Committee had a letter from a Mr F. B. Muff relating to the construction of a tobogganing slide on the Moor.

When it was Christmas holiday I used to take my toboggan up to the moor. My father being on business in
Norway brought back two louches which are high off the
ground with just a support for the rim. Even in deep snow
you were four inches above the snow level whereas a lot
of home-made toboggans had boarded sides all the way
up and that built up the snow underneath and they
couldn't go. I used to drag my toboggan right up to the
Cow and Calf rocks and I would come all the way down
past the grammar school, past the town hall and station,
and one year where it had been particularly frosty first and
the snow came on top of it I got right down to the rugger
ground and that would be a record. In 1922 the village
bobby he came to us and said that there was getting to be
more car traffic and that we'd have to go across to Curly
Hill. Well Curly Hill was no good 'cause it was all lumpy
and that brought it to an end.

16 March 1894

A letter from Miss Sharples of Craiglands, relating to swans on
the tarn. Mr Foster be deputised to purchase a female swan.

Resolved:
That the sides of the island in the tarn be made good.
Rushes and debris to be removed.
Footpaths at the tarn and near Old White Wells be repaired and
that Mr Foster be deputised to purchase a female swan.

April 1894

Application from Mr Jackson for an increase for the feeding of
the waterfowl at the tarn.

Now that the moor is public property, it is a melancholy
reflection that those who should be the very ones to uphold

the natural beauty of the place should be the first to attempt to alter its whole character. When we signed the petition to purchase the moor we gave no one permission to alter its character. The natural beauty of the place is a concern to both those who regard it as a residential place and to those who are determined to make it a popular resort; by which I mean a resort where health was not so much considered as band stands or Eiffel towers.

Look at the Tarn. They have erected a shelter there for £18-5-4, with the aspect of an old fashioned weather box. I half expect an old woman to come out in fine weather and an old man in wet. The pretty Tarn has been further spoiled by clearing out the rushes. Not content with that they have built a couple of islands, beautifully round, banking mud all the way round until they are as picturesque as the sewage pond in the valley. A shoddy imitation of nature. What would happen next. Years ago the Council wanted to pull down White Wells and erect an Eastern pagoda. Let the Board go back to Gas works and drains, go below the earth instead of spoiling the top.

– Mr Sievert

21 September 1894

Dr Rabagliati wanted a right of way from the south side of his property known as Tom Halls on to Ben Rhydding Road.

19 October

Dr Rabagliati be allowed a right of way from the south of his property condition on that he throw out land for the widening set forth on the plan prepapred and that he bear the expense of the construction.

19 November

Letter from Dr Rabagliati dated Nov. 13 declining to accept the terms of the board's offer.

1 July 1895

Footpaths opposite the cottages and Fire Brigade be asphalted, also paths inside gardens to cottage doors a privet hedge be planted parallel with the unclimbable rails adjoining the fire brigade station.

15 February 1897

Recommended
that damaged trees in Herbers Ghyll be cut and that the dead swan from the Tarn be stuffed and placed in the Museum.

Mr Dilly: May I ask the gentlemen why they want to go to the extravagance of paying two guineas to stuff the swan? Was it a very valuable swan, or was there something extraordinary about it?
Mr Horsman: (laughing) Yes, it was the only one we had.
Dilly: I shall move an amendment that the swan is not stuffed.
Horsman: But it is stuffed.
Dilly: Then let those who wanted it stuffing pay for it. It is simply throwing money away.

27 September 1897

Mr Dilly of the Middleton Hotel objected to lay 10/- a year for water to a WC and urinal on his premises abutting Stockeld Road on the grounds that the conveniences were largely used by the public. Seeing that the conveniences referred to are situated on private premises over which the Council had no control they could not agree to the request

Wharfedale Homing Society (Ilkley)

At the general meeting of this society held at the Lister's Arms Hotel last week, Mr T. Robinson presiding it was agreed to fly under the Yorkshire Federation. Mr J. A. Middlebrook was elected President; Mr W. Brumfit,

Mr J. Beanlands, Mr H. Searles and Mr Thackray, vice presidents. The races arranged for the ensuing season are: − Old Bird Races − Ambergate, Ashby, Rugby, Banbury, Didcot, Winchester, Bournemouth, Jersey and Rennes. Young Bird Races − Ambergate, Ashby, Rugby, Banbury and Didcot. It was decided to give a silver cup and medal for the best average velocity in the English Old Bird Races, not including Ambergate, and a medal for the best average in the Young Bird Races, not including Didcot. Members are reminded that subscriptions are due on April 1st.

AN ILKLEY PIERROT'S SAD END

James Crowther, a licensed hawker, living in a field near the stepping stones said he found the body of the deceased, Fred Oakland, at the far end of the field. He was fully dressed with the exception of his cap, which hung on some bushes. Harry Eugene, of Lynn, Massachusetts, stated that the deceased was a vocalist and a member of Howard's Pierrots to which he also belonged. He did not know his age, but should think he would be about 46. The company had been in Ilkley about four months and that was the extent of his acquaintance.

Coroner: How has his health been?
Witness: Well, he has been drinking lately. He complained of not feeling well.
Coroner: Have you any idea of what was the matter with him?
Witness: He complained of both his heart and liver being bad.
Juror Bellerby: Is it true he was suffering from *delirium tremens*?
Witness: I think there might be a little truth in that.

Petition from the residents in the locality of Harksworth Street in which complaint was made of annoyance arising from noise in the working of a "Steam Round-a-bout" on the land abutting that street. After conferring with the owner of that land Mr W.A. Johnson and pointing to him that it was sold on condition that no noisy, noxious or offensive trade should be carried on, resolved that the Council would not enforce the removal of the Round-a-bout this year on condition that the noisy music should be softened as much as possible and cease at 9pm and that it be not allowed another year.

Mr Dilly: Anyroad, I am very pleased to see that the main road is to be lighted as far as Wheatley Lane. I notice that we are going to put these lamps 70 yards apart, whereas at the other end they are 120 yards apart. Surely the lamps at the west end ought to be altered, especially by Middleton Road. It is very dark there.

The Chairman: Coming home again? (Laughter)

Dilly: Well I am continuously passing along there.

THE MOOR (6)

THE SWASTIKA STONE

Almost level with the Cow and Calf, a slight mile away, stands the Swastika Stone, and together they frame the town as if a Neolithic Lutyens had taken his bearings and placed the settlement between their geometry. There are markings upon this too, but they are guarded on three sides by an iron gate and tall iron railings, and if you wanted to touch them (and he does) you would have to pull away the rusty lock or climb up on to the rusting iron spikes and edge your way round to the fourth (open) side, where the rock falls sheer. The carvings are so tantalizingly near that this seemingly facile imprisonment seems like an Arthurian test, that should you grasp the metal and manage to inch your way around and enter upon the caged stone some secret might be imparted to you, that who manages to enter will awaken the stone's slumbering power. Perhaps it is not as easy as it looks. Perhaps it is the giant carrying rocks, leaping the Strid all over again. Is that what is required around here, a leap of faith?

He pulls at the gate hoping that it might swing open of its own accord, but it does not. He looks at the railings, wondering whether he could scale their height. It is a long time since he looked at railings, noticed their properties. Railings were a municipal thing for parks and ponds. There were railings in Ilkley, functional railings around the railway station, ornate railings round the bandstand, elegant railings planted along the Grove, tall railings circling Mill Ghyll fountain, half-sized railings running on

Skipton Road and Church Street walls. There are none of those any more; two world wars saw to that, and yet when you see them there is still the urge to climb them. He looks around. There is no one in sight. Foolishly he puts down his book and his pen and climbs up. He cannot climb over, but it is possible to edge around, to where the fourth, unguarded side lies. He starts to manoeuvre round, his feet on the lower rung. He does not look down, he knows enough not to do that, but as he grows closer to where he must swing round and pivot around the last railing over the drop his arms begin to shake, until, poised over the edge, he can go no further. He is defeated. He will have to go back. But it is iron he is gripping, a straight rod of it, and remembering the swing in his garden he grips hard, and placing his toe on the other side swings round. He is in! He steps on to the slippery stone and walks inside, gingerly as if he might break something. He touches the face of rock, crouches down next to the markings, places his hand upon them. They are cold, that is all, cold and unforthcoming. What if someone should come along and catch him squatting down behind these bars? How foolish he would look.

In the fifties, he remembers the sequence of tramps coming to his home – in Middleton Villas on the Skipton Road, the back gardens of which ran down to the Wharfe, a longish road along which men with old boots and battered hats would come, the string around their overcoats looser in the summer than in the winter but tied about the waist all the same, men with a touch of stale bread about them. They were not old all of them, indeed if he remembers correctly there was one could have been no more than thirty, with teeth and hands worn older than the rest of his body (he never saw his feet). From the front bay window of the drawing room he would see them coming purposely down the short drive, past the monumental pile of soot (which is why he so often looked out of the bay window in the first place, hoping the sweep might come again to add to the forbidden pile), past the front porch (down to the left of which, underneath the window, lay his holly house and his secrets), along the open side end to the cramped yard with the coal bunker and the dustbin and the dilapidated cage in which sat their large and unhappy rabbit, white and motionless, with watery pink eyes, where they would climb up the back steps and knock on the back door and stand, hat in hand, while claiming their right to a bite to eat and something to drink. They had a docile quality, these tramps, with an unaccountable ability to make outdoor life appear strangely domestic; ordered, unflappable, slow, reassuring. They had captured space too and held it somewhere beneath the ragged folds of their person. From their demeanour and the simplicity of their apparel came the seductive suggestion anyone could be a tramp, without worry, without hurry. Small wonder that children knotted handkerchiefs around garden sticks, setting off, not for adventure, but to reach another security beyond the turmoil of home. In the summer months they would be frequent, these tramps, and his mother would make meat-paste sandwiches and cups of tea laced with extraordinary amounts of sugar (five spoons please missus); perhaps three, four a month. Some would have walked the spine of England (south to north for the six months March to August and north to south the remaining September to February), following unconsciously the ancient travellers on the Icknield Way, searching not for flint nor for a place to settle, nor a way to the Irish Sea (though that would have been a possibility), but following the route that other tramps had laid before them. It was not uncertain, their path, for they followed marks, marks made by themselves and their predecessors, marks in the neighbouring streets and on the approaching walls, marks on the gate and very doorpost, marks denoting where each would be treated decently, marks indicating where work would be required, marks signifying a variety of options and warnings. *Food here. Overnight stay possible. Savage dog.* What these marks were, their configuration, the means by which they were drawn, he never found out, but certainly his was a house where a tramp knew what treatment he might expect (if not generosity then quiet decency), an odd job for a rare shilling, some weeding, some cutting back of nettles, or better still some moving of the precious pile of soot. He would scour the walls on the route to his house looking for these marks but he never saw anything that looked remotely like a sign, nor when he saw one pause before the drive did he catch him examining a particular brick nor stoop to make an additional mark on his departure. So where were these signs? And when were they made? Did tramps rise at night and make their marks under cover of darkness, was the Ilkley night a world of tramp shadows, was that what happened in every English town, its streets peopled by a ghostly parade of itinerant men working their way through sleeping towns and villages, padding softly on the residential pavements, scratching their marks while we slept? Or did they carry out their renovations in broad daylight, dropping down to tie their shoe, or feigning exhaustion, lean against that brick wall, that stone pillar, penknife in hand? Are they there still, not catalogued and annotated like those up on the moor but simply undiscovered, forgotten like the men who made them and who read their meanings with care? Wandering men making wandering signs. He wonders too what became of these readers of stone, this ragged migrating flock moving over England by dint of foot, pushing England slowly before them, moving almost as slowly as change itself. Certainly they are not seen now. No tramp comes to his own door, asks him for a slice of bread. Perhaps there are no marks any more, perhaps there is a lost legion of tramps looking for markings that have been built upon, knocked down, erased by modern glaciers. Unlike the megalithic dead, surrounded by their means of travel, theirs have been removed, and so, they cannot roam. They are the untramps, held motionless as the world races past, cut not adrift but becalmed, while lapping at their boots the water rushes past, carrying memory and future and what transpired before them.

He remembers one afternoon in particular, a regular visitor, a long brown overcoat tied with a length of tarred string, standing in the back yard in the drizzle, gloves with holes in the fingers (the first time he had ever seen such a thing), eating a sandwich. He had come at elevenses, knocked on the door and while his mother retreated back into the kitchen to carve the bread, had stood a pace back, on the stone step, with the rain running down on to the rim of his hat, arms hanging patiently by his side. What she put on the bread he cannot remember, but as she lifted the blade to the lip of crust, she had looked up and pointing to the space just inside the door where the mat lay indicated that the man should step forward, not to enter the room to sit at its table, but simply to absent himself from the weather. Like his mother the young tramp said nothing, but shook his head (the motion accentuating the cascade of water, reminding him of Nelson, the black dog, who lived upstairs), rejecting her offer, not to spare his mother's feeling or the kitchen's purity but in order to avoid what would be in essence a blasphemous communion. The tramp had shaken his head and stood, waiting, the boy watching his mother and the man, and the noise of it all, the rain falling, the bread being cut, the tea being poured and a slight breeze scuttling around his bare legs, carrying the man's smell in from the outside as she spread first the butter and then the filling, pressing the two halves together before handing that and the tea over to him. And he took them, the young tramp, took them with hands as old as his mother's but more ragged around the edges and thanked her and winked at him and went back down the steps into the yard where he set the cup down upon the wall and began to chew, patiently and thoroughly, as a donkey might feed under the dripping eaves of a house. And he remembers standing in the doorway watching the tramp as he stood by the rabbit hutch, lifting the cup, swallowing the tea, chewing the bread, unaware of the cage, the rabbit loping forward, watching the man and his half-gloved fingers and the thick slice of bread, his pink nose twitching through the rusty mesh of wire, the rain dripping and the tramp chewing, and all at once, on a gulp of tea, the tramp looked down and saw the rabbit, saw him large and white, trapped in an upturned orange box, saw his dank bed of straw and his four damp feet, saw the sad pink eyes and the sad pink nose pressed through the gap, saw his lovely ears and his large hind legs that could never stretch, never run, never dart away from danger, and he tore a whole strip of crust from his bread, tore it off with half the sandwich still attached and, bending down, pushed it through, poked it at the rabbit's feet, and as the rabbit hopped round it, turning his back on his benefactor to examine his unexpected gift, the young tramp put his fingers through and touched the silky white back, touched him and closed his eyes and then with a final swallow straightened up, set the cup back on the wall and nodding curtly walked down the drive and on to the Skipton Road.

ILKLEY (8)

OSWALD LISTER

He lived in Ilkley round forty years, his business as a plasterer and contractor, undertaking work in Yorkshire and parts of Lancashire. Soon after coming to the town, seeing others take the same bodged opportunity, with the Council wet behind the ears, he began building operations on his own, and ran swiftly into regulation rock: two houses on Bolling Road, Ben Rhydding pulled down by the local authority; by-laws undermining his foundations on Easby Drive; his houses on Victoria Drive closed to the municipal sewers unless he opened up his private purse; and around a parcel of land down by the old bridge his railings were removed for encroaching upon the public highway.

Thus denied he filled the land with materials he could not use, machinery he could not work, stone and iron and rubble thrown together in a sculpture of discontent, set by an artisan's eye, to be witness to those who would thwart him, as he was in his person. Broken, unsightly, heaped with rust and bounded by weed and nettle, the townsfolk walked past it and gave it a name, Paradise.

A staunch churchman and a stern walker to the parish church, he taught himself the laws of local government, sang his hymns, said his prayers and carried before him his legal papers knotted up in a red handkerchief, his dusty-feet brief, striding like a preacher with his unwanted message on to Ilkley's urban council corner, taking the ridicule and punishment meted out in pounds and pence and lengths of unregulated pipe.

Lister lays his foundations and scowls. He believes the Board to be men intent on lining their own pocket. He sees Ilkley built in their name and for their benefit. It is true what he sees, those nods and winks in Council chambers, the orchestrated meeting and the resolution passed, a glass of club brandy at a later date. It is not a full-blown conspiracy but a close-run thing, these men, casting their net around Ilkley's uncharted waters in expectation of good fishing grounds,

but there is still the hauling in

To the Council 14 September 1894: A letter from Mr Oswald Lister, Tivoli Place Ilkley. Those present at its reading, Mr Middleton (in the Chair), Messrs Barker, Dilly, Illingworth, Foster and Dean

Sirs,
    re the houses in Victoria Drive. It is not my intention to submit these plans to your Board again as it is quite evident to me that there is a combination on your board to continue disapproving them for the slightest reason.
    The building operations are still in progress and has been since 10 August on which date I informed you building would commence which it did on that date. I cannot give you the levels until they complete the plans which I have no doubt will be placed before your board in due course for disapproval as the order of the day.
    Will you kindly reply to the following query. Query. Does our board refuse to put in the main sewer along Skipton turnpike Road so that my property can be drained into it? I again request your board to lay the sewer in Skipton Rd so that my property can be drained into it. I refuse to have a sump on my property. I have seen plenty of that beastly filthy work at Ben Rhydding, I see it every week.
    Yours Truly
    Oswald Lister

Mr Holmes attending, of Messrs Robinson Scott and Holmes, advised the Board to seek an injunction to restrain Mr Oswald

Lister from proceeding in Victoria Drive until the Bye-laws of this Board have been complied with.

3 November 1894

The Committal of Oswald Lister, In the Chancery Division of the High Court, before Mr Justice Chitty, the case of Ilkley Local Board of Health v. Oswald Lister, plasterer, arising out of an action to restrain the defendant from building except in accordance with plans which had been properly submitted and approved in compliance with the rules. Mr Eustace Smith appearing for the defendant stated that he was prepared to give an undertaking not to proceed with the erection of any buildings until the plans were considered.

Mr Patterson: Will your Lordship grant an interim injunction?

His Lordship: You have Mr Smith's undertaking.

Mr Patterson: I would rather have the injunction. There is a local superstition that an undertaking is not as good as an injunction.

His Lordship: What has the court to do with local superstition? If a man breaks his undertaking he might be sent to prison. That is all.

Mr Patterson: It is in the defendant refusing such an undertaking that the motion came on. On the tenth he wrote a letter to the surveyor of the Board saying he intended to start building at once.

Mr Smith: Mr Lister has not attempted to build.

His Lordship: But he has threatened to build. Let the motion stand for a month.

Mr Patterson: May I ask my learned friend to say that the defendant will refrain from writing to local newspapers.

His Lordship: He cannot do that, but Mr Smith will no doubt convey your wish to the defendant.

Lister bangs his hand. He is out of pocket and without the inner circle. He sits at night at his stubborn table and writes in his stubborn hand, injustice burning in his heart. O the perversity of these men! He will have no truck with their municipal privilege, they are corrupt like the fat Pope of Rome, they mouth unctuous goodness and steal from under the people, they dress in pomp and hide their duplicity in the furs of ceremony. He is tormented by their brazen corruption, it cramps his stride and troubles his bowel. Come election time he strides out and nails his treatise to Ilkley's door. They cluster and read, and when the council gather before it, they rip it down from its plasterer's nail

December 12 1894

•

Ladies and Gentlemen – I think it might be interesting for you to have an outline of the spiteful proceedings instituted against me by the Board. I may say that if there had been an honest man sitting upon that Board these proceedings would not have commenced. The Board has no case against me excepting that I had commenced building before my plans were passed. Gentlemen the Board had sat on me for twenty months and I thought it high time to show them that I would not be sat on any longer. They combined not to pass my plans. When they got into court they had nothing to plead except that the people of Ilkley were superstitious and that I was a confounded letter writer to the press. His Lordship told them to do their public business more honestly and told them to go home and pass my plans. It is quite clear to me that the Board are afraid to face this case out before the election, they are anxious to get back to power again and then they will snap their fingers at the ratepayers. I have suffered the loss of £40 in interest through the Board's action on the materials lying idle on the land. I desire to ask the public of Ilkley if they consider it honest work for the Board to put in a line of sewers for the Chairman and William Holmes' property at a cost of close up to £200 and then in the same breath to refuse to spend £67 to put sewers in for my seven houses, but the Board prefers sumps, seven sumps. They have found those at Ben Rhydding to answer so well that they are desirous of extending the system. Of course anything is good enough for the working classes. The ratepayers may thank Thomas Horsman and William Holmes for this expenditure – two men who have violated the by laws more than all the rest of the men of Ilkley put together. The ratepayers would do well to get rid of Mr Horsman and Wm. Holmes. These men sit on everybody else's plans and bar the way to progress and good trade. Have no more of them, but allow me to ask you to support Dr Scott, John Gaunt, H. Moisley, O. Lister

Friday 18 January 1895

Mr Oswald Lister in the Chancery Division before Mr Justice Chitty, on a charge of contempt of court in publishing a circular to the ratepayers of Ilkley at the recent District Council Election. Mr Smith represented the defendant. Mr Farwell informed the court that the defendant had put in an affidavit saying that he had issued the circular when he was candidate for public office, that he had written it hurriedly and that he has since discovered that some of the statements were inaccurate particularly the observations attributed to the learned judge.

Mr Smith: I cannot not defend the circular but I must remind his Lordship that it had been put forward during the time of elections: it was only a small handbill, and had no way been posted about the place.

His Lordship: Something like 1500 copies were sent out.

Mr Smith: There is no evidence how many were delivered.

His Lordship: I do not see how his being a candidate affects this case or forms any special grounds for excuse. It is not a mere matter of abuse; the statements are false.

Mr Smith: He says he found he was mistaken but he thought at the time the statements were correct.

His Lordship: It is pure invention. It is a most serious charge. He says the judge told his adversaries that they were dishonest men. I hold that this is contempt which I ought not to overlook. I must make the order for the defendant's committal but I limit the time that he is to be detained in prison for ten days from the time he is to be taken.

Mr Farwell: I ask for costs.

His Lordship: Yes.

Lister joins the council, tries first to fix his grappling hook into their midst, to climb up over the council wall and join them in their playground keep, offers Paradise for sale. There is money afloat in the council, money and by-laws and the passing of men's intent, drains and sewers run into councillors' land, lamps lit near councillors' homes, roads paved near councillors' drives; more to the point there is £688 made from the Magerison Estate, and with the idle bundle landing on the council table Lister has hopes that they might direct their gaze to the old bridge and his iron-bedded land, and take Paradise lost unto Ilkley's own, Paradise found; remarks to Councillor Beanlands how handy this £600 would be for such a purchase. But they wash their hands of it. They do not have a spade dug in that particular turf and thus they do not need it turned. £600? Paradise is not worth that much.

But it is not this gnat which bothers the councillors, nor any other of the disgruntled petitioners and pleaders, it is the sight of land and the throwing up of building, the function rooms they do not have, the portraits that do not yet hang on the wall, no proper place for placard and foundation stone, no mute witness to who these men are. They need a museum of their own, for themselves and their future bones, similar in the measure of their authority to their offices of business and the fireplaces of their homes, but hallowed by a distant posterity which they themselves will fashion; they need a permanence to solidify their dignity, to gild it, give it room to breathe and soak the walls, not these cramped Grove rooms with no measure of their seat and their numbers and the enormity of their deliberations. They want a Town Hall, have wanted one for some time, but there is growing opposition fermenting in the town, opposition in the spending and the building. On part of the old Sedbergh Estate, opposite the new railway, there is land going, good land, suitable land.

They can buy it, it is said, for £1 a yard, but when the time comes and the auction is held, they do not, but let Mr J. T. Jackson snag the whole shooting match for £7,500, an estate with stables adjoining gardens, orchard and land, 18,140 square yards. And on part of the estate are a collection of greenhouses, greenhouses that Mr Horsman, nursery man and councillor, rents.

In March '97 a crowded ratepayers' meeting gets under way protesting at the part purchase of this estate from Mr Jackson (upon a section of which still stand those greenhouses) and the intention of the council to build their Town Hall. The meeting is chaired by a past ally of Oswald Lister, Mr W. Horn. In the front row, in the best seats (by virtue of their office), sit the very men against whom the meeting is arraigned, Messrs Horsman, Firth, Ellis, and Beanlands (who in a public dinner held days before could not resist, meat on his fork, wine in his glass, gravy on his mouth, dabbing his lip and vouchsafing that they would have their Town Hall, in spite of all the opposition). Alongside them, the newly elected Oswald Lister, uncomfortable in their proximity.

> The Chairman: I am pleased to see a number of councillors present and I hope the meeting will give them fair play. As you know we sent two deputations to Councillors Mr Horsman and Mr Hartley, asking the Council to call a public meeting of ratepayers to consider this question, and it is a sad reflection of how this Council conducts itself that they could not see their way to calling such a meeting. The Act which constituted District Councils is probably the most liberal and democratic measure of our age and one would have thought that a District Council would be conducted on the most democratic grounds, but the government of the Ilkley District Council is quite the reverse. I must say I think it very unwise to have such a number of councillors who have estates here and there and everywhere. Whichever way we look we have councillors with property and land waiting development. They can't make a road wider, longer or straighter but that it benefits one of them.

Mr Thornton: I would like to propose the following resolution. That this meeting condemns the purchase of the Town Hall site and opposes the completion of the Town Hall Scheme and proposes four candidates pledged to oppose it.

Mr Sunley: I will second the motion. As far as I can see there is no necessity at all for such a building: four nice square rooms are all the Council require. The Council claims that there has been no discussion regarding the Town Hall but that is very misleading. Certainly they have not discussed the matter in full Board because they know that reporters would be present and then the ratepayers would get to know about it. At election time these gentlemen come round and ask me to vote for them and promise me any mortal thing but 5s. (Laughter)

Lister: I must take exception to this remark. I did not go about the town asking anyone to vote for me.

A voice: What a big lie.

Mr Wood: I support the motion. I'll never forget the treatment we received as your deputation from the most important meeting ever held in Ilkley. The Council kept us waiting for over an hour, hoping no doubt that we would go away. (Shouts from the front row of 'No, no!') When at last we got upstairs it occurred to me that these twelve gentlemen who we had elected at the last election had got the impression that they were there for life. That they were peers of the realm, or bishops, or something of that sort, and that we had not elected them at all. I half expected to see them in robes and the Chairman sitting with a wig on, but I was disappointed to find that they just appeared to be ordinary men. (Laughter)

Mr Horsman then ascended the platform.

Horsman: Replying to questions concerning the purchase of the Town Hall site I and the rest of the Council hold that the price, when the land thrown in by Mr Jackson for the street's improvement was taken into consideration, is very reasonable, working out at about 28s per yard. I am sure that we could dispose of it at the same price if it becomes necessary.

The Chairman: Seeing that the land is deemed cheap at 30s per yard how did it come about that you let a stranger come in and buy it for 8s 7d?

15 December 1897

Buildings, Slaughterhouse, Fire Brigade, Hackney Carriage, Museum and General Purposes:

Street and Drainage:
that the lamps in streets mentioned in the minutes, to the number 103 be fitted up on the incandescent system.

Lister: I would like to propose an amendment that the matter relating to fitting up of an additional 103 incandescent lamps be referred back to committee for further consideration. I think that the poor people of this parish have as much right to incandescent lamps as anyone else whoever they might be.

Mr Ellis: The gas engineer said they were too exposed.

Lister: I place no value on what the gas engineer has to say at all. The lamps in question are no more liable to be blown out than any other lamps.

The Chairman (Horsman): If I recall at the committee meeting one of the places you seemed most anxious to have one fixed was at the bottom of Tivoli Place.

Lister: It's a lie and if you say so again I will pull you out of the chair and by the throat too.

Chorus: No! No!

The Chair: No you won't, sir. I think it's a great pity you don't know manners better than you do.

Lister: Well, I'm not going to withdraw the remark if that's what you desire. All through my time here I have been boycotted and my speeches suppressed. The Chairman has never treated me with respect.

The Chairman: I have given you as much liberty as any member of this council and more.

Lister: That is a falsehood.

Lister gathers his hat and coat and departs.

2 February 1898

Mr Lister moves the following resolution. That the Council authorise by public auction the greenhouses etc. now standing up on that portion of Sedbergh estate as purchased by the Council; and that the same be entirely removed by the 1st of April '98 and I hereby request that all deeds and documents relating to the purchase be read over to the Council by the clerk of the Council at the next meeting to be held next Wednesday night.

There is no seconder and the motion falls

9 April 1898

At the conclusion of council business Mr Crawley proposes a vote for Mr Horsman for the able manner in which he has fulfilled his duties as Chairman during the past year. Mr Middlebrook seconds.

Lister: I rise with a very strong objection to giving the Chairman a vote of thanks.

The Chairman: Quite right, sir.

Lister: I think, and I hope you will excuse me telling you point blank, that you sit there for no other purpose than to plan and scheme to rob your fellow townsmen.

Chorus: Order! Order! Shame! Shame!

Lister: It is no shame, sir.

Mr Crawley: I hope the reporters will take a special and careful note of this.

Lister: Yes, take a careful note of it; I desire you to do so. Gentlemen to sit and hold up their hands for a man to take something like £1000 worth of property and appropriate it for his own use – I refer to the greenhouses – is a disgrace to all civilisation and I don't care what man hears me say it, and I say it without any feeling or animus. It is not him personally, but his confounded infamous conduct. I always like to say what I have to say to a man's face and not behind his back.

Middlebrook: It's a cowardly and dastardly attack.

Lister: I tell a man to his face. What is cowardly in that? It is a notorious fact that Mr Horsman has not paid anything for rent upon this land upon which the greenhouses stood. I think, sir, the ratepayers will admit we are a generous set of vagabonds.

Chorus: Order! Order!

11 June 1898

A letter was read from Messrs Berry, Robinson Scott & Holmes authorising the production of minutes and any other documents that may be necessary to be produced at the Assizes in the forthcoming action for libel and slander Horsman v. Lister.

Chairman. Now then, gentlemen, vote.

Lister: Yes, with both hands.

LEEDS ASSIZES

Friday 29 July 1898

Before Mr Justice Day. Acting on behalf of Mr Thomas Horsman (Rosemount Nurseries) were Mr Tindal Atkinson, Mr Scott Fox: Mr Wallace represented Mr Lister.

On the case being called Mr Wallace asked his Lordship if he would see him and Mr Atkinson privately. Wallace informed his Lordship that he has induced his client to withdraw the charges and to express his regret. In addition for the further protection of Mr Horsman the defendant has agreed to enter into £100 bond not to repeat the libel.

Mr Justice Day: It is a most desirable settlement. I have read the pleadings and feel bound to say that had the case gone on there is no doubt that the jury would have visited the conduct of the defendant with very heavy damages indeed.

The following day, Saturday 30 July 1898

Mr Lister requests to be allowed to make an application which Mr Justice Day is willing to hear.

Mr Lister: I desire to ask my counsel Mr Wallace if it is not a fact that over and over again I refused to give an apology to Mr Horsman and also that I would not consent to permit Mr Wallace to apologise on my behalf, and yesterday when the case was called, I placed in my learned counsel's hands nine reasons, and nine very strong reasons too, with a request that he would state the same before your Lordship. Mr Wallace said that to put the nine reasons before the court and jury would mean absolute ruin to the plaintiff Mr Horsman and that he could not to do it without Mr Atkinson's consent. He saw Mr Atkinson who refused and I then requested Mr Wallace to place my reasons in your Lordship's hands. I take it for granted that my counsel did not. I think it is my duty to request Mr Wallace to pub-licly repudiate the statement published in the newspapers that I tendered an apology. I all along maintained that the publication and utterance made by me was made with per-fect truth at the time that it was made and it was only on Thursday when Mr Wallace's junior showed me the agree-ment signed by the then chairman William Hartley which said agreement reserved the greenhouses for Mr Jackson, that I asked Mr Wallace if I was bound by that signature obtained at an illegal meeting. Mr Wallace says it binds you absolutely. Under those circumstances my Lord I consider it quite wrong to let it go forth that I in any sense uttered an apology.

He produces another document.

Lister: Would you Lordship permit me to state the reasons?

His Lordship: I do not want to hear your reasons. There is one piece of advice I would give you. Make no more of these applications, here, in the newspapers or in any other place.

Lister: But my Lord will your Lordship permit me to explain.

His Lordship: No, I will hear no more.

1 Piccadilly, Bradford, 2nd August 1898

Dear Sir,

Enclosed we send draft bond herein for your perusal and approval on behalf of the defendant, and shall be glad to receive the same back at your earliest convenience. We enclose a copy of the order made at the Assizes –

Yours respectfully,

Robinson, Scott & Holmes

Ilkley, August 2nd

Horsman v. Lister

Gentlemen,

I write to request that *you do not sign* any document or agreement, bond or anything, or subject matter relating to above on my behalf, as solicitors acting for me in the above cause.

Yours truly,

Oswald Lister

Halifax, August 8th 1898

Dear Sirs,

Mr Lister has returned the draft bond, with a statement that he positively refuses to sign it, and at the same time requests us to ask you to send your account direct to him. Mr Lister sends a long string of reasons why he declines to sign the bond, but we do not think any good will result in giving you them.

Yours truly,

Dickons & Aked

Wednesday 10 August 1898

Before Mr Justice Day. Mr Tindal Atkinson on behalf of the plaintiff Mr Horsman. Mr Lister represented by neither solicitor nor counsel.

Atkinson: All I ask, my Lord, is that you should fix a date on which the bond should be signed.

His Lordship: Within a week?

Mr Atkinson: Why not tomorrow?

His Lordship: (smiling) Oh! Oh! Mr Atkinson.

Atkinson: Here is the bond. Mr Lister is in court now. There could be no better opportunity.

His Lordship: Are you going to sign it?

Lister: I refuse to sign it.

His Lordship: Very well, I will make an order that you do so within twenty-four hours.

Atkinson: And also pay the costs of this application?

His Lordship: Certainly.

Wednesday 17 August 1898

Before Mr Justice Phillimore. Mr Scott Fox moves on the behalf of the plaintiff Mr Horsman for an order for the committal of the defendant Oswald Lister to prison for not signing the bond.

Lister: I only agreed to withdraw the charges mentioned in the statement of claim and entered into a bond not to repeat them. I never agreed to have put into that bond the words 'or similar charges'.

His Lordship: You have escaped very heavy damages through the undertaking of your counsel that you would not repeat the libels or slanders complained of. You cannot have your cake and eat it. It would be an idle undertaking if it did not pledge you not to repeat the libel 'or similar charges'.

Lister: When Mr Wallace finished I desired to say a few words and my solicitor pulled me down.

His Lordship: Very wisely I think.

Lister: Unfortunately.

His Lordship: Fortunately I should think, but I cannot help the foolish ideas you got into your head. Your solicitor treated you as a naughty child and hushed you down.

Lister: My solicitor never once said I could not prove my case. I have a duty to perform myself.

Lordship: What is your duty?

Lister: To stick to my word like a man and an Englishman.

His Lordship: That is all nonsense. You are really very silly. I am very sorry for you.

Lister: It is no use wasting more time over me. My mind is made up.

His Lordship: Very well, the order must go. You may consider yourself in custody.

Lister: How long for?

His Lordship: Until you arrive at such a state of mind as will enable you to sign the bond.

Lister: If that's the case I might as well sign now, but I would rather do the six months than sign it. (Laughter)

Mr Lister signs reluctantly.

ILKLEY URBAN DISTRICT COUNCIL

5 October 1898

Lister: Then there is the case of lots 5 and 6 purchased from Mr J. T. Jackson for the Town Hall. I say when lots 5 and 6 were purchased from Mr Jackson for the Town Hall, and Mr Arthur Holmes solicitor to the Council, brought the agreement on July 1st 1896, and laid it on the table before the Council, the clerk to the Council was not permitted to read it over, neither was any member of the Council permitted to read it over, and the chairman did not read it over, the consequence of this was Mr Horsman picked that document up off the table and handed it to Arthur Holmes. Mr Arthur Holmes took it away and on July 8th 1896, seven days later another agreement was sent to the Council from the solicitors which contained a clause reserving the greenhouse to the vendor, but the agreement of July 1st did not contain such a clause. This was a gross conspiracy to deprive the town of the greenhouses which they had and did resolve to buy . . .

Mr Crawley: We have had weeks and weeks of this and I am not going to stand for it any longer – jaw! jaw! jaw!

Lister: I am not out of order.

Mr Ellis: I have distinctly told you that you are.

Chorus: Chair! Chair! Chuck him out! Chuck him out!

Lister: But I am not going to be chucked off like this. I say without hesitation that if the ratepayers knew half the dirty transactions that were carried out in this room they would rise up in open rebellion and some heads of department would do well if they did not get lynched.

The members all at once jump up, they put on their hats and coats and leave the room.

Lister (alone): Forty members will not stop me from speaking.

Letter from Reservist Newton

From Mudder River Dec. 8th

Dear Percy,

We have arrived here safe and sound after a severe struggle/we have had three battles Belmont Gras. Pas, and Mudder River. They are all well fortified places and the fighting was most severe. We took this place after 27 hours continuous fighting. It is a sort of pleasure grounds, swings, roundabouts, shooting galleries, boating and drinking. You can bet we had some fun when we took it – looting and taking what we wanted. The Lancers were in first and when we got there they were nearly all drunk. We were all on chickens for dinner, every man cooking his own. We had to move on account of the smell of the dead Boers and horses. We were drinking the water out of the river for two days and then found 42 dead Boers in it with stones tied around their necks who had been put in to poison the water. I will write from Kimberly if I land safe. They are saying they will send all reserve men home when Kimberly is relieved, and you can bet I shall be glad to be back at the post office. Your true friend

    Tom

ILKLEY URBAN DISTRICT COUNCIL

7 December 1898

Crawley: Sit down!
Lister: Get away, you soft head—
(Cries of Order! Order!)

Trooper Ballardie

[January 1900] At present we are off the coast of Portugal have just come down from the troop deck where I am pleased to see the moon is rising. This is the first night we have had it so it will be lovely in the evenings about the time when we get into the tropics when I suppose we will all sleep on deck. Whenever I get into the tropics we are going to have a large canvass sail filled with water to bathe in and by George how I will enjoy it. Many and many time I sigh for the delightful bath at home. There are about 500 of us on board and each man has a horse. I can tell you its no catch cleaning out the stalls; you have to get into each stall with a basket and shovel and jolly well scrape it clean. It is not so bad just now, but when the warm weather comes in I expect it will be awfully sickening. It is very funny to stand at one end of the boat and look down to the other when you see about 200 horses heads sticking out.

    As I am going on guard at 10 o'clock I am going to finish my letter now. This morning is simply glorious, warm bright with a lovely sea, During one of these days we had it so rough a tremendous amount of crockery was broken and heaps of fellows tipped out their hammocks

148

Wednesday 14 March 1900

Mr Lister: I should like to protest against the notice that has
been posted on the Church doors authorising the audit to
take place at 10.15 whereas the overseers had received
notice to attend at 2.20. Surely the overseers ought to have
intimated on the notice that the Ilkley accounts would not
be taken until 2.30?

Mr Rich: I had authorised the issuing of notices. The audit did
start at 10.20, but for the convenience of the overseers a
note had been written at the foot of the notice that they
need not turn up until 2.30.

Lister: Then the overseers ought to have informed the public.
What sense or reason is there in Ilkley ratepayers coming
down here and having to wait all this time? I do not blame
you Mr Rich, in the slightest. I blame the overseers.

Mr Horsman (one of the overseers): It is not the duty of the
overseers to notify the ratepayers as to what time they
should be here. They have got to take their time from the
public statement on the church door.

Lister: That is the most senseless piece of argument. You were
notified not to be here until 2.30 and as an act of courtesy
you ought to have notified the public to the same effect. The
overseers have been remiss.

Mr Horsman: Not at all.

Mr Rich: Come, come, Mr Horsman, don't interrupt Mr Lister.
Allow him to finish.

Lister: Now to business. On the face of it there is a tremendous
lot of juggling in these accounts. Take my advice and burn
the books.

Mr Horsman: Burn you.

Lister: Call the clerks and overseers together you have been
accustomed to sup and dine with, and tell them in plain language that the game is up. I object to the assistant overseer's
claim of £18 10s. 2d. for preparing voters' lists. I maintain
his salary covers every duty and when I demanded to see
the vouchers and revising barrister's certificate Mr Pate told

me I must first get Mr Horsman's permit to see them. I wrote to Mr Horsman but have been refused to examine them.

Horsman (*who had been out of the room a few minutes*): Certainly I refused. No ratepayer has any right to see them.

Lister: I claim the right to see them.

Mr Horsman: Mr Lister has appeared before the revising barrister and not withstanding all his representations and budget of law wrapt up in a red handkerchief, that gentleman gave a certificate that the accounts were correct and perfectly legal. After that neither the Local Government Board or anyone else had any right to see them.

Lister: I admit he signed the certificate but I will go further and say he had no power to do so.

Horsman: Rot!

Lister: Furthermore I accuse Mr Horsman of taking away a sheet of paper containing my notes.

Mr Horsman It is a most abominable lie. I have never seen the paper or touched it.

Mr Lister: It was a sheet of foolscap. It was here before you left the room and it is not here now.

Mr Horsman: Well, I have not touched it.

Chairman: It is a very serious charge to make against a member.

Mr Lister: Yes it is and a most disgraceful piece of conduct likewise. I say he has taken it out.

Mr Horsman: I have only been out for a very necessary purpose. I have not seen the paper and I appeal to members sitting opposite to say whether they have seen me take it.

Mr Lister: There had been no one out but you and it is nowhere to be found.

Mr Crawley: Are we going to submit quietly to these accusations, Mr Chairman?

Mr Lister: He is the only person that has been out the room and it is gone.

Mr Firth: You have no right to accuse by inference.

Mr Lister: It is a clear accusation, isn't it?

Mr Firth: But it is not clear proof.

Mr Taylor: It is a very serious thing for members to have to run the risk of being accused of theft.

Mr Lister: If a man does wrong then he deserves it. Don't you pull my coat, Mr Horsman. I'll smack you in the face if you do.

He raises his fist and glowers.

Chorus: Order! Order!

Lister: According to the terms of Mr Pate's appointment he is not entitled to receive any remuneration above his salary.

Horsman: He is off his horse and rambling, and only doing so for a purpose.

Lister: I am not rambling. I desire to see the vouchers and invoices respecting this £18 10s. 2d. paid to Mr Pate.

Horsman: Mr Lister is just trying to mislead the auditor and likewise the public. I will take good care that he does not see these invoices and vouchers for as long as I can help it. (Turning) You are nothing but a coward and a snake in the grass.

Mr Rich: Now, now, Mr Horsman.

Horsman: You are a coward and want sending to—— Jericho.

Lister: They are going to send me to the front.

Horsman: The sooner you go the better.

Mr Rich: Now, now, Mr Horsman.

Horsman: Mr Lister has no right to go into anything beyond the half year's accounts under audit. I am a big ratepayer and I object.

Lister: And I am a little ratepayer. The payment is an illegal one and it is the duty of the auditor to disallow it.

Mr Pate: Mr Lister knows well enough that it was sanctioned by the ratepayers.

Lister: If that be true why am I refused to see the churchwarden's book that contains the particulars of the appointment? Can I see the appointment?

Mr Pate: No, you shall not see it. The sneaking slinking hound that you are.

Horsman: Why don't you give in. You know you haven't a leg to stand on.

Lister: I have two good ones. I don't shuffle my feet along the street like some folks. Now, sir, have you decided to allow that £18 10s 2d. to Mr Pate?

Mr Rich: Certainly.

Lister: Then I must ask you to state your reasons.

Rich: Give me your objections in writing and then I will deal with them.

Lister: You will get them from the newspapers.

Rich: I prefer to have them written down properly.

Lister: Very well. I will oblige you. That is all I have to bring before you.

Lister gathers his papers and books and ties them in a large red hand-kerchief. He notices Mr Horsman looking quietly on.

Lister: You see, I have got the handkerchief yet.

Horsman: It is not worth much.

Lister: Oh, but this is an old heirloom. What would you give to have sufficient cheek to walk through the streets like this.

Horsman: Well, you lick all I've come across for that. Evidently you have come down here for a day's outing.

Lister: Yes, but it's been a longer day than I anticipated.

Horsman: I hope you miss your next train.

Lister: Will you be light porter for me? I'll give you sixpence.

Horsman: I should want you to put a seal on it, because if there was no seal you would swear I had stolen something.

Lister: May I wish you all a pleasant afternoon.

Lister takes up his handkerchief and departs.

Trooper Ballardie

[April 2] I saw a most magnificent sight tonight – a terrific lightening storm unaccompanied by any thunder or rain like some great artillery duel taking place in the heavens, whole clouds being silhouetted against a vivid sheet of gold while great zig zag pillars of lightening rose from the earth. It was very vivid when I dropped off to sleep and was still in progress when I woke the next morning.

[April 3] We had reviled at 2 o'clock this morning. We fully expected to come across some Boers today so to rest our horses as much as possible we walked them. It is jolly tiring as you have to lead a horse carry a heavy rifle 100 rounds of ammunition besides a haversack stuffed

and water bottle. When the sun gets up it does make you perspire. Altogether we did about twelve miles today and halted for the day beside a large lake in the veldt but the sun had dried most of the water up and left a great expanse of glistening white sand, with only a small corner of deep water. Here the heat was terrific and as we had no tents we rigged up shelters with our rifles and blankets, using our bayonets as tent pegs. I am looking forward to seeing the Ilkley paper. What is the idea at home about our returning, do they think that peace will soon be declared?

LEEDS ASSIZES

4 August 1900

Before Mr Justice Bruce. Mr Tindal Atkinson appeared for the plaintiff, Mr Horsman. Mr Lister represented himself.

Mr Atkinson: We will not be content to proceed on the bond alone. It has now become absolutely necessary to take every precaution possible to restrain the defendant.

Lister: I desire that the matter be gone into in its entirety. It is only right between man and man that it should be. I make my charges openly and in court and I ought surely to have the privilege and right to bring witnesses before the court to prove them.

His Lordship. That part of the case has already been dealt with.

Lister: Is it no use a man coming here and trying to win his case?

His Lordship. I don't think it is, under the circumstances.

Lister: Then I must submit to you.

His Lordship: You see, all this was decided in chambers and the order stands. There seems no doubt that you have broken your bond and repeated this slander.

Lister: I appeal to Mr Horsman to join issue with me, and let us have the whole case thrashed out in court. If Mr Horsman is a man he will accept my challenge in a manly spirit.

His Lordship: Mr Horsman has already been prepared to accept your challenge and you withdrew. You have repeated this slander after you had undertaken not to repeat it, and there can be no defence in such a case.

Lister: I would not have executed the bond if Mr Justice Phillimore had told me there was no alternative.

His Lordship: You might have gone to prison if you had preferred it. (Laughter)

Lister: That would have been folly.

His Lordship: There is no question here to submit to the jury. It is a question of damages. Have you anything to say to the jury why they should not award damages against you?

Lister: Yes, my Lord, I have.

His Lordship: What damages do you think you ought to pay for this slander?

Lister: None whatever, because I can prove my case up to the hilt.

Atkinson: Even now, when the defendant is faced with the fact that he cannot defend the action, he persists in repeating the slander in open court.

Lister: It is not slander. You have only got to look at the matter of Mr Horsman as overseer. Mr Horsman has acted most discreditably. He had assessed his own property at about the quarter of the rate which the property of other people had been assessed. There is no equity of the system, no equity at all.

Mr Atkinson: I must protest, my Lord. The defendant is repeating the slanders yet again.

Lister: Oh I beg your pardon, Mr Atkinson. I did not realise you were judge and jury, as well as counsel. I hope you're getting sufficient pay.

His Lordship. You are wasting the court's time, Mr Lister.

Lister (warmly): Have you no sympathy at all with a man who goes as a public representative to the District Council, and tries to do what is right and is fearless and sticks out, and does what is right to the best interests of the township? I challenge Mr Horsman to join me on this issue.

His Lordship: He has done so once. He is not bound to do so again.

Lister: Am I to submit to an apology I don't agree with? It is very wrong – very wrong indeed. (Laughter)

His Lordship: You are not improving your case.

Lister: Very well, my Lord, I will sit down. I have nothing more to say.

The jury, after a brief consultation, returns with a verdict for the plaintiff of £100 on the bond and £100 damages.

His Lordship. You must not repeat these slanders.

Lister: Then I suppose I shall have to let him sit in the council chamber, and let him take what money he likes out of the pockets of the ratepayers, but I am not prepared to do so.

Lister takes his large red handkerchief, smooths it out upon the solicitor's table and collects his large bundle of documents upon it. He ties it up in his familiar knot, and with the court watching, he leaves the court.

It was the last time they saw him there; his time in the council drawing to a close too.

ILKLEY URBAN DISTRICT COUNCIL

October 1900

Lister: I beg to move a resolution to condemn the action of the three overseers Messrs Crawley, Middelton and Horsman in trying to take advantage of the ratepayers of Ilkley in convening an illegal meeting held at the Parish Church Vestry on the 30th August 1900 and to further point out that the resolution passed at the above mentioned meeting is null and void and of no effect and that no increase of salary must be given to Mr Pate, the assistant Overseer.

Mr Horn: I will second. When a class of gentlemen attend a meeting who are not in the habit of taking part in public meetings, it might be safely assumed that some special interest had drawn them together. I have nothing against Mr Pate personally you understand. I have always found him very civil, very obliging, and I am sorry that physical infirmity has taken such a hold on him, otherwise I feel sure he would not have allowed such unjust assessments to be made as has been made. The struggling working man who had his rates taken out the clothing of his children had been assessed at five and a half and six per cent; whereas those who lived in large houses and were best able to bear the burden of taxation were assessed at one and a half per cent.

Lister: The meeting was illegal.

Mr Horsman: It was perfectly legal.

Chairman: Whether it was or was not it does not concern us. It is simply a waste of time to discuss the matter further.

Lister: It's no use giving a sly wink at Mr Horsman.

Mr Horsman: I was asking the Chairman if he would allow me to speak and he said he wzould not. That is the wink he gave me.

Chairman: You are too ready with your innuendoes.

The continual bruising he received tempted him to retire from public life. But in April 1909 he stood again, drawn to action no doubt by the rising splendour of the new Town Hall (erected, in defiance of all his rantings, not five hundred yards from his front door), and the likelihood of how this self-regarding munficence would generate further municipal malpractice. He was returned with a majority of 58, the voters recognizing the need for such a fierce uncompromising voice to be heard in the midst of this growing corporate complacency, and Oswald Lister the benchmark, stubborn, fearless, unable once set on course to turn from his chosen purpose (no matter the reefs that lay ahead that might sink his craft), but sadly, swift illness took hold of that fearsome pair of lungs and stilled him. In December of that year, on a Monday, he contracted a chill which led quickly to pneumonia. A week later he was dead, dying shortly before 3 o'clock Monday morning. He left a widow, four sons, and three daughters.

At the funeral the Councillors present were as follows: I. Dean, J. Dinsdale, J. T. Jackson, J. C. Naylor, J. W. Dixon, L. M. Wilkinson, H. Mott, J. W. Benson, A. Eames. Thomas Horsman did not attend.

And in private they rubbed their hands, nodded to each other
    over the wooden table, their rehearsed winks
their rehearsed winks brought out as he had pulled out his hand-
    kerchief and spread his papers out defying their complicity
defying their complicity with an anger funnelled by tight com-
    press of the municipal gorge, so strong he could not help
could not help himself, could not stop the flood of anger he felt
    surging forward as he saw them
as he saw them floating their Ilkley stock upon this company,
    which was commerce and benefit for them

They got the better of him in the end, bought his plot of land from
his executors for a knockdown price, Lister under the hammer for
£200, and once appropriated, took it down,

Paradise Removed.

[February 10th 1900] Prince Christian and Princess Victoria of
Schleswig-Holstein paid a visit on Tuesday afternoon on behalf
of the Queen to the wounded at Ilkley Hospital. The men in the
surgical ward who had actually received wounds numbered
three hundred and twenty-nine. Many of the men had lost limbs
and all the others had been severely wounded. All appeared very
cheerful.

Trooper Ballardie

[April 5th] We are now in a standing camp awaiting the
mobilisation of a column of 12000 (?) men. About midday the news that the enemy was in the vicinity was
brought in. The Sherwood Rangers and South Notts.
Companies of the 3rd Battalion and the 1st section No 3
(the inlying picket) of the Hussars were immediately
mounted and sent out. The remainder of the Hussars,
including my section, were grazing about two miles away
and could not be mounted for about an hour. It is just

my usual luck not being sent out with them, as I had to lie in camp all the afternoon doing nothing.

I was lying in this tent about eleven o'clock at night being generally flooded out when I heard our men return and jumped up to get the news. They had been in action; They found the Boers who numbered about 200 and managed to surround the kopje where they were. On average each man fired about a dozen rounds, and the artillery three or four shells, when the enemy put up the white flag. Lieut. Williams then advanced to meet them and was immediately shot down, after the white flag had been shown. Another lieutenant then borrowed a rifle from a man and shot the man who showed the white flag. The kopje was finally taken at the point of the bayonet. Poor Williams, he was such a nice fellow – one of the best. We have caught a little springbok and I remember only this morning he came up to us when we were feeding it on condensed milk and asked a lot of questions about it, and now he is lying dead in the hospital wagon. This springbok is an awful neat little thing, quite young, and it only stands about a foot high. It was caught by one of our fellows when we were watering down at a spring.

[5 May 1900 Ilkley] A meeting held in the large room behind the coffee tavern to consider what steps should be taken to celebrate the relief of Mafeking whenever that much desired event should take place. Mr Dobson in the chair said it was the duty of every resident to celebrate this long looked for relief. Himself and several other tradesmen had met and talked the matter over and had thought in their own minds that a procession, tea and sports and games afterwards would be a good way of honouring the event. Blackpool Southport and other health resorts could get up very successful demonstrations of one kind or another and why not Ilkley? In Ilkley they were very good at proposing anything but few things were carried to their successful issue.

[April 20th 1900]   About midday I was called up on to the top of the kopje as a sentry and shortly afterwards we saw the whole camp strike tents and start moving off towards Boshof. The Bucks (38th Co. I.Y.) reported that they had seen the enemy advancing, and had fallen back, so McKillop at once sent a galloper into camp for instructions. He soon returned with the order that we were to hold the kopje until the last man had left camp and the whole column had got clear away. The Boers then opened a hot fire on us from the shelter of a ridge of rocks, and to this we cheerily replied, blazing away for all we were worth. We heard bullets whistling all around us, but as none of us were being hit we were rather enjoying ourselves, until we heard a devil of a row and found out that the Boers had started shelling us with big guns and also with pom-poms. By George they did hum a bit. I was smoking all the time I was firing, and managed to get through four cigarettes before we were ordered to retire.

The news came half-past nine Friday evening, and by ten they were collected around the Post Office. Newsagent Dobson received telephone messages from both Bradford and Leeds newspapers that the news was correct; by eleven, the telegram was stuck on to the Post Office window. Mafeking had been relieved.

Now they made their own town war, shopkeepers opening up their stores and handing out the explosives: Roman candles, squibs, crackers, rockets, jumping jacks set off in the midst of the crowd, while above them, on the new railway bridge, they fired up the boiler and ran an engine and tender backwards and forwards over fog signals placed on the line. Cordite and burnt powder smoke hung in the air, Ilkley sniffing the splendid spectacle of war.

[20th April]   We then got the order to retire and did so in splendid order. We got our horses round to the rear of the kopje, dismounted and made our way up, where we found the remainder of the Hussars under Major Gasgoigne, potting away at the Boers who had just occupied the kopje we had just left. We had good cover here and lay behind the rocks, potting away at them for some considerable time, having no casualties so far, their shooting being miserably poor, although some shots seemed to whistle terribly about our heads. So far I had been enjoying the novelty of the thing immensely, when the enemy opened a heavy fire behind us, having done a flanking movement on our right, occupied a large kopje, got round behind it, and occupied another kopje almost dead behind us. We were thus under a heavy fire from three sides – in front, in rear, and on our right flank. When I saw and heard the bullets go pop and spit all around me, I believe I asked myself why the devil I had ever joined this crush, but there was no time to think, I had to find cover somewhere, so I lay flat on the ground, and crawled about twenty yards, until I got behind a low ridge beside Lieut. McKillop. We went on shooting at the Boers behind us, until McKillop suddenly said, "Hello! here's a fellow killed". I looked round and saw the poor fellow shot through the temple with his head in a pool of blood, and at the same instant I felt as if I had had the whole of my insides blown to pieces. It was the most awful thing, the pain being excruciating, and I was unable to tell whether or not the wound was mortal. I remember saying to McKillop – Good God I'm shot. The pain however did not last long and I went on firing, firing another three shots. I then began to feel dizzy, and asked Major Gasgoigne if I might retire. He told me to drop my rifle and retire on the horses, but I didn't like to leave my rifle, got to my feet and staggered to the edge of the kopje.

The matron begs to acknowledge the receipt of the following gifts sent during the month.

From Mrs Atkinson, grapes, oranges, knitted stockings, 7 yards of print; Mrs Beanlands, Miss Crewe, Mrs Gant and Mrs Stoppard dripping; Miss Brice cake and eggs; Mrs Cooks and Mrs Turner beef tea; Mrs Knight brown flour and sweets; Mrs Moon piece of beef; Mrs Smith (Hebers Mount) milk and jam; Mrs Hudson *Sunday Stories*

Trooper Ballardie

No. 2 General Hospital, Wynberg   6 May

When I got to the edge of the kopje I felt so terribly weak and dizzy that I fell down and rolled under the shelter of a large boulder, where I was quite safe from the bullets. I think I lay there about a quarter of an hour and saw men creeping back, so I clutched hold of my rifle and walked down to the foot of the kopje. From the nature of my wound – I was shot through the stomach, the bullet passing through my left thigh – I was unable to crawl, and had to stand upright all the time I was descending the kopje, and it was a high one. I think it was almost beyond a miracle I hadn't 30 or 40 bullets through me; they were simply splashing around me like raindrops. Arriving at the bottom of the kopje, the scene was a bit sickening. The Boers had been firing right into our horses and ever so many of them lay there dead, lying in little pools of blood; the remainder of the horses were terrified, rearing, kicking and struggling. When I got to the flat veldt again I looked around for my horse, but could see nothing, as my eyes got completely blurred by a thick yellow haze and I felt so terribly faint that I had to drop my rifle. Then, amid all the shouting, I heard my name called out and stumbled up against my horse. Then someone lifted me into the saddle, shoved the reins in my hand and when the horse started moving, my head got quite clear again and I knew exactly what I was doing. My horse had been shot in the mouth, under the chin, the bullet passing upwards through its tongue and out through its right cheek, carrying away with it a piece of the bit with it, and it was terribly fidgety and restless. Then we formed up in some sort of order and got the word to retire. Two or three riderless horses then passed, and my own completely broke away and bolted with me. Then a horse in front of me put its foot in a hole and came down, throwing its rider yards ahead and bringing down several others. My own horse which was right behind it, jumped clean over it and went on with its rush. It was just at this moment that my near stirrup was shot away and I also lost my off stirrup, and as I had no grip whatever with my knees, I had to hold on to my saddle with the right hand while trying to direct my horse with the reins hand. It is as well that it took it into its head to follow the others as I had absolutely no control over it whatsoever. All this time we were under a heavy fire from the kopje which we had just evacuated and from the kopje past which we had to go to retire on the column. It was during this time that most of our casualties occurred. After about a mile of this rush, my horse jumped a donga, and as I could not stand the pain any longer I lay on its neck and rolled on to the ground.

I immediately scrambled on to my feet and started to walk in, but one of the Leeds troopers (Leather) came up, dismounted, handed over his horse, and started carrying me, although I insisted on his going on and leaving me, as I really thought I was a 'goner' by this time. However he would not hear of it until his strength failed him and he had to lay me down, when two other fellows, Bagley and Gutch, dismounted and between them I struggled for about half-a-mile until a doctor rode up and I was lifted into his saddle, while he led the horse and the other two held me on, sitting sideways. One of the Kimberly Corp.'s officers also had a try at getting me away sitting on the saddle in front of him while he held me on, but his horse started, rearing violently and I had to be helped down. Dozens of other fellows also offered to give up their horses to me, although all this time, in fact until we came across the doctor, we were under a heavy fire from the rear and right flank . . . The sun was setting as we reached the ambulance wagon and then I had a terribly painful jolt of ten miles over awful roads, along with seven other wounded men. It was a treat that journey. Two of the men were suffering from concussion of the brain and were raving, while others were sick and others groaning and all were wanting water, which the orderly was constantly handing round. We got into Boshof about four hours after we had been shot. I had been losing blood all that time and had absolutely nothing to eat since five that morning. I had no chloroform while being dressed, and four doctors had to hold me down, while Lord Methuen spoke to me and told me that "we had made a very plucky stand of it." Then after an injection of morphia, some beef tea, I was laid in a tent along with three others, on a stretcher, and tried to get asleep. We had a candle lit in the tent all night with a special orderly, as we had one fellow suffering from concussion who insisted on getting up and "fighting" and "going home", &c. . . .

Taken altogether it was a novel sort of experience, while it lasted, and highly enjoyable, although after you have been hit you begin to think what a fool you have been to go in for that sort of amusement. Now that I am all right again, I shouldn't mind being under fire again in the slightest.

[16 June 1900] 8 o'clock on Saturday night a report gained currency that Trooper Jack Ballardie, eldest son of Mr J. de C. Ballardie, manager of the Ilkley Wells House Hydro, was expected home that evening from South Africa, where for some three or four months he has been doing his country's duty with the Yorkshire Hussars Company of the Imperial Yeomanry, but

had been invalided home in consequence of wounds received in the abdomen.

Trooper Ballardie failed to catch the 3.45 at King's Cross as intended, and journeying by the 5.45 it was eleven before he reached Ilkley. Fortunately he had telegraphed to his parents that he had missed the first train and knowledge of this spread rapidly from mouth to mouth, a crowd of extraordinary magnitude awaited his arrival. Directly he alighted at the station he was hoisted shoulder high and in this way carried the whole distance to Wells House. Some thousands of people were gathered in the Railway Station, and the hustling was so severe that it was almost a miracle someone was not killed or very seriously injured. Several people were thrown down, kicked and bruised, and one or two females also fainted. A landau was in waiting for Trooper Ballardie's convenience; but this (those who were carrying him) altogether ignored. The Town Band played "See the Conquering Hero Comes" and on the other side and in front of Ballardie marched the "Highland Brigade" in full uniform and with lighted torches. The wildest excitement everywhere prevailed and cheering and shouting was most enthusiastically indulged in. "Long Tom" also took part in the procession and directly the Hydro was reached a succession of shots were fired in Ballardie's honour. Hundreds poured into the corridors, and when Ballardie disappeared into one of those drawing rooms, the feelings of these assembled found vent once more in "See the Conquering Hero Comes" and "Soldiers of the Queen", songs which had been sung over and over again during the march from the station. Ballardie afterwards came to the door and thanked the crowd for their hearty and enthusiastic welcome, and spoke a few similar words from one of the upper windows. Within the hydro he was subjected to a very tiring round of hand-shaking and had also to endure the caresses and kisses of numberless females. He remarked to our representative that he had entirely recovered from his wounds and was in the best of health.

Interview took place on Mr and Mrs Ballardie's silver wedding anniversary. Mr Ballardie is a naval architect and very early in his career went out to Ceylon, residing in the district of

Dimbula, where Trooper John de Caynoth Ballardie was born a little less than 24 years ago. Here Mr Ballardie was engaged as a coffee planter, and after returning to his native Glasgow, eventually took over the management of the Peebles Hydro; from there migrating to the Harlow Manor Hydro, Harrogate, and finally to the Ilkley Wells House. By profession Trooper Ballardie is a chartered accountant, and up to donning the khaki was engaged with Messrs Price, Waterhouse and Company of London. After being wounded he sailed from Cape Town on the *Pavona* on May 8th and arrived at Woolwich on June 8th.

> Interviewer: I should think you are mightily pleased to get home and be out of it?
> Ballardie: I don't know about that. Certainly it is not all "beer and skittles" and getting wounded is to say the least a little bit off; but bar getting wounded, it is a grand and intensely interesting experience and I am glad I went out. In pecuniary terms I have gained nothing. All I have brought back beside my equipment are a number of bullets and little mementoes of that sort, and my wounds; the scars of which I shall carry to the grave.

The summer grows, the sun rising. Ilkley in is heat. The Wells Hydropathic establishment is now the epicentre of romance. Private Ballardie, rested from his wounds, is in the thick of it once more, besieged by admirers who hope to fell him anew with their hopeful glances. He moves about his father's fort peering at the moor, or the town below, waiting for the cavalry, growing sluggish on tea and Gentleman's Relish, venturing out under cover of dark, when the air has cooled and the streets emptied of the skirted enemy. It is a fierce heat that Ilkley bears. It seems he has known nothing but heat ever since they left the coast of Portugal. He is tired of this drawing-room life.

THE MOOR (7)

Thursday 12 July 1900

not in the winter months, when the town is wrapped up, nor the spring, when there is sponge enough in the earth to soak some of the danger, but when the town has its parasol out, in the dry spell, the earth hard and sharp like flint, horses fly-swatting, shop hours idle, dusty skirts sweeping along the cracked ground, the river moving like congealed blood its banks revealing fish gaping their mouths fighting hard for oxygen, and men too, in the bowl of the long heat, listening as the metre of sluggish water beats the rhythm of their own parched circulation.

the moor is brown with bees in their heathered holes, yet there is a breeze up there and at night the air is cool and down by the river too, but in the day they cannot climb, nor until the wage has been earned laze for an hour by the waters' banks; work they must, attend to school and to business, business that is good in this temperature, ice cream and soft drinks and the cool of the alehouse, and up on the edge of the burnished heather the shrines to cold water

skinned carcass hanging in the butcher's frame, a crate of unwashed milk bottles outside the dairy, a dog asleep in the door-way frame, an empty tin of Ilkley Wells toffee lying in the gutter, the shopkeeper idling with his broom; excessive heat on the Tuesday, Wednesday, Thursday looking set to follow, and in its breadth, windows thrown open above and below, blinds drawn; in the garden a hammock, in the yard an old armchair, the back door idling open, work suspended, lying in the darkened bedroom in the still of the afternoon, or fashioning desire under heat's heavy hammer, and in the midst of this complicity a fluttering breeze, the curtain billowing in and a cool upon the body that is as unpredicted as it is refreshing, and the dog raising his head as the shopkeeper sweeps his broom dust out, sees it lift and swirl along the pavement, hears the toffee tin stir, the breeze pleasant on his face, but growing muscle, unexpectedly bitter, yes a taste in the air, and looking up to the horizon, a line of a dark thing above the moor, galloping over the prairie blue, like the ten-day charge of a herd of bison, as the thundering black billows up, filling the sky with its rolling ink, the bedroom, the cobbled yard, abruptly chill, the languid body cold but curious and wrapped in a bedspread moving quickly to see the first large drops fall, as the wind turns and the trees bend. There is pleasure in this, pleasure too in that scent that rises up from the baked pavements of summer; and as they breathe in the perfume, bathe in its promise, the sheen will bring to all their dusty skin as the thunder moves up close, shakes the rock above, those darkened shapes stabbed by light,

and so a cloud bursts on the moor

bursts over the tinder of grass and the hard crust of earth, as if the giant walks again, running with his stone dropped, foot crushed, and in his anger tearing the sky with his huge hands. The water begins to run, down the hard rivulets and channels, little stones and little waves of sand moving running with it, the rain harder now and harder still, as it reaches the steeper slopes and begins its rush before the town below. They hear it . . . and close their windows, shut their doors, move inside. They know of rain, know the storms that lash the moor, know the treachery of the swollen river, how sudden the change of mood, but it is not the river this time, and they do not expect it.

it comes armed with rock and branch, knives of its own making, to carve afresh the channels, swift strokes, cut deep like African skin (and which in time will settle widened, lovely on its face), but now, newly sliced, pours out its thick cloudy life, spouting rock and boulder and branch towards the newly built town. It has not been long in the making, this Ilkley. They can look at their roads and chart the map of their progress, see the grace of their houses, the width of their streets, the wealth that is accumulating; they can count the businesses started, the lamps lit, the pavements laid. There is order here, order in the timetables and opening hours, order in the clubs' rules and societies' minutes, order in the municipal bulbs dug in and the municipal trees planted out, order in the old stuffed swan and the new fire engine, and, even with Mr Lister present, order in the council. It is a modern town, growing in modern confidence.

and the rain gathers. The earth is too baked to absorb it. It can only direct it, to the town over which it watches. That is all right. This town knows about water. This town sits by water, made its name on water, sells water by the bathful. The first company formed was nothing else but water. This town *is* water. Water is the Ilkley Cure. So now it is the town's turn to be plunged under, to come up gasping, to be plunged under again. From Backstone Bech to the east to Herbers Ghyll in the west, the water pours. On the western edge of the moor, down Spicey Ghyll, the water tears across Westwood Drive, throwing out the culvert and carrying the road before it, leaving a hole ten yards across. Now it has the steep drop of Parish Ghyll to guide it and this it swarms down, surging round house and over garden, sweeping boundary walls and pillar boxes away, boulders, branches, trees, all this churning soup carried downhill, branching out along arterial Princess and Wilmot Roads, down again, Eaton Road, Oakburn Road, Albany Walk, Riddings Road, before embracing the town's dignity, boiling along the Grove and down Brook Street, sometimes breast-high, splashing against the lamp-posts, leaping up like seaside spray. In Bolton Bridge Road, at four o'clock, two hours after the storm started, a wall and a shed collapse undermining the foundations of Mr Brogden's coachbuilding paint shop, just off the centre of town. Mr Brogden senior is away on the St Margaret's choir trip but his sons Alfred and Edward and Robert are there working as usual. Business is business whatever the weather. Hearing the crash Edward moves his mother into the house, while Alfred goes back to warn his fellow workers, kneeling down, looking through the hoist, calling to the smiths below. As Edward comes back he sees the roof of the paint shop fall in, burying his brother beneath it.

Coroner: Can you suggest anything that might have prevented your brother's death?

Edward: If he had not gone back to warn the other men he would have got clear away.

Juror: Have you any reason to doubt the stability of the building?

Edward: The last time we had a flood the water came through into the bottom shop and we had to break a hole through the cellar to let the water out. If the foundations of the shop had been further away I don't think it would have come down. Every storm dashed stones and rubbish against the building.

Juror Mott: How far is the building from the brook when there is no flood?

Edward: The water laps against the foundations of the shop.

Juror Mott: Is it the same with the cottages at Chapel Lane?

Edward: No, there is a wall on that side.

Juror Hood: What space is there for the water to run down?

Edward: Four or five feet.

Juror Hood: That is sadly insufficient for the weight of water that comes down that stream. I am surprised that the Council ever passed the plans.

Juror Dobson: Surely the lightning had as much to do with the building falling. The water was pressing just as fully against the Chapel Lane cottages as against Mr Brogden's shop.

Juror Hood: Oh no. He says there was a wall between the cottages and the stream.

Coroner: I think the jury may dismiss the idea of lightning having anything to do with the building falling.

The jury hand over their fees to the fund started in aid of the sufferers through the storm.

Two hours, the town transformed. The river did its best, took away the water as fast as it could, and though it rose seven feet it did not break its banks. But oh, what was left. Buildings washed away, roads torn up, boulders left like tumbleweed strewn over the ravaged street, Ilkley a frontier town again, blown in by a hurricane from its high prairie. In Chapel Lane there is sludge up to their armpits, the smell of sewer gas overwhelming. Trippers inspect the ruins, the rubbish heaps at the back of the houses picked over, mementoes of the disaster. At the bottom of Church Street, out of Mr Curwen's house, thirty tons of rubbish are removed, seventy-two loads carted away from the low-lying sidewalk at the front. The bridge and culvert under Ben Rhydding Road collapsed on the moor side entirely; the culvert under Hangingstone Road, a great hole in the middle; the new reservoir above the Cow and Calf, great cracks in the sides, the stream blocked with tons of rocks; the bridge at the bottom of Herbers Ghyll destroyed.

(Mr Dobson of Craiglands: £400 worth prize poultry.
Mr Horsman: damage to his nurseries at £700.
To Mr Ingham: damage £500.
Mr Brodgen: his machinery and stock, three carriages sent
in for repairs and his property £1,500.

On Saturday and Sunday a number of ladies took collecting sheets in various parts of the town, by means of which £170 was collected from trippers alone. The Ilkley Town Band gave a concert at the top of Brook Street on Saturday afternoon and Saturday evening and Mr Howarth's company of Pierrots gave the proceeds of their concert on Wednesday evening to the same cause.

The remains of Alfred Brogden interred at Ilkley cemetery (a coffin of polished pitch pine with brass fittings) close to the spot where, walking a few days after the flood, his father found his account books.

And (he cannot help it) a last stutter from Oswald Lister:

ILKLEY URBAN DISTRICT COUNCIL

October 1900

Mr Lister then proceeded to move that Mr Horsman be notified to take up pipes laid in the old water course which is now laid in the ditch along the South east Boundary of his garden in Bridge Lane and further that Mr Horsman be given seven days notice to open and clear out the said water course and that if he fails to comply the Council do the work and charge Mr Horsman with the cost thereof. Also to notify the Wharfedale Estate Company Ltd to take out the present drain pipes and to erect a walled in water course through that portion of land at the west of Castle Road and to carry it forward to deliver into the old water course and to junction with the water course in Mr Horsman's garden.

The Chairman: Under what Act do you propose to proceed?

Lister: I don't think an Act is necessary unless an act of justice between one man and another. There are gentlemen sitting round this table, professing to watch over the interests of the ratepayers—

Mr Horsman: That means Thomas Horsman.

Lister: It is most cruel the amount of destruction caused by the flood to those cottages at the back of Bridge Lane and in the cellars in Cunliffe Road and which was all brought about by the blocking of this culvert.

Mr Horsman: I have nothing to do with it. It's only a matter of personal spite.

Lister: I have no personal spite.

Mr Horsman: You know you have.

Lister: I have no spite against the Wharfedale Estate company.

Mr Horsman: Then why should you have any spite against me, then?

Lister: On account of your contemptible conduct, that's how it is.

171

Mr Stanfield: Should this not be referred to the Street and Drainage Committee? We're going to be here all night.

Lister: If you're tired of staying, there's the door.

Mr Geo. Smith: The matter has been dealt with by the Street and Drainage Committee. Mr Horsman has very generously allowed us to construct a surface water drain through his land.

Lister: If that is so then the least that could have been done was to place the plans on the table. It is a most disgraceful thing to be done by anyone.

Mr Fletcher: It is not.

Lister: Excuse me, Mr Fletcher, but I don't interrupt you, and I hope you will have the gentlemanly conduct to keep your mouth shut. I don't want to saddle blame on wrong shoulders, but I was not aware it was the Council's doing.

Mr Horsman: I propose that other resolutions standing in Mr Lister's name be dealt with by the committees to which the matters belong.

Lister: (jumping up) No! No!! He has not given proper notice.

Chairman: Mr Horsman is on his feet. I must ask you to sit down.

Lister: Before I will sit down I will create a scene. Mr Horsman has no right to get up in that way.

Mr Horn: Seeing that Mr Lister has not moved his resolutions can Mr Horsman get up?

Mr Horsman: My resolution is—

Lister: I object.

Chairman: Sit down.

Lister: I will not. I refuse.

and Herber's Ghyll returned to form, the watercourse hollowed out, its orchestrated timidity replaced by wilderness and grandeur

ILKLEY (9)

From J. Bertram Private Secretary to Mr Carnegie
June 22nd, 1903

Dear Sir,

Responding to your appeal on behalf of Ilkley, Mr Carnegie will be glad to give three thousand pounds to erect a free public library building for Ilkley if the Free Public Library Act be adopted and the maximum assessment under it levied now (so that there may be money to stock the library when built) producing two hundred and twelve pounds a year asserted by you.

A site for the building must also be given, the cost not being a burden on the penny rate.

[17 November]   Recommended a scheme involving total expenditure of £10,000 including a grant of £3,000 from Mr Carnegie. Premium of £100, £50, £20 for the best design submitted.

21 April 1904

The Committee inspects sixty competitive designs with the assessor Mr Bulmer. The designs are numbered, so that no one may know from where they came. 1st Prize to design 53: it is what they want, design 53, it places them in the centre of things: on the left side the King's Hall, for amusements and concerts and meetings of town import, on the right the library for the town's education and growing knowledge, and guiding them both, the Town Hall rooms and the council chamber, with its panels and its dais and its sturdy table of records. There it lies, on the first floor, up the flight of stairs. They have their pride architectured now, pride in the growing stature of the town and their own place in it and they require the capture of it, to put themselves in the circus of municipality, that they may parade about the town advertising their own attractions, perform their tricks in public. Step up, see that gavel banged and the ring-master set the lions in the ring; wood-panelled be their tent, and gold chains their lion's mane. In time pictures will be commissioned and their florid faces, their sturdy gaze will stare out, their faces glazed with the same expression, trying to mask the skin of self-advancement under the greasepaint of selfless authority. Vision is not like that. Vision to some degree is always a matter of self-interest. So now it is

Resolved

that the building be erected for the sum estimated by the competition.

The Chairman opens the sealed envelope containing the name and address. The author of design No. 53 is Mr William Bakewell, 38 Park Square, Leeds. Motto 'Economy'.

April 1905

A petition of ratepayers is presented asking the council to postpone such a frivolous erection on the grounds of a) severe depression in trade b) large number of empty houses in Ilkley c) abnormal increase in the Poor and education rates d) the special 'war' taxes.

The council look askance at these complaints, rejecting not simply the nature of their argument but to the validity of the protesters themselves. They plot each ratepayer signature against its ratepayer value.

545 people on ratebook

45 neither owners nor occupiers
9 owners who are not occupiers
4 duplicates
2 illegibles,
a total of 605,
the assessable value represented by these petitioners being:

Unquestionable £17,688
Questionable £1,992

15 May 1905

That the council consider the present a favourable opportunity for erecting the building for the following reasons 1) that the land which was purchased by sanction of your Honourable Board having laid idle for over 8 years at a cost to the ratepayers of £340 per year for interest and instalment on loan, the Council consider it now quite time that the site was used for the purpose for which it was purchased 2) that the scheme can now be carried out in conjunction with erection of the Free Library for which Mr Carnegie is giving £3,000 3) that the price of building materials and labour locally is now very reasonable and not likely to be cheaper at any time 4) that almost the whole of the money will be spent in Ilkley thus providing business and employment for local tradespeople and workmen.

10 June 1907

recommended that the tender of Messrs Smith and son Derby be accepted for supplying a one dial clock striking hours only to be fixed in the tower of the public offices.

Mr Jackson reports that he has had an interview with the Revd

Dr Collyer who intended to sail for America on the 5th October. Recommended that Wednesday the 2nd be fixed as the date for opening the library by Dr Collyer.

(who when a boy learnt his trade at the steady beat of the Ilkley hammer beating metal into softened shape hammering horseshoes. Later in America he travelled the towns and farmlands about Chicago (remembering Ilkley) and softened men's hearts beating on the anvil of religion had them waiting in line to be shoed in the calling of the Lord

Dr Collyer is coming! Dr Collyer is coming! It was all they had, Dr Collyer, their man of learning, their man with vision and horizon in his eyes: Dr Collyer, born in Keighley in '23, worked in a cotton mill over at Blubberhouses and learnt the blacksmith's art down on the Leeds Road, working with Jackie Birch across from the Crescent Hotel: married an Ilkley woman, Harriet Watson, buried her and their child: married again a year later and left for America straight: worked in a claw-hammer factory but threw it down to preach across the dusty farmstead of Kansas and later in the heart of Chicago, where in the midst of its great silos and its meat and canning factories he felt the breath of Rombald soft on his neck and wrote a great unfolded history of the town. They love Dr Collyer, love him for his flowing white locks and his wise old face and the strange western lilt to his northern voice, love him for his sermons and his wide goodness and his calling upon Ilkley as the place of all his apprenticeships. He receives their petitions and deputations with grace, admitting always his debt

(Mr Barker who visited the States in 1877 and wrote him asking if he might visit: Collyer answered, prompt.
We are at home and shall be very glad indeed to see

you, don't go to any hotel but come right here. All Ilkley folks are my guests by right of nature and grace. Just take a carriage and bring your traps. I know your name in connection with the town; though you must be one of the new men, but new or old an Ilkley man is as welcome as the song of a skylark

Mason work stone from the Council quarry.
Excavator mason and Bricklayer, George Smith, Hawthorn Cottage, Ilkley.
Iron founder and Smith, Redpath Brown and Co., Salford.
Carpenter and Joiner, Thomas Smith, Skipton Road, Ilkley.
Slater, R. and J. Nelson, Leeds Road, Ilkley. Also plumber and glazer.
Painter, Hampshire, Leeds Road, Ilkley.
Library £2,466: 17: 10
Public Offices and Hall £7,814: 16: 5

The building goes on apace, the Town Hall, the King's Hall and the Free Library, see the scaffolding and men walking past, men climbing about its precincts. The slater, R. Nelson, has climbed all these buildings, his tenders thrown out to catch every passing building, scaling Ilkley's masts with ladder and nail, holding the blue slate in his hand, lapping it in layers; he rides upon his calling as Collyer took his on the prow of an Atlantic ship and a Unitarian pulpit, seeing the municipal bow plough upon Ilkley's sea, the valley filled before him. Every roof you see has had his hands upon it

(In January, four men, Frank Carter, William Mitchell, John Clarke and Joseph Spence, were hoisting a 5cwt cornice stone at the north end of the Assembly Hall portion of the building when the scaffolding gave way hurling the men and the stone to the ground. Carter and Mitchell were pitched over the hoarding into Station Road, the stone landing on Carter's thigh and then rolling across his head and face. Both men lingered for a minute or two before dying

Still, if the Town Hall is to be completed they must deal with particulars

4th Sept. A silver gilt key, in Design No 1 commissioned to give to Dr Collyer. On the 9th Sept 1907 Mr Earnshaw, a local tradesman, submits a design for Illuminated Address intended to be presented to Dr Collyer on his opening the Library, the design including photographic reproductions of Dr Collyer, Mr Barker, Mr J. Jackson and the Town Hall buildings also Ilkley views viz. The Saxon Crosses; Brook Street in 1807; Ilkley Old Bridge; Ilkley New Bridge; Mr Earnshaw to supply the address for £12 plus £2. 5. 0 for scroll case.

Messrs Potts and Sons had reported having completed the new clock in the public office. Recommended that the clock be started by Mr Jackson at 3 o'clock tomorrow afternoon.

The New Clock in the tower of the public office, Station Road was started by Mr J. J. Jackson at 4 o'clock on Sat 24 August.

Ilkley Orpheus Glee Union are hired at a cost not exceeding £2 2s. Recommended that the building be decorated and illuminated on the opening day. 200 copies of the Hymn 'O God Our

Help in Ages Past' be printed for distribution on the occasion. Friends of Dr Collyer will be welcome, with endeavours made to accommodate them on the platform. Members of the Council and others taking part in the proceedings be notified of the arrangements and that each gentleman be invited to be accompanied by a lady

The building is not yet completed, but as Dr Collyer has accepted the invitation on the understanding that the function will take place in September and that he has arranged to leave Liverpool for New York on the 5th October, the council have no other alternative but to have the library portion opened now. He arrives in a carriage accompanied by his niece, a guard of honour flanking the entrance formed by members of the fire brigade under Captain Powell, councillors swelling their collective chest. He is presented with Earnshaw's key, embossed with his own portrait and topped by an awkward replica of the Town Hall itself. He takes the clumsy thing in his hand and unlocks the door. He enters. Ahead of him two veiled busts stand (the work of an Ilkley woman, Miss Frances Darlington) one of Andrew Carnegie, the other of himself.

'It had been decided that these rooms should be adorned with these portraits in order that our children and their children should keep up acquaintance with him.' Says Dr Collyer: 'It is well done, and will stay well done. Time will only ripen its features.'

They have discarded their acquaintance now. Not for Robert Collyer the warm shelter of the small hall, or the dignity of the oak-shelved reading area, where glass-fronted bookcases of Ilkley's history are kept, cuttings and pamphlets, parish records, topographical works, regimental memoirs, Collyer's own collected works. Not even the shelf above an inner door where hangs some inappropriate Royal Navy bell or wheel (he cannot remember which). Along with their benefactor he has been imprisoned behind a meagre square of glass in the cold walls outside, two recessed cells on either side of the entrance, their faces peering through the opaque neglect to the grim reward of the bare station opposite.

Dr Collyer stays with Mr J. T. Jackson, he who sold the council the land (and kept the greenhouses), laid the foundation stone and is now its Chairman. A dinner is given in Dr Collyer's honour at the Wells House Hydro, after which a torchlight procession played out by the Ilkley Brass Band and accompanied by a huge crowd accompanies them up to Elmleigh, Mr Jackson's residence. They love their celebrations, their ceremonies, these Ilkley folk, the doffing of hats and the waving of handkerchiefs. They love the open-air address and the throng of listeners, the light of torches, the rhythm of drum, the pass of a procession; they love the open air; they love the open air. It is where after all celebrations must take place, for it is in a crowd where a man is equal, where he can assume a place no greater, no smaller than his neighbour. Flags and hymns and brass bands here. Mr Bellerby, the moustached band leader, struggles to the front with a huge Union Jack but returns it to the master of ceremonies when he realizes that all the other bearers are small boys. They toil up the steep hill blowing their trombones and trumpets, banging their bass drums, their notes dissipated at every breath until at length, at Kings Road, they falter, exhausted. Mr Bellerby boulders his way to the fore once again and bringing his cornet to his lips rallies the band. Dr Collyer raises his black Puritan hat and disappears inside.

Ilkley's religious conversion is now complete.

29 October 1907

Two offers for the library. One from Mr John Waugh offering 194 volumes of the *Gentleman's Magazine*. One from the Swendenborg Society offering to present 60 volumes, being copies of the writings of Emmanuel Swedenborg and others. Both offers accepted with thanks,

58 Volumes from the Revd Siston Smith
36 from L. Learoyd
A typewriter bought
Mr L. Pate: Boswell's *Life of Johnson* 4 vols., Wardell's *Historical Notes of Ilkley, Rombalds Moor etc.* Also a letter press and stand offered for sale.

By 4 May the shelves were full; the Reading Room and Museum opened to the public on and after Monday 11 May 1908

12 May 1909

Librarian reported an issue of 32,203 volumes from 20 July 1908 to 31st March 1909

He sits for a time on the opposite side, eating a cake from Betty's (a Yorkshire conceit, but fashioned like so many successes here by the immigrant), crumbs falling over the rim of the paper bag, pastry flakes on his knee, watching the people walking past the long edifice of the Winter Gardens and the Town Hall and Library each with its own foundation stone and tablet bearing these men's names, men who sat and delivered, and accounted in their particular and proud way, the sum of Ilkley, the pioneers. They had fought for money, their own and the town's, and did not care for spending unless it reflected well upon them (and sometimes their pocket); who because of pride and self-importance wanted their town to be as good as any other, who wanted to name it Ilkley and see it flower by the Wharfe, who saw the moor as the town's weight, the town's conscience, who wanted to run the town, bear its importance on their shoulders while other men lived and bred within it, who gave the town, in their selfish way, matters which it needed, not a collection of houses, but a place to reach an understanding, bridges to cross and paths to walk upon, great events celebrated as town, as people, as an entity of its own, watched as the people passed them by, as all history is passed, without a thought to it unless it rears up or is ripped from your unsuspecting hand. They pass now, their inheritors, pass without a thought to these men and the simple things they did that mattered, pass without a thought to them and their plans, the expenditure they laid out, the ground they injected, who came one day with their gleaming shovels and chains of office, they themselves their own small band of admirers, their long overcoats buttoned tight over their self-importance, dug the trowel in the mixed cement, laid the stone which bears their mark. The river gave it cause, the moor importance, the railway wealth, but the Town Hall, the Kings Hall and the library have given it depth in stone and in exhibition and in print. It has a history now, a past, a present, a future, on the day when Ilkley learnt to read.

Call them down, then, call them down, the Dobsons and Donkey Jacks, the Listers and Horsmans, let their names ring, let the bells sound Jackson and Eames and foolish Bellerby, to mark their beginning and their end. He knows none of them and yet holds them in sentimental affection, how they marked Ilkley's map, 'the routes they took, the resolutions they passed. They know him not these men, have no inkling of him and his thoughts, and would disregard what he says with scornful bluff or indifference.

And he would like to build something that would last, a thing that arcs and spans sturdy like a bridge and showing rust on its surface, making the connection, to name that which he encompasses without their permission, without their knowledge, to grasp the entity of a town, how it is led by those who rouse it, how it can turn against its keepers, how deceptive is the taming. It is cruel to tame a town, it needs its movement, losing spirit when enclosed by anything else other than its energy.

O Ilkley, the love of this blue-slate town. Let him chip a piece of gritstone rock free and carve their names upon it, let him throw it upon the waters of the Wharfe, let it sink, let the river rush, so that they may hear its passing once more, taste its peat, feel its endless strength. It is their town this Ilkley and these are your men and your women, who built it, who raised their children within its compass, who were sent away to die far away from it or to be swept away through its hard embrace. This is your town, yours, as is every other town and everyone who belongs there. Despise them not, these towns, these villages, the petty walls they throw up, they are ours, and under them rest our bones. They fashion us, the lilt on our tongue and the look in our eyes.

ILKLEY PUBLIC LIBRARY
F. S. JACKSON
1905

THE KINGS HALL
J. T. DIXON
1906

And in the centre

18 DECEMBER 1912
F. S. JACKSON

No Co-operative Society can successfully compete with

BEANLANDS & SONS LTD

BROOK ST

in supplying the Public with Genuine and Fresh Goods at
Small Profit Prices The Stock comprises
TEAS GROCERIES PROVISIONS
Perfumery, toilet requisites, patent medicines
Proprietary Articles
BEERS WINES AND SPIRITS
The purity and freshness of all goods may be absolutely relied on
They deliver all goods by their own Vans Free of CHARGE

There are two classes of people now in Ilkley, those who pay and those who wait for payments. Money has been coming up from Bradford every day of the week, and will come now until the old machines fall silent. Three eras of woollen splendour, the First World War, the Second World War and in the Fifties Korea: and for all that time, from now till then, the names that turned Bradford mills, pocketed Bradford tills, the Cunliffes, the Listers, the Cloughs, the Binns, Henry Price the fifty-shilling tailor, so called because that was the average weekly wage, Whitakers, Fattorini the jeweller, and the Muffs, owner of Bradford's greatest department store.

LEGAL NOTICE

[14 August 1909] We, Henry Maufe, heretofore called and known by the name of Henry Muff, of Red House, Bexley

Heath in the County of Kent and of the City of Bradford, Director of Brown Muff and Company; Charles James Maufe heretofore called and known by the name of C. J. Muff of Homescroft, Ilkley, in the County of York and of the City of Bradford, Director of Brown Muff and Co. (limited) and Frederick Broadbent Maufe heretofore called and known by the name of F. Muff of Warbeck, Ilkley, hereby respectively give public notice that we, being desirous to revert to the old form of our surname, on the 30th day of June 1909, respectively, formally and absolutely renounced, and abandoned the use of our rais surname of MUFF and then reverted to, assumed, adopted and determined thenceforth on all occasions whatsoever to use and subscribe the name of MAUFE instead of the said name Muff for ourselves and our respective issue

Dated this 12th day of August, 1909

Henry Maufe (late Muff)
Charles James Maufe (late Muff)
Frederick Broadbent Maufe (late Muff)

> When in Ilkley on the Wharfe
> He is known as Mr Maufe
> When in Bradford sure enough
> He is known as Mr Muff

Ilkley people never paid bills. My father used to send a bill off and someone would come in and say, my husband only pays bills twice a year and unfortunately yours came in just a little bit too late. It was rude to ask for money, you might lose the business.

Bradford called the shots then and, though moved to Ilkley (known to some as Harrogate for beginners), they belonged still to Bradford. Bradford ways and Bradford money its own aristocracy now

(Joe Fattorini used to go to the Box Tree Restaurant, used to entertain all his guests there, used to go in with his briefcase and hand it over and when the meals came they served up all this delicious food, and then they took the lid off Joe's plate and there would be this black pudding, bought from Bradford market

[*March 8th*]   Henry Sutcliffe well known Bradford wool merchant found dead in a train on its arrival at Ilkley. Travelling on the 5.24pm express from Bradford, which reaches Ilkley at 5.50pm.

"Born in trouble and criticism, it has continued in that particular nursery to the present day. That is the unfortunate career of the council's Municipal Orchestra."

– William Dobson speaking before the members of
the Ilkley Chamber of Trade.

On the other side of the Town Hall from the Library lies the Kings Hall with its dress circle and marvellous pink icing boxes running all around in the shape of waves and on each one a plaster-cast bust of an artistic genius. Later a Winter Garden was addded with a wrought-iron and glass ceiling and a wide balcony above where one could sit and take tea. Above, at the top of Wells Road, on the edge of the moor, in the middle of a small park stands a sturdy bandstand with lights and wrought-iron railings and surrounding flowerbed. And in all these venues appeared the Ilkley and District Council Band, decked out in top hats and tails, managed and conducted by the whiskered Wardle S. Bellerby, owner of the saddlery down on Brook Street. He is a walrus, Wardle Bellerby, and waves his baton over the town in an expression of indignant belligerence. His daughter, the fair Ida, plays the piano. She plays for schools and concert parties, and practises at home in Tivoli Place where Oswald Lister and passers-by might be soothed by the Chopin and Liszt rippling through the window. She plays the piano well, too well for this rude town. Her talent should take her further. Ida Bellerby, O Miss Ida Bellerby, legs of piano and shape, fingers of pianissimo, heart of fire. Her father is in charge and she must bridle at his limited authority.

On 24 June 1910 the Kings Hall Management Committee receive a letter:

From Mr Henry Seargent dated 24 May complaining of Mr Bellerby's conduct in abruptly requesting three ladies to stand up in the Kings Hall on the occasion of Mr Hibberts Lecture on May 21st. Mr Seargent attended the meeting and stated that he called Mr Bellerby's attention to the matter at the time and afterwards went into the booking office to discuss it with him when Mr Bellerby requested him to leave the hall. This statement was supported by a youth named Buck, but neither of them knew the ladies mentioned nor could they give any clue as to their identity.

Mr Bellerby explained that on the occasion in question there was a large audience present and that several persons had not found seats when the lights were lowered for the entertainment to commence. He was requested to find seats for a lady and a little boy and noticed two vacant seats on a certain row, being the fourth and fifth chairs from the corridor, the first three chairs being occupied by three youths who he requested to stand up whilst the lady and boy passed to the vacant chairs. He was not speaking to any ladies at the time when Mr Seargeant inferred. The three youths requested to stand up by Mr Bellerby, E. Horner, N. Lee, W. Mellor attended the meeting and corroborated Mr Bellerby's statement, each stating that all Mr Bellerby did was to request them to allow the lady and the boy to pass to the vacant chairs and that Mr Bellerby did not speak or request any ladies to stand up at the tone mentioned. Mr Seargent stated he was satisfied that he had made a mistake, withdrew the complaint and tendered an apology to Mr Bellerby.

Poor misunderstood Mr Bellerby. He frets, Mr Bellerby, frets at the constraints of office, at the constraints of his pay, frets at the unreasonable pettiness of officialdom, and the blessed public, prying, poking, always finding fault: the quality of the band, the choice of music, the choice of film, the seating arrangements, his dress, his abrupt manner, the till receipts, the quality of the film equipment, the lateness of the opening of the doors: Mr Bellerby has to bear them all.

22 March 1911

Application from Mr Bellerby for an increase in salary. He to be paid a salary of £52 a year as manager of the Kings Hall and £39 a year as Musical Director of the Season Band.

Resolved that Messrs Hibbert's terms for supplying films, machine and an operator for Cinematographic Performances in meetings be accepted
a) for a matinee and evening performance 5 guineas
b) for evening only 4 guineas

That in future the charge for private boxes in the Kings Hall during Cinematographic Performances be 6/- each box.

30 November 1911

Resolved
that the Kings Hall manager to arrange Mr Hibbert two lectures to be given.

22 July 1912

Clerk submitted correspondence he had with Hibberts Ltd with reference to the unsatisfactory Cinematograph Exhibitions in the Kings Hall and it was resolved that a Pathé Cinematograph Machine be purchased – advertising for a secondhand machine.

24 September 1912

The new Century Film Company offer with respect to hiring of films be accepted, subject to them agreeing to provide a capable operator.

9 October 1912

Kings Hall Agent reported that the arrangements for giving Cinematograph Exhibitions were now complete.

Invitations to all council members to attend the opening on Saturday the 12th inst.

2 November 1912

Miss Ida Bellerby be engaged as pianist in connection with the Cinematograph Exhibitions and that the Kings Hall agent be instructed to visit the premises of the firms from whom the Council hire films in order that he may personally select same and that he use every precaution in selecting only such films as are suitable for a high-class exhibition.

Bellerby re-appointed 1913, 14th Feb., at a salary of £80 Manager of Kings Hall and Annexe. But Ilkley has a new musical director, Mr Henry Jason. He wants an extra horn player but the Committee demurs. However, new uniforms for the band are purchased.

9 July 1913

The Town Hall and Band Sub-Committee resolved that the Musical director be authorised to engage an additional violinist and horn player for the Municipal Orchestra.

18 July 1913

Librarian reported the receipt on July 11th of the Books bequested to the library by the late Dr Collyer and forwarded by his executors books comprising archaeology, antiquities, history and topography of Yorkshire and 249 volumes a special bookcase be obtained for shelving the collection in the

Reference Department. Messrs Deans and Mennell of Ilkley construct and erect a new bookcase.

25 August 1913

Various complaints against Mr Bellerby have been received, of a serious nature.

Resolved
    that Mr Bellerby should act as manager for one month and provided his conduct of business is satisfactory his services to be retained, but if in the meantime complaints are received of a similar character that Mr Bellerby be given notice forthwith to terminate his engagement.

4 October

A quantity of pepper thrown amongst the audience during a Cinematographic Exhibition.

9 December

resolved that for 1914 season an Orchestra of 17 performers be engaged. Also Hired were:

The Honeymoon Co. July 21st, 22nd, 23rd
The Love and what then Co. 25th, 26th, 27th
The Mo LLusc Co. Aug. 28th, 29th, 30th
Arthur Hare and Co. (in A Pair of Spectacles and Sweet Lavender) Sept. 4th, 5th, 6th.

14 January 1914

Bellerby dismissed from all posts. The Clerk instructed to advertise for applications from suitable candidates for the position of Manager of the Kings Hall and Winter Gardens at a commencing salary of £150 per annum.

Bellerby is lost. His daughter has left him too, for Leipzig, where she is being taught the German piano.

Committed an assault on Mr Eckersley, Clerk to the Council (god to his own god, and an absolute stickler)

> (It may be remarked that the Clerk to the Council is a very capable man but he is of a very autocratic nature and will not brook any interference or any contradiction of what he says.

Councillors come and go but it is Eckersley who administers the rules, Eckersley who feeds the paper into the municipal machine. There should be an Eckersley saloon and an Eckersley general store; his cousin should be sheriff. Eckersley it is then who transmits the council's decision to the maligned Bellerby, and as Bellerby remonstrates, Eckersley sets his face in a grim smile and adds his own autocratic pennyworth to the effect that if he had his way, he, Eckersley, would see to it that he never worked in this town again. Bellerby broods. He has been deprived not merely of a part of his living, but his role in public life. Is it not the band that draws the crowd on a summer's day, is it not the band that livens the winter nights, begins romances, cements engagements, is no less than father to half the young marrieds in the town? Who played when Dr Collyer arrived, who welcomed Trooper Ballardie's return, or sounded the celebrations on the coronation of King George? The band, and who led the band, who chose the music, who laboured night and day for the band, for the Kings Hall, for the musical attraction of this town? Bellerby marches on the Town Hall armed with his redundant baton. Climbing the stairs he skulks along the council corridors, working up his head of steam until Eckersley emerges out of the office, dry papers in his bony hand. Wardle S. Bellerby pounces, and catching hold of Eckersley's coat drags him to the banisters, holds him over, pulling on the knot of Eckersley's tie, Eckersley's lank hair hanging down into an empty space. Wardle S. Bellerby shakes Eckersley, shouts in Eckersley's ear, giving the clerk the distinct impression that he is about to be chucked over the side. Eckersley squeals, cries for help. The council office door is flung open, officials running out. While others send for the police, two councillors rush to Eckersley's aid, prise Wardle S. Bellerby's fingertips from the clerk's collar and urge him back to the safety of his office. They hold Bellerby fast until the police arrive, when he is arrested and spends the night in jail.

Mrs Halbot of the Leeds Branch of the National League opposing Women's Suffrage addressed the members of the Ilkley Branch of the Women's Unionist Assoc. in the Grove School, in respect to the League's attitude to women's suffrage.

She emphasised the grave responsibility of the vote and held that the vote should be placed in the hands of those best fitted to use it. The average man was better politically informed than the average woman. Such questions as the housing of the poor, sanitation, sick nursing and hygiene came within the daily life of a woman. This is why anti-suffragists pleaded for better representation than women had at the present on all Boards of Guardians, County Councils, Borough Councils etc. On such questions as finance, shipping, mining, making of treaties, and the army and navy a woman could have no practical knowledge.

Those who have seen most of his Majesty since he came to the throne notice that during the last eighteen months or two years he has changed. He is more genial, jokes and laughs more, and is very pronouncedly the friend, rather than the father and the King, with his sons. The reason for this according to the *Lady's Pictorial* is not far to seek. The King is in far more robust health than he was. His digestion was for some years the source of great trouble. He suffered frequently from dyspepsia and was very often on a milk diet for weeks at a time. Now his Majesty is very well, and usually eats and drinks like other men, save that in the matter of spirits and wines he is more temperate than most, even in these characteristically temperate days.

[7 August 1914]   For some months Miss Ida Bellerby IRAM, a well-known Ilkley musician, has been studying at the Leipzig Conservatoire of Music, and a week ago the Conservatoire closed for the summer vacation which she had arranged to spend in Dresden. She obtained her ticket with this object, but finding the railway station full of soldiers and no English about thought it best to go and see the Consul who advised her to take the first train for home. She accordingly got her ticket changed and caught the last train out of Leipzig for Flushing. The train was half an hour late and she began to think that she would never get away. At the German frontier her passport was examined and here an interesting incident occurred. A German posed as an Englishman but was found to be a deserter.

From Leipzig to Hanover Miss Bellerby travelled with seven German soldiers who were proceeding to join their regiments. She was in the last compartment and through the window at the back noticed that as the train entered Holland big gates were put across the line. Someone stuck a British flag in the carriage window and as they passed through Holland all the soldiers saluted and cheered it.

They had a very rough crossing. Even when they were reaching Southend their troubles were not over, for the regular captain had been called away, and the Dutchman acting as captain did not know English and neither showed a light. Just as they were going into Southend a battleship came alongside and through the megaphone the order was given that if a flag was not hoisted fire would be opened. The vessel proceeding on its way, a live shell was fired, but wide of the ship, and this caused the captain to stop and hoist the Union Jack.

Miss Bellerby arrived home without her luggage. She thinks the Germans a fine people, and it is her impression that they wanted anything but war. In proof of this she mentions that there were riots in Leipzig against the war. Her experiences in Germany have been in every way pleasant, and she is only hoping that the war will soon be over, so that she can get back to her studies.

WHO'S AT WAR

The Diplomatic Situation

The diplomatic situation is one of extraordinary confusion, for, though nearly all the Great Powers of Europe are at war in two groups, each member of the group is not necessarily at war with each of the others. The present position is thus:

Great Britain	at War with . . .	Germany
Germany	at War with . . .	Great Britain, France, Russia, Belgium
Austria	at War with . . .	Russia, Serbia, M'ntegro, France
France	at War with . . .	Germany, Austria
Russia	at War with . . .	Germany, Austria
Belgium	at War with . . .	Germany
Serbia	at War with . . .	Austria
M'ntegro	at War with . . .	Austria

That distribution of hostilities may be expected to undergo modifications during the week

Ilkley Development Association

Mr Eckersley suggested that this was the opportunity for advertising in some of the leading dailies with a view to extending the Ilkley season. Cr Thompson had said they had spent Sat. afternoon calling upon the proprietors and managers of four or five hydros, and several had shown a disposition to support any movement of this nature. The next day he spent another couple of hours in interviewing tradespeople on the subject and had had rather a disappointing afternoon. The feeling was that it was too late to advertise. A few of the tradesmen appeared very apathetic. They were ready enough to complain, but did not seem at all inclined to assist with the advertising. Councillor Bray proposed that they advertise with a view to extending the holiday season. There was still six weeks to run and no doubt many people who contemplated going to Scarborough, Whitby and others, coast resorts would be changing their minds. Ilkley had benefited considerably through being close to such towns as Leeds, Bradford, Keighley and Shipley. Owing to the war many people were restricting their holidays and instead of going away from home were spending days at places like Ilkley. The Council are being asked to extend the engagement of the Municipal Orchestra for a further period of two weeks.

Amalgamated Society of Carpenters and Joiners. Ilkley Branch.

August 16 1914. In Bank £6 – 16 – 6. In Treasurers Hand £1 – 15 – 4

28 August

Ilkley Municipal Band season finishes with a concert in the King's Hall on Sunday evening. Members of the Development Association were anxious that the band performances would be continued for a fortnight longer, but the District Council have not seen their way to fall in with this suggestion.

GERMAN BRUTALITIES
ATROCITIES COMMITTED IN BELGIUM

At Linsmeau where a German officer was killed during the fighting, terrible vengeance was taken out on the village, although none of the civilians took part in the hostilities. The Germans gathered all the male inhabitants together and divided them into three groups. Those in one were bound and eleven of them placed in a ditch, where they were afterwards found dead, their skulls fractured by the butts of German rifles.

On Monday August 10th at Orsmael, the Germans picked up Commander Knapen, very seriously wounded, trussed him up against a tree and shot him. Finally they hacked his corpse with swords. An old man in the village had his arm sliced in three longitudinal cuts; he was then hung downwards and burnt alive. Young girls have been raped and little children outraged, and several inhabitants suffered mutilations too horrible to describe.

At Aerschot on August 18th in one single street the first six male inhabitants who crossed the threshold were seized and shot at once under the very eyes of their wives and children. They compelled the inhabitants to leave their homes and marched them to a place 200 yards from the town. There without more ado M. Thielman, the Burgomaster, his fifteen year old son, the clerk to the Legal Judicial Board and ten prominent citizens were shot. The Germans then set fire to the town and destroyed it.

LORD KITCHENER APPEALS FOR MORE RECRUITS

At the Kings Hall, on Monday evening, opened not three years ago for concerts and gatherings and entertainment, surrounded by fairy-tale pink and velvet curtains, where in the stage such pleasant fantasies had taken place, there is a table and several chairs. The crowds push in, busy with excitement, enthusiastic.

A united choir, drawn from all the places of worship and conducted by Mr T. Ackroyd, led the singing of English, French, Belgian and Russian national anthems. At the rear of the platform hangs a Union Jack with emblems of warfare on either side of the proscenium, ancient spears and shields, and more recent firearms, mementos from Private Ballardie and his kin. Mr Dobson is in the chair and next to him Captain Mercer, organising secretary of the National Service League. Dobson rises, and straightens his waistcoat. He is a large man and filled with the import of duty. A hush falls.

"This meeting has been called as a result of circumstances that are without parallel in the history of the world. We are at death grips with the greatest tyrant of all times, a human monster, who while assuming love and affection for his people is prepared to sacrifice one million of their lives and render thousands of homes desolate in order to assuage his avaricious and wicked desires. I hand you over to Captain Mercer."

Cheering. The Captain rises, a thin man and filled with the import of duty. He looks upon the crowd, the workmen of Ilkley, and feeds them his bittersweet spoon.

"My feelings here are a mingling of pleasure and sorrow. Pleasure for the thrill of pride because I know our soldiers and sailors will uphold the best traditions of the British Army and Navy. Sorrow because of the many brave fellows who have fallen. Thus far there has been a noble response to the nation's call, but many more men are needed. The question is, is Ilkley going to rise to the occasion? I notice that the Cumberland Rugby Football Union had recommended their clubs to continue to play football as long as possible. All well and good you might say but is this the way in which the young men of England are going to maintain the nation's honour and glory? Playing rugby? If that is all these young fellows think of their country, they ought to be tabooed. I hope that the young women of this country will have nothing to do with young fellows who are content to play cricket and football, to leave the nation's work to others."
  "Put golfers in there, Captain Mercer."
  "I look upon golfers with the same contempt."

This is the outing to beat all outings, this is the outing for boys leaving school, for apprentices and young men. This is the outing for restless undergraduates and bored railway porters, this is the outing not in charabancs nor the Bradford walks, this is the outing to beat all outings, the one that will keep the winter fires warm in later years, the one that will preserve his youth, his need for comradeship. This is not Britain, not Germany, not even poor little Belgium, this is the outing to beat all outings, a rucksack for a bucket and a gun for a spade, bedraggled trophies dragged home from the beach of the German trenches, to place on the mantelpiece, to finger summer's dream. Killing? Death? What is killing and the witness of it compared to carrying your chum to safety and lifelong friendship, as it was in the schoolyard, as it was stealing apples or skating on the tarn; this is the giant come again striding across the landscape, supreme and confident; this is the boy leaping from rock to rock, skipping the stepping stones, pedalling fast, this is a young boy with a catapult, hiding in the long grass, frightening the horses and your maiden aunt too. This is boys' work.

11 September

The recruits are sworn in. Two companies raised, each of about 120 men. They leave Ilkley on Monday afternoon, and march to Keighley by way of Silsden and Steeton. Leeds Road, Church Street, and the Skipton Road laden with relatives and friends. They stand on the sidewalks, those wives and sweethearts, mothers and fathers too, swallowing their unseasoned apprehension, wishing them God speed and a safe return with cheery voice, the band marching the men through the town on to Addingham, where they leave them, playing 'Auld Lang Syne' on their polished brass handkerchiefs.

Their men spend the night at Keighley Barracks and leave for Halifax by the 9.30. By Tuesday afternoon they are in Portsmouth. Their camp is situated at Wool, near Wareham in Dorset; a village of 800 inhabitants it has now in its vicinity around 6,000 Kitchener's recruits.

We are sleeping fifteen to a tent and occasionally have to drink tea without milk. When we left Ilkley we were under the impression that on reaching Halifax we would be provided with our uniforms but instead we were sent on to Wool in our ordinary clothes. As most of us took very little beyond what we stood up in numerous packages of underclothing additional suits and overcoats have since left Ilkley at very urgent request as a good deal of rain fell during the first few days. I have only come across one girl since we landed. All the same Wool appears to be a very old world sort of place, with thatched cottages and the district is full of charm and beauty, with moors and hedges of honeysuckle and fruit in abundance. I never saw so many nuts and berries in my life.

They have read about them, seen cartoons in the papers regarding their plucky weakness, understood what the Hun bully can do, and suddenly they are come in their midst, a party of forty-six Belgian refugees turning up on Ilkley's doorstep on a dark Wednesday night in October, women and children mostly, but with three males too, wrenched out of their masculinity, to stand helpless before a people they do not know and women they can no longer defend, bandanas around their neck that Wharfedale might expect to see on travellers and visiting fairground lads, but not tied with the knot of apprehension that these folk bring; sons and daughters with unpronounceable name tags, women with crude, short-cropped hair, or tied back tight, as if to speed haste, sabots on their feet which clatter on the platform as they clamber down and seem to the watching eyes of the town very clumsy and inelegant. They stand outside across from the Town Hall in a rude huddle, talking incessantly in their own tongue, as if their language is their last defence against their unknown fate, their few reminders of the former life tied in thin bundles before their feet. A young Belgian woman, Florentine Van Nieuwenhuyse, who is in the service of a Miss Wood, is on hand to explain the arrangements that have been made, where they will be taken, but far from raising their spirits this seems to plunge them into a state of dejected quietude. Now even their language has been breached. The children cling to their elders as if convinced that they are to be wrenched apart, and they in turn look down in despair, unable to realize, however unlikely it may be, they are amongst friends.

It is true. No flag-waving, no cheering, no bands and no speeches, the crowd too big and curious for comfort, but for all its aspiring elegance, its mansions, its chauffeur-driven cars, Ilkley has a rough heart and can recognize itself in garb like this: the town is not that old; they can remember where they came from, remember the thatch before the slate, the candle before the gas, the mud before the macadam, remember too the awful flood and how caprice can sweep all before it.

There are no buses to take them further, so arranged private carriages and cars begin to arrive, like on a first night, and matronly usherettes open the polished walnut doors on to the leather uphol-stery and help them aboard in their twos and threes, patted down with a rug over their knees, and they are driven to the coal fires of their strange new homes.

Refugees under the care of the committee were as follows: kept by private hospitality 1 with Father Galli; 2 at Mrs Haigh; 7 at Mr J. T. Jackson's; 8 at Wellington Road by Ben Rhydding Wesleyans: 2 at J. Whitakers. The majority to Ilkley's Charity Hospital.

It stands in the heart of the town, looking out over dipping lawn and trees, an oddly fanciful affair, its austere crenellations topped with pyramid roofs and fairy-tale turrets studded with slits for fairy-tale arrows. At its centre there is a three-sided courtyard with more apertures aloft, to defend the needs of the wounded, a building of prosaic purpose made fantastic, leading the sick into a land of med-ical make-believe; the ambulance as coach, the doctor as knight, the nurse as princess: Ilkley's (and Yorkshire's) first charity hospital, opened in 1862 by a curate named George Fenton, and set back from the Grove where across the way Mr Heap sells pianos and bicycles, Ellis Beanlands stacks his groceries and millionaires' wives take tea in the elegance of the upper rooms of the Imperial Café. Soon after the outbreak of war it is converted into the largest Auxiliary Military Hospital in the country, Auxiliary Military Hospital No. 1.

A workroom for Belgian women is to be opened next week where they will meet twice a week to sew for the Belgians soldiers abroad. It is hoped that they might later also work for themselves, preparing an outfit to take back with them to Belgium.

[16 October 1914] on Friday we went to a route march to Lulworth which is about ten miles from here. The scenery was splendid and the cliffs chalk, through one of them being a tunnel. We had to climb down one of the cliffs to the sea, where we had a bather. We could see Portland Island and the prison. By the time we reached camp we had done twenty miles on two slices of bread, but we had a good feed then and 7s pay (What! what!!)

Rev Glennie
St Margaret's Vicarage, Ilkley   14th Dec. 1914

Dear Sir,

I paid a most interesting visit to the Bovington Camp last Monday where I received a most hearty welcome from QM Sergeant Heppell and our lads. A hurricane of rain and half a gale prevented me from seeing as much of the camp as I would have liked. But I made the acquaintance of Col Hayden who invited me to tea. During the tea the Colonel said "Vicar I want to ask you a favour. *Send us some more of your Ilkley boys. They are some of the best lot in the Battalion.*" I replied that I was afraid we had sent them all. "Oh have another look round the neigh-bourhood – *we must have some more Ilkley lads.*"

Now Sir I want to appeal to any Ilkley lad who has not yet gone but who still means to go, and wants to know what regiment to join. *Join your pals of the 9th Duke of Wellington* and on these grounds.

1. You could not have a finer set of officers to serve under
2. You could not have a nicer set of mates to serve along with
3. All the initial drawbacks connected with the Bovington Camp are a thing of the past
4. The Battalion has today marched into billets at Wimborne, 16 miles away
5. It will return to Camp when the huts are finished
6. It will then find a splendidly equipped institute, subscribed for by Ilkley friends, also a fine YMCA recreation tent and Picture House
7. The men are already having their khaki kit served to them
8. The Camp is a healthy one and is free from many of the ordinary temptations of Camp life
9. In other words the Camp has at last got its proper equipment and that normal military training will soon be in full swing.

So rally to the colours boys, and help keep up the high reputation that the lads of Wharfedale have already won in the Dorsetshire camp!

It is strange feeling he has, that they should have gone to Wool, stranger still that very soon after arriving there they should march to Lulworth Cove, and swim about Stairhole and Durdle Door, for this is the journey he would make, every year from Skipton Road Ilkley to the Launches West Lulworth (which he might have still in their possession had not someone played a tricky game) with his parents and his brother, their dog, their cat. A long journey, two days slow driving, sleeping overnight in the old Lanchester, pillows against the window, blankets over knees, lonely headlights marking the long hours by occasional solitary sweeps, the cold and cramp creeping in under the covers. He had never imagined that at any time others from Ilkley might have made that journey, found themselves taken from the shelter of the moor to such another place where rock and water rule, white rock which crumbles, water that in its blue sparkle is almost as treacherous as the Wharfe.

The wooden bungalow in which they stayed was built by his grandmother, and had, amongst other things, thin prefabricated walls which screeched when you ran your fingernails down, which he did, every night. Across the way the hills leading over to Warbarrow Bay, protected by army flags and danger signs for unexploded shells, lying in the long grass waiting to burst and destroy; one careless step was all it took. He felt that was what his family was like, an unexploded shell, lying there small and innocent-looking, hiding in the long grass of his family's garden, imagined any one of them taking the wrong step, imagined it blowing up, destroying them all.

He remembers the heat of the bungalow when they came back from the beach and the smell of baked furniture; and in the kitchen the milk bottle, standing in the sink of water, the water warm, the milk slightly turned. After supper, as the dark gathered in, the Shambles foghorn would sound, a long way out, and on the three-legged table distant plays would seep strange mists from the brown Bakelite radio. He remembers them, the plays, how they would envelop him, unable to see across the room, how outside voices coming up the path would add to their unsettling dimension. One play he remembers above all, of a man going swimming in the sea with one of his own children and her best friend, an only child, and how the fierce current swept them far out and how, with his strength failing, he had to choose between saving his own daughter (one of three) or the only child. And Michael Airey had floated in his mind small and bobbing and reaching for help, how Michael might have swum to his arms, how Michael was the one he could have saved, how he could have brought Michael ashore alive and grinning; but how, in the end, Michael was the one he left behind, Michael fished out and laid out cold and limp, how they stroked back his damp dead hair and closed his eager eyes, and how he moved away from him, as Michael lay in the long grass of his memory, an unexploded shell.

All the men of Ilkley to Lulworth and all the Lulworth men to Ilkley, climbing up the Cow and Calf, making their mark on Ilkley stone, while Yorshiremen skim flat Dorset pebbles on the calm surface of the cove, all the men moving one town to another, from hamlet to city, from seaside town to hillside fort, from smoking-chimney Bradford to paddle-boat Weymouth, black funnels spewing out on moor and water, Wool men to Whitby, Southampton men to Scarborough, all of us, man woman and child biting into that lettered rock, our names running through the nation's stone, carved on bark and scratched out on rounded pebbles, all of us sharing in the physique of this isle, our footprints on it all, all the men, all the women, all the girls and all the boys toing and froing, picking up our stones and throwing little pieces of our history out upon the water

Ben Rhydding Council School, closed for three weeks: an outbreak of scarlet fever. One child had an attack at home; the parents did not know it. He went to school in the peeling stage and infected the rest of the scholars.

Mr Dawson: These outbreaks seem be a hardy annual around here. It is about time something is done about it. Ben Rhydding is more like a colliery village than the enlightened place it is supposed to be.
Fletcher: It is the duty of the parents to notify the medical officer.
Dawson: It is bad drainage and rotten closets.
Mrs Reith: How many cases are there?
Fletcher: Twenty-two.
Dawson: We think more about our pigs and calves and our stud horses than we do about our children.

Mix some Woolwich Powder with tincture of iron or essence of lead and administer in pills (or shells). Have ready a little British army (a little goes a long way) some Brussel Sprouts and French mustard. Add a little Canadian cheese and Australian lamb and season with the best Indian curry. Set it on a Kitchener and keep stirring until quite hot. If this does not make the patient perspire quite freely, rub the best Russian bear's grease on his chest and wrap in Berlin wool. Dr Canon's prescription.

PS The patient must on no account have any Peace soup until the swelling in his head has quite disappeared.

To the Editor of the *Gazette*

Sir,

The appeal of the Belgian Refugees now sharing the hospitality of Ilkley has met with a most hearty and generous response. Therefore the Hospitality Committee, gratefully acknowledging the splendid response made by Ilkley to the appeal, make now another appeal to the good sense and judgement of the public. The desire to show affectionate interest in the little stranger children is natural enough, but there is no real kindness in putting sweets into their mouths and pennies in their hands whenever they are seen. The constant eating of sweets makes them ill, while the too frequent bestowal of pennies comes dangerously close to forming the habit of begging. Similarly to offer drinks to the men is meant as an expression of good will, but it is no true kindness – quite the reverse. The very light wine or beer which the Belgian peasant drinks at home are totally different from the strong drinks offered him here, and he is not prepared for the difference.

Further, it is, to say the least, embarrassing if not positively demoralising to be stared at and followed and regarded as a sort of show whenever one goes out of doors. Since it is not possible to talk with persons whose language is not understood, there is no object in crowding round the Belgians, and it would be far kinder to pass them quietly. This applies with even greater force to the soldiers who, one regrets to see, are so much the objects of attention of too many young girls. It must not be forgotten that in European countries girls do not go about with the freedom which they use here. The kindly meant but indiscreet friendliness shown by many young women and girls towards the soldiers is liable to be misunderstood, especially as their conversation in most cases cannot be understood at all.

They have suffered much. They have lost almost everything. Let us see to it that they do not lose their self respect.

W. Dobson Chairman of the Refugee Committee; Helen P. Ragliati Chairman of the Ladies C. Hospitality to Belgian Refugees

MEN WHO ARE MAKING HISTORY – we are showing a series of remarkably fine portraits of Lord Kitchener, Admiral Jellicoe and General French. They are produced by a new process which gives a very fine rich tone, and the price of 1/- each is exceedingly reasonable. Orders may be received for these at SHUTTLEWORTHS' Great Fancy Repository, Brook St Ilkley

War disturbs regular trade: the brown overall is hung up, the notebook closed, and pencil behind the ear left on his familiar desk. The railway carriages bang shut empty, porters deserted for the trenches. The town is awash with ghostly feet, only the echoes of fortitude and past pleasure remain. They carry other burdens now.

[20 November 1914]   Private James Clarkson son of the late Mr William Clarkson, North-eastern engine driver, wounded on the

8th of November, a bullet hitting him just below the left eye, passing through his tongue and lodging in his jaw.

When the Germans saw a bit of steel they cried Mercy! Mercy!! Goodily English! and screamed like pigs.

and Private Arthur Homes, a porter at Ilkley Railway station.

The Germans are going to have another go for Calais and London. They will get there (I don't think). Never mind what the papers say about them. They can also shoot as well. Not as well as we can but good enough

He is engaged to be married to Miss Olive Wilson, niece of Mr and Mrs Myers. The banns have been put up and he is expecting to come home on leave any time now for the ceremony.

Chaplain Waggett
Sept. 17 1915

Dear Mrs Myers,

Lance Corporal Holmes went away to Base this morning. He is doing well in my ways. He is most patient and good and in complete possession of his mind. He sends renewed messages of affection to your niece. Captain Owen of his regiment gave me your name. And I have to lay upon you a most difficult task of affection and wisdom. For in spite of what I have said and of the strongest hopes that dear Mr Holmes recovers his full strength, he has suffered the most grievous loss. Both his eyes were pierced by fragments of a bomb, and it was totally impossible to save them.

I pray God to give him comfort in this great affliction and sorrow. I honour and love Mr Holmes more than I can say.

PS. Dear Holmes does not yet know of his loss. The doctors forbade his being told in his present weak state. Care must be exercised in writing to him till we hear his general strength is much recovered.

The Troutbeck Hydro, unoccupied for years, is made ready for the reception of about 200 men as a training centre. Other large empty houses are to be utilized.

Leeds Bantam Battalion of the West Yorkshire Regiment billeted in the town. The Council lets the ground near the river at a nominal figure for drill purposes also will allow the troops to use moorland for field training.

And across the moor they drag sacks and pluck sphagnum moss anew, the saviour of the another age, now dragooned into this bloody service: ponies and carts waiting, donkeys bearing baskets of dank green, peasant work this harvest, watched by Belgian refugees, to be taken to be sent across to the front, to place on wounds, where bandages and remedies are scarce: the Ilkley Cure.

Private Norman Dobson of the 2nd Battalion, Duke of Wellington's (West Riding) Regiment killed. Eldest son of Mr and Mrs Ernest Dobson. Killed in action Feb. 24th now buried in a little mound near the brick kiln on the Zellebecke road, north of Ypres. And his friend A. Watt.

I shall never forget him. I shall welcome a speedy end to this awful war, and if it is my luck at any time to go back to Zellebeck, you can depend on my doing up of Norman's grave.

Corporal Swales, son of S. Swales of Cowpasture Rd

[*Friday 7 May 1915*] On Saturday night we went up to the firing line and had to pass through a town that had been bombarded. Jack Johnsons were flying around, but we got through with only one killed. We camped for the night just outside and the place was then all on fire. We had just got breakfast when a Jack burst in the middle of us, killing four men, wounding four and killing five horses. We were then shelled out of one place and another. Nobody has any idea what it is like. I shall always look upon this Sunday as a nightmare.

We left the firing line in the evening and came back through the town. The gases from the shells and the smell of dead men and horses nearly choke you. I wonder how it would feel to be out of hearing of the guns, in Ilkley again.

Mrs Rabagliati, the chairman of the Women's Suffrage Society, said that Women's Suffrage is at present like a dog which has buried its bone. It has no use for it at present, but when it wants it, the dog knows where to find it and can dig it up. Our bone is ready and we know where to find it.

OUR STRICKEN BRAVE [*4 June 1915*]
Trooper Ellis (killed in action)
Sergeant Harold Holt (killed in action)
Sergeant Jon McRink (gas poisoning)
Sergeant Frank Barnes (gas poisoning)

Military Cross for Captain Cuthbert Euan Charles Rabagliati of the King's Own Yorkshire Light Infantry and the Royal Flying Corps. Youngest son of Andrea. For conspicuous gallantry and skill on Sept. 28 1915 when accompanied by Second Lieut. Vacour; they carried out a reconnaissance over Valenciennes and Douai. The award reads:

They had to fly in thick cloud for nearly the whole distance and several times their plane got into a 'spin'. The pilot however succeeded each time in righting his machine and they reached their objective and carried out their reconnaissance at 2,800ft under very heavy fire.

[Feb. 1916]   Ilkley is well in range of the Zeppelin raids therefore it behoves us to take all precautionary measures possible.

When Zeppelins or other enemy aircraft appear a warning will be given. This will consist of sounding a buzzer – a long blast of two minutes followed by three short blasts of fifteen seconds.

On hearing the signal householders are warned to turn gas off at the meter. The gas will not be turned off completely by the Gas works as this might be dangerous in the case of people leaving taps open.

Public lighting has been reduced to the lowest possible minimum. In connection with public buildings the glazed roof of the Kings Hall Annexe has been treated with Duresco and the glazed roof of the electricity works has also been darkened. At the Ilkley parish Church the windows are painted with Duresco, a green paint which gives a sufficiently subdued light.

a green light all over Ilkley, a dim green dulled; green the colour of their hymn books and their praying hands; green glowing from their surplices and from their candlelight; green shining down on the dance floor, glinting on the Winter Garden trumpets, green on her hair and on your collar, green the colour of her modest shoulder and your dress shirt, green the colour of eye and looking glass, green the colour of day, green the colour of night, subdued, and muffled and putrid like a lifted coffin lid

For Men in Khaki
For Men in Blue
For Men in Mufti
For Women, too
Swan Fountain Pen
IS THE BEST
May be Had at Shuttleworth's Fancy Stores
Brook St, Ilkley

Private Eric Joseph Scott shot in the face by a sniper on March 2nd and walked out of the trenches to the Field Dressing Station succumbed to his wounds the following day. Only son of Mr and Mrs Tom Scott, 11 Weston Road. 20 years old. His father is an old soldier and went through the Egyptian War.

Weston Road is just off Church Stret, and No. 11 the fifth house on the left, the last one in the block, two up, two down, the door in the centre. It is a short road, Weston, the houses on the left mirrored by their neat counterparts on the right, and still served by a cobbled alleyway at the rear. Proximity, then, outside privies lined up like sentry boxes, backyard washing eyeing backyard washing, sounds of domestic life sounding through the walls. When storms came they would cover up mirrors and open the back and front door so that the lightning might pass safely through, while the children would sit on the stairs and listen to the cannon roar above. An intimate street, as many are, the ragged tears of life hung out on the Weston washing line for all to see. It is very Ilkley Weston Road. At the top, where it runs off Church Street, stands the fish and chip shop, Harbour Lights; over the way, the curve of the Crescent Hotel, the first rim of Ilkley's hum; beyond, the moor, always the moor. But turn around and look down, to where the unseen river lies, and it is almost as if you are standing on the edge of a great cliff, that between you and the woods of Middleton on the other side there is nothing but space. It is true, this curiosity that possesses Ilkley, the solid sense it has of harbouring the desire for permanent flight, the great flowing movement that swirls in and out of the town's formal structure. It taunts you with that promise, holding you fast as it rushes by. And it is here, on a morning that Private Scott walked out of the door, kissed his mother, embraced his father, tipped his hat and bade goodbye to his neighbour, roughed an infant's head, clapped a younger, envious youth on the back, promising him a souvenir or two, raised his hand to who knows how many, here that he would have turned and seen Ilkley for the last time, the sum of it on this little road, the small black-bricked houses, the great sweep of the Crescent and, leaping into it all, the flight of air; green and wood and sky, and at the back the solid rock of the lonely moor on which he had built his life, which he had trusted. And Ilkley let him go, as all our towns let their sons go, and this son, he marched away, never to see his Ilkley, his sweetheart or his life again, marching to where the look of Ilkley was lost in his eyes, the comfort of his small home impossible. How could he remember the configuration of his silly old town and the balance of its easy ways, the simple symmetry of the cobbled stones and the hills beyond. How could the world have changed so, and how could he ever return?

April 7th
ILKLEY PICTURE HOUSE
A Romantic and finely illustrated drama,
Little Blonde in Black.
Also *Another Man's Wife* and the Twenty First Episode of
THE EXPLOITS OF ELAINE, *The Ear in the Wall.*

Wu Fang, the Chinese Master Criminal, lays further plans to kill Craig Kennedy, the scientific detective, and so secure the Clutching Hand's millions. He has sworn an eternal vendetta, not only against Kennedy, but also against Elaine and her friends and devises a scheme to bring about the death of either Kennedy or Elaine's Aunt Josephine. Kennedy learns the secret of this and there is a denouement very different to what the Chinaman expected, though he is eventually able to forestall the police who Kennedy has summoned, and they arrive to find that their bird has flown. The super-grip of this episode however is where Kennedy tricks the wily Oriental at his own game, but the incident is too good to give away and should be seen.

Next week's episode is *The Opium Smugglers*.

Tin foil for the wounded sent to Beanlands. Amount so far collected 1qr 23 lbs 1oz.

July 7th, Ilkley Tribunal: Two Conscientious Objectors appear, both claiming exception. The first is an Ilkley draper and fancy dealer. He has advised them for so many occasions, his customers, for their times of joy and their times of sorrows, but it is what he wears upon his sleeve that concerns them now.

C: What do you think about the war?
Applicant: It is a very sad affair.
C: Are you prepared to protect yourself?
Applicant: I would rather be clear of it. I do not know what I would do in a tight corner.
C: Would you protect your wife?
Applicant: Yes.
C: Then you are of the same opinion as all of us. Application refused.

Next, a commercial traveller residing in Ilkley.

C: You are brother of the last applicant?

Applicant: I am. I belong to the Plymouth Brethren. My conscience does not allow me to take up arms and kill anybody.
I would rather be shot.

C: Would you be prepared to take non-combatant service?

Applicant: I want to be entirely free from the military element
but I am prepared to do work of national importance.

C: Someone has to do the fighting.

Applicant: It is a most unhappy position to force a Christian into.

C: Do you mean to say that those who are fighting are not
Christians?

Applicant: I did not say that.

C: If you were a Quaker we should know it was part of your
religion to be opposed to war.

Applicant: I would be very happy to engage in munitions work
or anything else for this country, except take up arms.

C: Applicant passed for non-combatant service.

The Best Guide Books
MAPS
PLANS &c.
Messrs S
Great Book, Stationery and
Fancy Repository
Brook St (opposite Crescent Hotel)

Mr F. B. Maufe received a telegram on Saturday afternoon inti-
mating that his eldest son Major Stathan Broadbent Maufe, West
Yorkshire Regiment, died of wounds on July 5th. Educated at
Uppingham and Clare College, Cambridge. Two of his brothers
are also officers in the army, one being in the Wharfedale
Howitzers. He was 29 years of age and married.

[Sept. 8 1916]   The Hall, Ilkley. Sir James Oddy and Lady Oddy: The death of their only son Captain James Leslie. Worked with his father's firm of James Oddy, Junior worsted manufacturers: went to the front April last year, wounded July 12 following; going back in May was wounded a second time: had been in action about three weeks before receiving his last wound.

[Sept. 15 1916]   Captain Lister Holroyd, elder son of Mrs Holroyd, Hangingstone, Ilkley. Last week we announced that Captain Holroyd had been badly wounded in the face, arm and leg on Sept. 1st. Now comes the still more sorrowful news his death has occurred from these wounds. A prominent rugby player played for Ilkley and also Yorkshire.

Private Humpty sat on a bomb
Private Humpty was suffering from
The effects; notwithstanding, the medical men
Sent Private Humpty back to the Army again.

Wounded Horses Flag Day has been arranged for tomorrow.

JUST RECEIVED FOR THE
COMING WINTER SEASON!
A FINE SELECTION (SMALLER) OF

ZAG-ZAWS

ROYAL PICTURE PUZZLE

SHUTTLEWORTH

THE TOY AND GREAT
FANCY REPOSITORY

In connection with the Strength of Britain Prohibition Movement, another meeting took place in Ilkley. There was a very poor attendance and in deploring this fact Mr Hanuam said that the use and sale of intoxicating liquor, both in the army and civil life, was a source of danger and weakness and was hindering us winning the war. Seventy per cent of the food value of what beer contained was destroyed in the process of brewing.

ILKLEY PUBLICAN'S DEATH
BECAME UNCONSCIOUS WHILE VISITING THE BREWER

Robinson Whitehead went out about a quarter to three the previous afternoon to go to the Ilkley Brewery. He was brought back in a cab about six o'clock. He then could not walk and did not say anything.

THE THEOSOPHICAL SOCIETY

Nearly the whole earth had now been explored and mapped out by travellers. In a short time there would be no unexplored regions left, but after the physical world had been thus conquered there still remained a subtler region into which few explorers had so far consciously ventured. The great majority of people did not as yet believe in the existence of such a country as the Land of Dreams, but Miss Pattison believed it to be a real region which only awaited its discoverers.

The best time for sleep is between ten o'clock and two o'clock, as then the life currents are negative and the Land of Dreams experiences will be most vivid. Anaesthetics, alcohol and opium were what we might call the backdoor entrances to the Land of Dreams, but anything that tended to injure the physical body tended also to destroy the connecting bridge between sleep and waking consciousness.

A Red Letter Day in the Town's History

[24 August 1917] Youngest son of Mr and Mrs F. B. Maufe, recently awarded the Victoria Cross arrived home yesterday for a few days furlough.

> "Under intense military fire this officer on his own initiative repaired unaided the telephone line between the forward and rear positions, thereby enabling his battery to immediately open fire on the enemy. He further saved what might have been a disastrous occurrence by extinguishing a fire in an advanced ammunition dump, regardless of the risk he ran from the effect of gas shells, which he knew were in the dump."

He is only nineteen years of age and still a boy, yet in his manner and bearing and utter lack of vanity and pride he is the embodiment of everything a true hero should be.

From the pen of N. N. W. an Ilkley soldier at Vimy Ridge

Twas Easter Monday, nineteen seventeen
When nature was touching the hedges green
That the lads of the British army won
A battle with bayonets, mortar and gun
The barrage begins with a sudden roar
As shells from out eighteen pounders pour
Then over the top our brave lads leap
And steadily forward begin to creep

The Curtain of fire then forward glides
And star shells gleam from many sides;
Machine gun bullets whistle all around
And brave men's blood drips to the ground.

How the battle was won I cannot say
But I know that there was a price to pay;
Many a life was given that morn
And for mothers and wives new sorrow was born

Ah life is sweet while it does last
But at its best it may soon pass;
For on that day many crossed the bridge
And reached their Heaven – via Vimy Ridge

Friday 7 February 1919

The Ilkley Belgian Hospitality Committee provided the Belgian refugees still resident in this district with a farewell party in the Kings Hall Annexe, as most of them were leaving Ilkley for their own country the following morning. Mrs Rabagliati, president, read out a number of instructions for the guidance of the Belgians leaving on the morrow. She said it was Mr Gordon who first proposed they should invite some Belgians to come to Ilkley. He said the suggestion came from his wife. The people of this country had opened up their hearts to the Belgian people. Mr Jues Lammerling remembered with heartfelt gratitude how they were received in Ilkley on their arrival, thanking them all for their four and a half years. They left in a saloon by the 11-15 train to which several vans were attached containing their luggage.

Arrangements have been made for the famous Belgian Cellist Madame Fernande Kufferath and party (including Mr Harold Craxton, who usually accompanies Madame Clara Butt) to visit the Kings Hall, to aid the fund of the Belgian Order of Jerusalem assisting blind soldiers, orphans and widows.

Ilkley War Memorial Public Meeting held at the Kings Hall.

[23 March 1919]

Mr Eckersley: The committee has decided to recommend a monument should be erected on the triangular piece of ground at the junction of Bolton Bridge Road and the Grove. Mrs Cooke is willing to let us have it for £1,250 and the monument itself would cost between £2,000 and £3,000. It is fitting that the men who died have a fitting monument to their name.

Mr Baynes: I can't see the wisdom of it. £3,500 for a useless memorial when the widows of those that have fallen have to eke out an existence on 21 shillings per week. Their wives and children should be provided for.

Mr Tennant: I'm in favour of a monument but strongly object to buying the land.

Mr Mott: Shouldn't the memorial should take the form of something more useful, like say a swimming bath? Swimming baths have been talked about for the last ten years in this town, and they will be talked about for another ten years before anything is done.

Mr Talbit: What about a cross?

Mr Eckerseley: What about a cross?

Mr Talbit: I thought it might be appropriate to have a cross. On the moor.

Mr Eckersley: Not everyone can get to the moor.

Mr Maufe: I move that the report of the committee be adopted. Canon Wood seconded. Carried.

Their sons are dead, their sons are dead, dead in every town, in every street, brothers and fathers too, but most of all, their sons are dead, and they bury them, their mothers and fathers, a block of stone for many, stuck in front of empty ground, and speak their name wishing that it was their sons standing, staring down at them. Their sons are dead, their sons are dead, they never thought, holding them soft or cuffing them on the side of the head, watching them grow and misbehave in this proud town, that their country could lead them away to such an orchestrated land of torment, to be so paraded on stations and waved goodbye on trains simply to vanish, as if they meant nothing but a quick spray of blood wiped clear of weary eyes. Their sons are dead and they write poems and plant flowers and trees and hope that God understands it all, for they do not. This is the house of the twentieth century, and this tremor has cracked its foundation, tilted the structure askew: we can no longer maintain our balance within its walls, cannot help but bang against its sides, fall about in disorder, topple out of its windows. Their sons are dead.

Mr Jenkinson entertains seventy discharged soldiers and sailors and repatriated prisoners of war belonging to the Ilkley district in the Wesleyan Hall.

I wonder if any of the men present took part in that memorable Sunday afternoon sending off in August 1914. Much water had passed under Ilkley Bridge since then but amidst all the rough and tumble of it and the great adventure they had made, they had been spared to return. Oh! What a shake up the old world had had during the last four or five years, and what was more it was not going to be allowed to slip back into the old groove.

They gave him wings
To Fly O'er Land and Sea
But Thou dids't whisper and those wings
Have carried him to thee
Wainwright, Gifford Ernest. 2nd Lieutenant RAF
Died of his wounds in France, October 14 1918. 20 years.

Healthy Exercise
for Girls and Boys
Skipping Ropes
Wood and Iron Hoops
Battledore and shuttlecocks,
whip tops
Marbles, Golf Clubs, &c.

Prior to the war English children were mostly acquainted with toys "Made in Germany". We are determined that the words Made in Germany shall never again be seen in English shop windows, or any article of German origin we can possibly make do without, and we can do without anything German if we like.

With the new Ilkley industry of toy making, Mr Cooper sets out with the very patriotic idea of providing as much employment as possible for discharged soldiers (but has only been able to secure a few of these). The staff of thirty employees he is commencing with will consist of ten men and twenty girls, the latter possessing some training and experience in the handling of tools and machines gained as munitions workers. Possibly Ilkley may one day become as famous for its toy making as Nuremberg

and for the men wooden legs and wooden crutches, marble eyes, and gutta percha hands.

25 November 1919

Resolved
that the Council offer to maintain the eleven War Graves in the cemetery and grant permission to the Imperial War Graves Commission to erect headstones where necessary and to waive the payment of fees in respect thereof:

THE MOOR (8)

PROFESSOR MODLEY

Physical Culture and Massage
Classes for Ladies and Gentlemen and Children
Private Tuition Arranged
Boys Classes Sat at 10 am 2/6 per week
Girls Classes Sat at 10 am 2/6 per week
Boys taught Breathing, Self Defence, Gymnastics etc.
Girls taught Deportment, Skipping Rope, Dance etc.
Full particulars apply Prof. Modley, 6 Regent Rd Ilkley

Professor Modley, gymnast, acrobat, professional strongman, ran the indoor swimming baths, the only bathing area in the town open to all, its water and its heat provided by the Ilkley Brewery company nearby.

[Friday 6 February 1920] A display was given today by Prof. Modley and his pupils. Professor Modley, the local physical culture expert, and his pupils provided a very interesting display in St Margaret's Hall on Friday evening. Miss Annie Wall and Miss Modley went through a series of exercises with the Whiteley developer followed by a broadsword and fencing exercise by Miss Wall and the Professor. A demonstration of Ju Jitsu methods of gripping throwing etc. was shown by Prof. Modley with his son Albert (who became a music hall star, learnt fencing with

his father, which gave him the cut and thrust, the parry and the lunge needed for timing. He started work as a butchers' boy for Dalton's and greeted people he met with his very own catchphrase. "It's a grand place for a bike, Ilkley, it's all downhill.")

Later there was a skipping competition for the girls. Moba Gell was the winner with 260 jumps. She was still skipping when this number was reached but Professor Modley wisely stopped her to prevent exhaustion. The principal event was a boxing event. Percy Blaimire and Robert Gale took part in a blindfold boxing competition causing roars of laughter.

Professor Modley used to demonstrate the efficacy of his regime by performing an unusual demonstration on the Cow and Calf, standing on his hands for over half an hour.

Professor Modley climbs the moor and, pulling himself up on to the Calf, walks to the edge and turning round, raises himself up on his hands. His head is held close to the names written on the rock (Ilkley is awash with names, names on benches, names on the rocks, names in their memorials, names on foundation stones, their little letters their only mark), lifts his right leg into the air and with the other following with professional ease begins his upside-down vigil over the town. Spectators crowd about, walking out from the hotel to the east, standing above him on the Cow, looking down at his wiry quivering frame. Professor Modley cannot see them for he is facing the other way, to where he sees the town inverted. Where it once lay below this rock, anchored by the silver rope of the Wharfe, Ilkley now floats above him, suspended in the air like some great wandering Zeppelin that they so guarded against, so majestic were they in their flight. He can see its portholes and the fumes from its exhaust, he can hear the whine of its machinery, see its passengers promenading on its misty decks, taking them they know not where. Some will be carried to other waters, others who will jump ship, fall overboard, or be set adrift, some are stowaways, some will never leave, some are content to place their feet upon its sunset railings watching the vessel drift, some wish to mount insurrection, storm the bridge, seize the captain, change Ilkley's course. Whatever, they are all marked by this vessel, suffer this vessel's journey; the horizons they see are from Ilkley's decks, the lifeboats slung out from Ilkley's sides (not enough for all).

The indoor swing was replaced with an outdoor variety, which was taken out down to the little wood halfway down the garden and hammered into the earth with long metal spikes. It was green instead of red, but possessed of the same genes as its bucking cousin. In Ilkley's municipal gardens and in the kindergarten to which he walked every morning he had only known of swings with chains, but here in the space of a week he had discovered this new, faster breed, the outdoor swing with metal-rod arms. He climbed aboard and discovered quickly two things about metal rod swings which set them apart from the chain variety: 1) that their rigid arms gave the seat great stability 2) that when propelled to the limit by long hard swings, as a golfer might following through, these rods would eventually deliver the occupant clean out of the bunker in which the seat racked back and forth, up and over the frame, describing the swing in a perfect 360-degree arc.

This was astronaut stuff before the world knew of the word, and as he swung hard and climbed, urging himself on to when, suspended on top, he broke the crest, he felt as he never felt before (before he knew what it was and what it would be in later years), an eclipse of the soul, with the swing and his body melted into a moment, his head at his feet, his feet at his head, everything mixed above and below, travelling through the forbidden air weightless, entering into a world of such incomparable and dangerous beauty that he had to lie down on the grass for twenty minutes afterwards to quiet his bumping heart.

This he accomplished on day two. Days three and four he spent circumnavigating his new globe with frenzied energy, pausing only to walk unsteadily back home for lunch and tea, careful not to spill the beans to his mother. Day five he revolved facing the other way (not as good). Day six, boredom. Day seven he made his first attempt to marry iron swing quality 1) to iron swing quality 2) i.e. to square the circle upside down, and thus be upright at its apogee when he should be upside down. He quickly found however that it was impossible to obtain sufficient momentum starting from an inverted position. Such a feat could only be accomplished by changing position when flight seemed imminent. However the very act of changing over, of placing his head on the seat and kicking his legs up was tricky, and even when he had mastered it (day nine) it also provided an unwanted brake to the enterprise. Week two was spent idling on the ground, upside down, thinking what the trick might be. The Strid and the giant had the answer.

The trick was, oh yes he learnt the trick, was to discard timidity and be bold, take the leap. When the moment came, in the pull of the final backswing, when he knew that on the next run the rods would take him over (and he grew to recognize that moment, the way the links seemed to settle back in themselves, his body almost perpendicular to the ground), the trick was to grip the rods with his hands as he hurtled down, and without thought except to the will of it, flip himself up, head hanging free, legs wrapped around those iron rods, hands clenched tight below, swooping down, flying up, his body stretched out like one of those figures he had seen in his brother's Greek story book, reaching for the sun, rearing up to that time of perfect stillness, when heaven and earth met and he was standing motionless in the air, legs apart, arms raised, the wooden seat above him, the metal frame below, defying gravity and sense, a boy grown a hundred feet tall, like Rombald of old, ready to stride across the landscape, to take it all in his hands and fashion it as he might. At that moment the world lay before him, every future stitch of it, to be woven and worn any way he wanted.

And then, of course, he fell back to earth.

SHOULD ILKLEY HAVE A SEASON BAND?

[15 February 1924] Born in trouble and criticism, it has continued in that particular nursery to the present day, was the

description given by W. Dobson of the career of the Ilkley council's Municipal Orchestra before the members of the Ilkley Chamber of Trade.

Last year the band had cost £530 and receipts had amounted to £217. The last two years the band had run at a serious loss. The penny rate which was available for this purpose produced £256 but if they allowed £260 they would still find there a deficit of £53.

On the six weeks run there was a total loss on the band of £52 3s 4d. J. R. Feather said he didn't know what the rest of the members of the Chamber thought but he himself thought it was time for something fresh. He was in favour of letting the bandstand, either for nothing or to the highest bidder. For their number they were a good band but they only had twelve performers. The weather of course was disastrous but 'the band we have had has been a washout'. We should either mend it or end it. We either want a better band or not at all.

Mr Tennant brought forward the suggestion for utilising the penny rate available for the public purse by securing visits from three or four good military bands. Mr McEvoy said he did not see why the site near the Tarn should be utilised and recalled the performances of the Pierrot company which formerly appeared there. J. Tomlison remarked that some health resorts were paying as much as £250 a week for military bands the whole season. The Ilkley Orchestra was not suitable for outside performances, though it was all right for the Annexe.

Mr Dobson said he was not going to speak either for or against the band. The question would come before the band committee. However there were several factors against the success of a band at the present band stand. On a fine summer's evening the people got too far away over the moors and they lost the collections. On warm muggy evenings it took all one's time to sit through a performance because one was worried about the midges. Later in the season, as the days shortened they could not sit to the end of the performance on account of the cold. On wet days the band conductor would come and ask him as Chairman whether they were to play in the Annexe. They would delay the decision until the last possible minute and after they had decided upon the Annexe on account of the rain, and the band had begun to play there, the sun would come out and people would be asking 'Why is the band inside?' Or the opposite might be the case; they would start to play at the band stand on a fine evening and half way through the performance rain would come on and people would go away and only half a collection. Until some provision was made for a place where the band cold play wet or fine, the band would not be the success they would like.

Mr Dean asked whether the Chamber was satisfied with the general condition of things, especially the King's Hall. If they were not how could they conscientiously support the present members for the next election. For himself he was not a believer in municipal trading, for they never ran anything at a profit and unless they ran things at a profit they would come to a dead end.

Dobson: We are selling gas, water and electricity, we're cleaning away refuse and dealing with sewage. That is municipal trading.

Dean: I am not in favour of the council running pictures. The Council were not elected for that purpose. I'd like Mr Feather to recast the accounts for the year ending March 31 1923 dealing with the King's Hall and Public Library.

Feather: They are available to anyone in the Ilkley Public Library. The expenditure on the King's Hall and Winter Gardens amounted to £5,839 18s and the income £5,126 18s 1d. The account show a loss of £712 19s 11d. The receipts from plays during the year amounted to £1,089 12s; from cinematograph exhibitions £3,224 5s 2d, private lettings £676 17s 10d, advertising £12 10s, and other receipts £123 12s 3d. The amount contributed to the Exchequer by way of Entertainment Tax was £1,144 7s 7d.

[Friday 22 April 1927]   Glorious Easter weather has given a good start to the Ilkley holiday season. A striking feature was the remarkably early hour at which the motor traffic began to throng the roads. Loaded motor coaches were passing along the main road at six o'clock and as the morn-

ing wore on the traffic increased to a pouring stream which continued without intermission until long after dark; the path from Dick Hudson's to Ilkley during the afternoon presented a scene of a continuous line of pedestrians.

Not just the Bank Holidays the dedicated walking. At Whitsuntide the Bradford walk, a journey of 32 miles from Bradford by way of Shipley, Menston, Burley, Ilkley, Askwith, Weston, Otley, Pool Bank, Yeadon, Apperley Bridge, Greengates, to Peel Park, with collections and concert parties along the way, Ilkley in particular. The turning point was down Stockeld Road and over the Ilkley Old Bridge. Ramblers came here too, not in their ones and twos but in their hundreds, in their thousands, held rallies to celebrate their need to roam, to possess the moor at a time of their choosing, today, tomorrow, a year from now, knowing that it was there for the taking, you and the moor: speakers came too, stood on the rock and bellowed to the listeners below.

[Sunday 15 June 1924] At the Cow and Calf on this Sunday, Dr Joad addressed a gathering of 2–3000.

If you come to think of it our towns, more particularly our towns in the North East, they are the ugliest, foulest, collection of buildings that have ever disgraced any civilisation. They are a filthy monument to the spirit of mean profit-making which produced them. We have the ugliest towns of any country in the world and we also have got the loveliest countryside.

But when we go to the fields and woods we find ourselves up against the sportsmen, a sportsman being a man who takes his pleasure in depriving birds and beasts of their lives. The scale of values is all wrong. We need legislation that gives crowded industrial workers of this country some chance of going to the moors and mountains and enjoying solitude and loneliness and exhilaration that come from these heights. Certain areas should be set aside as naturalist parks, from which the sportsman be excluded.

The heather is very dark here, and despite the stones of the twelve Apostles, human order is suspended. Across on the way, towards Bingley is altogether a different sight. Down over towards the Aire and on the hills to the south-east you see them, rows of back-to-backs set out like onions, with blooming roofs and well hoed streets, as ordered as any well tended allotment, bursting their pale blues and reds in the sunlight directed from the wild above; industry's kitchen garden. He stands there, looking at the houses, not simply enjoying the distant geometry displayed, but the way they appear to be piled on top of one another, like produce in a harvest festival, the sunlight slanting down on their blue-slate roofs as from a great church, how those men and women were regarded as a type of crop, grown on an industrial soil (and the diseases and deformities that sprang from that). He stands and tries to imagine the columns of smoke that must have been seen from here on a clear winter's day, a hundred thousand coal-fired funnels floating in the sky, imagining too the slow awakening of the moor as, on those spring and summer days, they began their Bank Holiday toil, the hill quiet at first, and then, out of sight, a slight hum walk as the first walkers set out, slow burning as a newly lit fire, a scrunch of paper and a small square of twig, as the thin smoke rises and the fire takes hold, larger logs now as Bradford opens up its gates, marches down its cobbled streets to the heathered base of it. Now the fire licks as they start to climb, crackles and takes hold as the stamp of boots shakes the earth; now it leaps high, touching the back of the chimney as they burst over the lip of the hill into their steady march. It is burning full now, fuelled hod upon hod, a streaming line of them stretching back like advancing troops, their numbers overwhelming, the peat-pathed moor echoing to their hollow drumming, gathering pace as the fire roars as they cross Rombald's height and, seeing the town laid out before them, race down to evaporate into Ilkley's keen and willing air

Thousands more came by road in crowded buses, in cars and on cycles. From noon onwards the cafe and tea houses were thronged, but perhaps the most remarkable scenes were in the evening with the long queues for the homegoing buses. Special services were run to Leeds, Bradford and Keighley. At 7 o'clock the queue for Bradford counted 1,700, and for hours the buses were leaving packed to the doors every five minutes, the crowds seeming to grow no less. It was after 11 o'clock that the last of the holidaymakers departed. In the meantime thousands had walked back over the moor to the Airedale towns.

On Tuesday morn sheets of paper, cardboard boxes, orange peel, blown and scattered on the moor.

THE ECLIPSE [29 June 1927]

They danced through the night and at the Pavilion cafe, perched pagoda-like behind White Wells, ate ham and eggs at four o'clock, the Cow and Calf crowded and becoming more so every minute, hauling themselves up for they knew not what. 'The More We Are Together' they sang and then, as the dull light spread through an overclouded sun, 'Am I Wasting My Time on You'.

Then the dark cold spread, no flashing lights or cheers in this age, the dead still lying in their hearts, the living eclipsed, frozen as the animal, in Red Sea apprehension. The rabbit beside the stoat, the fox stilled in the chicken coop, oh they know the dog fight and the hawk's claw, the bark of gun but in this great gloom they see, for the length of it, their own animal immortality. This brings their hush and listening we find the more we are together, the more we are together

I am down and out and in debt. I cannot go on any longer.
Love to everyone. xxxx
Jack Ongar

ILKLEY (11)

MARY LEAROYD

Good response for clothing for the Middleton Sanatorium.

[1929] Clothing for patients undergoing treatment for consumption in winter marks the difference between a chance of life and little or no chance at all. Something like 1,000 men and women pass through Middleton Sanatorium in the course of a year. Men are coming from the distressed areas bringing little more than they stand up in. Their homes can furnish them with no more. Their clothing might be sufficient if they could live in warmed rooms. But to fight consumption they must have uncontaminated air. Their only protection against the cold therefore is clothing, and the clothing they bring is not sufficient.

They come here still, the sick, to Ilkley, if not for the water then for the blessed air. There's not much to choose between them any road. It's all they are allowed to do, to fight this thing, sit and breathe this cold climate, look out from the window to the town with its coal fires and its chimneys, sit quiet in this stone vessel and let nurse wash the cold air over them, pulling charity's jumper over their pale and shivering frame. The name of consumption is solitude

Misses Jarvis and Brown Handkerchiefs and bed socks; Mrs Weatherhead new mufflers; Mrs Walton magazines; Mr A. Lister clothing

Some thirty-five years ago I had as a friend Mr John Turney. He was interested in astronomy as I also was and I therefore made and mounted for him a big 10 inch equatorial telescope, driven by clockwork, the mirrors of which I ground and polished myself. A year ago he died suddenly.

Last night January 20th 1929 I and my wife were just composing ourselves for sleep. The lights were out and the doors and the window were bolted. Suddenly my wife said that she heard a voice speaking to her and saying "Turney Wood. Look! Look!" and then a word she could not make out and then the voice continued "Five forty-five!" and then the word "Declination." We asked for the explanation of this but the voice, which was faint, said that the communicator was weak and would come again.

This morning we were discussing this remarkable experience when the letters, just delivered by the postman, were brought to us. One of them was a circular from the British Astronomical Society containing the announcement of the discovery of a comet and we read with amazement that the position of the comet was Right Ascension 5 hours 40 minutes, North Declination 20 degrees, as indicated by the message on the night.

This remarkable experience shows that my friend has neither ceased to exist, nor has he lost interest in his friend on earth, nor his scientific pursuits. God be thanked who thus permits a corner of the veil to be lifted.

Spence's Garden		Silverwell Cottage
0.19	Rainfall during the month	1.07
17	No. of days on which rain fell	11
49	Maximum Temperature	48
8	Minimum Temperature	8
29.4	Mean Temperature for month	29
15.10	Hours of sunshine	[—]

It was the coldest spell since 1895. The town skated and slithered and stoked its coal fires. By day the tarn was packed so tight, it was scarcely possible to glide for more than a foot without locking into another's skates, while at night, with the younger ones abed, they illuminated the tarn with electric arc-lamps and let romance take its turn. On Sundays coffee was served on banks decorated by frost-shaped flowers spun fantastic by the wind, which splintered at the slightest touch. Underneath the hump of the old bridge nine inches of ice clung to the river and down by the treacherous slip of the stepping stones a dam of broken ice piled up three feet in height. Boys disregarded history and common sense and slid towards it on a polished frozen slide, the water gliding unseen below as they bent their legs and dug in their heels and glided in cold purity, their breath and shouts warming the air. Snowballs and snowmen, ashes on the road, the cold keen and quiet, the weather, like the town, captured in a sparkling time, held in a frozen charm.

(It takes that, doesn't it, a time of utter cold, a sudden wreath of mist or one long baked day, walking back through a familiar street, it needs the weather, a cooked or frozen moment to burn the taste of a town on your tongue, to seal it upon you like a branded calf, to know that you are the town and the town is you, in the steps you take and the air you breathe, recognize the transportation that has taken place, that here is your island and you the Crusoe, thank God there is food and water here and a friend too otherwise you might die of starvation, wither on the town's barren vine, yes, you are the town, bear its mark but within your heart you hope this is not all true, that you are bigger than these streets and houses and the people behind the windows, you could leave, catch a train, your future parcelled up on the rack, your mother's cake already half chewed, discarded, your cloying lover's name vanishing on the carriage window's falsely drawn heart

The frost lasts for a fortnight. Ilkley thaws, the winds die down, the war ten years gone now. The graves are not as young now, but still tended, more mother and father than wife and child, the memorial fresh and though not soft to touch the names are, those small brass letters on which can be traced the little steps they took, names that pushed a porter's trolley or followed a father's footsteps, pressing their brushed, waistcoated attention on some attending bride, a future of pounds, shillings and pence carefully weighed or thrown to fickle fortune, the people they knew grown now, not wrapped up like they are in the cloth of time, the waving sweetheart a wife, patient with another's embrace, some other's child feasting on her breasts; a mother not emptied completely of her need, but breathing the sad fragrance of him every day, in the rooms he ran, the yard he played, remembering the time he broke a tooth or the china cup or simply held her hand, a child then and in that proud and saddened moment a child no more, a man, and then, inexplicably, no more at all. Good that she does not know what she bred him for, what he thought, what he saw, what he had to do, how he died, that there is this clean monument and these tiny letters to keep her memory clear. Ilkley is alive. Her sons are dead.

> *[March 31st]*   Police Constable Sowerby was coming from his allotment with his two little girls when one of them was hit by a small stone which the boy had shot from his catapult. The boy said he had aimed at the chimney of the cobblers shop but
>
> missed
>
>
> elastic on Saturday,
> catapult on Sunday
> trouble on Monday.
>
>
> James Heyworth, a telegraph messenger. Fined 2s. and 1s. 4d. costs.

The summer brings fine weather, which as June moves to July and July to August elongates into drought. Holidaymakers, day-trippers, weekend revellers leave their marks.

Attention was directed to the danger of accident to persons walking on the Moor by reason of broken bottles which are strewn on the Moor, particularly after each public or Bank Holiday and it was

Resolved
    That notices be placed on the Moor requesting users not to leave empty bottles lying on the Moor; and
    That the tenant of the Moor Refreshment Pavilion be requested to assist the Council in their endeavours in this direction by increasing the amount of the deposit on bottles which are returnable.

The townsfolk stand on the riverbank watching boys throw themselves from the New Bridge and wonder whether there would ever be a swimming pool. Cricket leagues and tennis matches and golf are played, the earth hard and dry, thirsting for another thunderstorm. Mr Dell the boatman counts his coins and prays it will not come. On some of the afternoons there is the bandstand while in the Winter Gardens the Ilkley Orchestra plays, twice on Sundays, for tea and dancing. There are two cinemas in the town, the New and the Grove, and there are the many drinking houses, the Royal, the Crescent, the Lister Arms, the Star, the Middleton, the Midland, the Wheatsheaf, you would be hard pressed to tap them all of an evening. It is not such a small town, then, there is entertainment here, and, if you're looking for it, the chance for evening romance, or, if the company is inclined, sex, given or paid for, in doorways and on cold moor benches, in unlit basements and darkened archways, hasty all. Girls go to dances and set their caps, some take themselves to public houses and set their price, not only Ilkley girls but from other towns, Otley, Addingham, Skipton, and the houses in between. There's a fresh crowd in town most Saturday nights, men with a bit of money in their pocket, girls with a bit of flirt in their hair, and if not that, then off to the films with a friend and see Gary Cooper. Or a play.

July 5th.

Kings Hall   Commencing at 8 o'clock
The Great American Comedy Thriller

THE MONSTER

by Crane Wilbur
Produced under the personal direction of
Miss Olga Lindo
Brilliant Young West End Actress
Prices 3/6, 2/4, & 1/2 Including Tax

Between Thursday 11th and Saturday 13th July a group of travelling players come to Ilkley, Mr and Mrs Lindo's Touring Company, a second-rate troupe playing Britain's minor halls. The play is an American melodrama and features a remote country house, a dark and stormy night, a mad scientist bent upon mutilation and a distressed damsel. It is grotesque and frightening and the characters clutch at the extremity of their passion at every curtain fall. The young Marion Wakefield is fresh and lovely as the darling French heroine, Mr Frank Lindo terrifies the audience as the insane Dr Ziska, while to captivate the feminine heart there strides their lead actor, rugged reckless Philip Drew, of American origin like the play, whose good-looking star is on the wane, a Wild West shock of hair, an overwhelming presence and tendency to drink too much between curtain calls. As the play opens, he is on stage masking his true identity beneath a false beard and a swathe of tattered clothes – an actor playing Red Mackensie, the hobo detective, a make-believe tramp.

They have travelled much, these players, Torquay, Grimsby, Bognor, Rochdale, Eastbourne, New Brighton, Reading. They are pleased to have left Reading, for on June 22nd there, an hour or so before the evening's performance was due to start, Alfred Oliver, the owner of a small tobacconist around the corner from the theatre, was found dying behind the counter of his small well-run shop, bludgeoned to death by an unknown assailant. But they have left all that behind them, that and a pair of Mr Drew's trousers which disappeared strangely that night out of his travelling basket. By the time they get to Northampton in three weeks' time, Philip Drew will become the prime suspect in that murder and will become, for a short time, emblazoned in the footlights of the press (after which he will sink into bitter, boozed obscurity). But he does not know this yet, nor do his audience know of his history and the murder that will catapult him into the fatal limelight. And there is another thing none of them know, for in this audience is another who will bear the brunt of an another awful savagery, Mary Learoyd.

She is a strange and lonely looking woman. From the photograph that looks out from the yellowing paper he can tell how tall and ungainly was her walk upon those streets. He recognizes with a degree of alarm the similarity between her looks and that of his own mother, not solely in the particular configuration of eye and mouth, or style of hair, though all those pertain, but rather in the look with which she faces the world, both benign and puzzled, at ease and discomfited, unworldly and yet knowing enough to find much distasteful. It is an expression which indicates an awkwardness with one's body, one's age, ones sex, an intelligence which has been half woken only to be thoroughly starved, as the body's food is similarly wanting; all undernourished, so that in the final count, though well intentioned and wishing for good, it is partial and ultimately unloving, like a parched flower unable to flower and bloom.

She was born in Halifax around 1894. Her family moved to Ilkley in 1899 or thereabouts, when she was five. Her father is a building contractor, responsible for much important building work in Ilkley including the houses on the estate, where they have made their home on Sedbergh Park Road, a steep curve of a road that branches off the broader, straighter Cowpasture Road, just up from the railway station and the Town Hall and the Library (to which at its conception Mr Learoyd donated books). Their house is called Little Gables, a small semi-detached house stuck on the sharp rise of the hill. She lives there with her parents, both infirm, and her aunt. Above lies the moor, below the pleasant familiarity of the town, and as she passes to and fro a ragged patch of waste ground, steep and long grassed, the stump of a large tree standing in its bedraggled centre.

The Lindo players leave, for Maidstone and Nottingham and appointments with the police. Ilkley has a good summer. The roads are filled with overheated cars, dripping oil, gushing rust. Sudden rains come, as sudden rains do, violent. Storm water fills the library gutters, cascades down into the building itself. The Wharfe rises, Mr Dell ties his boats fast and watches the ropes take the strain. The roads turn black and treacherous. On the thirteenth of the month Police Inspector George Marsh's son Leonard, aged sixteen, takes his motorbike out and skidding out of control near Mickle Ing Bridge is killed. On Friday 23rd Sarah Ackroyd, a friend from Bradford, visits Miss Learoyd and together they visited the Ilkley Parish Church. Mary's father, who is ill, is Hon. Treasurer of the Church Council and she empties various alms boxes in his stead. After this is done Mary suggests they go to the pictures, for she likes the pictures, sitting there in the dark, the bright dangerous world an invention swirling harm-lessly around her, but Sarah who lives in Bradford prefers to remain outdoors. It is what people in Bradford do when they come to Ilkley, remain outdoors. Being a friend Miss Learoyd agrees readily but vouchsafes that she will probably go to the pictures by herself the following evening. 'I wish you were staying with me for the week-end,' she says. She sees her friend off on the 9.45 bus, but before Sarah gets on Mary asks her if she could lend her three pounds for her forthcoming holiday in Jersey.

She kept house and my father gave her £1 a week. Her only extravagance was with clothes, used to get them at

Lingards and Brown Muffs. She had nothing to do with
the pound per week except dress and save for holidays.

– Eric Learoyd

She walks back that August night, up Cowpasture Road, turning
right up past the waste ground to her little house, her aunt and her
sick mother and father awaiting his operation, a small dwelling
enough for four adults, but smaller still with the many permuta-
tions it had to house, one couple, two single women, two invalids,
one ageing aunt, three women, one man, one father, one mother, one
sister, one sister-in-law, one niece, one daughter. Mary has a brother
married, a sister wed, she has seen two other siblings die eleven years
before, at which time she decided to stay with her parents in the
aftermath of their distress; twenty-four then, thirty-five now. There
is a recent picture of her, taken in the back garden, sitting half upright
on a wooden bench, feet curled, looking for a moment like that
younger woman again, grown too big for the confines of that domestic seat, waiting for the moment when she will stand up upon its edge
and take flight under her own wing, but other photographs show an
acceptance of what has become her lot, tinged with not regret but
sadness and distant longing. It is not that she is alone. She has her
friends. There is Doris Baker and Mary Ellen Dance and Miss Hodgson. There is Mrs Sugden and Mrs Hemingway and Sarah Ackroyd,
all of whom live in Bradford. (It is Mrs Hemingway with whom she
is going on holiday. They have rooms booked in a Jersey farmhouse.)
Men friends are fewer on the ground. There is William Caldwell, a
railways clerk, and like her a member of the Ben Rhydding Operatic
Society, and there is Mr Bird of the GPO, a divorcee, who has shown
interest in her, but the attachment it is believed is mostly on his
side. No one else, apart from Mr Elliott, the verger at the church. She
is very friendly with Mr Elliott. It began when her father took
charge of the alterations to the church and she came to visit. Since
then she has become a frequent visitor, not only to the church, where
she spends her time repairing the cassocks and surplices, but also to
the verger's house, for evenings of parlour games and parlour talk and

parlour music. Two, three times a week it can be, very often on Sunday and Tuesday. Yes, she is friendly with the verger.

Saturday morning, the 24th, and a lively start to the weekend. Business is good; there is bustle out on the street. Saturday morning becomes Saturday afternoon. Mary Learoyd out in the morning is ready to go out again. She does a lot of going out, does Mary Learoyd. Perhaps that is what they all do, these ladies then, call in from shop to shop, house to house, take tea, meet in a café, stroll down by the river, examine library books and lengths of material. She calls at Mr Elliott's house, 29 Wilmot Road, which is on the other side of the railway line, not five minutes from her own home, where she helps Mrs Elliott cut out a pattern for a dress. Mrs Elliott asks her to stay for tea but she says she cannot, as she has to call in at her father's office and do some more shopping. She leaves his house, they believe, at five thirty, but it may be earlier, for at four fifteen her friend Mary Ellen Dance meets her walking along the Grove. Mary Ellen suggests that she go to the Grove Cinema that night, as she has already seen the picture and can recommend it. Mary Learoyd says that she is expecting friends and that they will all go together. (She is not expecting anyone, least no one her family is aware of.) Mary Ellen watches as her friend turns down into Brook Street. Four fifteen? Five fifteen? Before the Elliotts? After the Elliotts? Perhaps they all have their times wrong. It is so fluid, this coming and going, this day to day calling.

Mary Learoyd goes home. She makes tea for her father, her mother, no doubt. Six, seven, comes the evening. She looks at the paper. At the New Cinema is the film her friend saw, Harold Lloyd's comedy *College Days*. Over at the Grove Picture House, Fay Wray and Gary Cooper are set to star in *Legions of the Condemned*, preceded by Claire Windsor in *The Modern Flapper*. She leaves the house once more. She is wearing a pale blue beret and green dress, a light tweed coat of a brown mixture with a leather collar and leather pocket straps and leather straps on the cuff. A black leatherette belt goes round the dress and a string of imitation ivory beads hang around her neck. In the buttonhole of her coat she has placed an artificial flower of yellow and green. At 7.30 she enters Mr Dobson's shop in Brook Street, and buys a copy of the *Radio Times*. She laughs and jokes for a minute, and though Mr Dobson laughs and jokes back he is struck by how unusual is her behaviour. As a rule she is much more reserved. At 8 o'clock Ernest Tilsey sees her coming from the direction of Dalton's butchers, and about 8.20 her aunt Maud Elizabeth Rogers

> was coming from the Railway Station and walking in the direction of home when I saw Mary. She had just crossed from the library to the station. I spoke to her but she did not say where she was going

followed almost immediately by her friend Mary Ellen Dance who catches sight of her. Mary Ellen

> was standing in the queue at the New Cinema. I saw Miss Learoyd passing along Brook Street, walking slowly along. She appeared to be waiting for someone. I waved my hand to her and she waved back and smiled. I did not see her again. I had a lady friend with me, Mary Sheldrake. She has very fair hair, practically the same colour as Mary

Brook Street, the library, the station, the Grove, up and down she goes. At eight thirty Fanny Fisher, just out of the first house at the New Cinema, thinks she sees her going up Brook Street, while a little later, Mary Mennell, now an usherette, flashes her torch down the aisle and thinks she sees Mary Learoyd sitting with Miss Dance in the back of the 9d. stalls, but she is mistaken. That is Mary Ellen's friend, Miss Sheldrake. Eight thirty, nine thirty, ten o'clock, ten thirty; one, one and a half, two hours. Having been seen by half a dozen people Mary Learoyd is seen by no one. She is not at home, she is not in a public house, she is not walking the streets, nor at either of the cinemas. Where is she? And who is she with? Herself, alone? At church?

At ten thirty, though, a maid, Alice Murray of Park Crest, Sedbergh Road, sees Mary Learoyd standing near the telegraph pole opposite her house. Mary is with a man. Alice knows it is Mary from the clothes the woman is wearing. The man has his arm around her. Ten minutes later Flora Hannah Evans, also of Sedbergh Park Road, is walking up the road in the company of her husband when she sees a couple about halfway between the houses which adjoin the wasteland, standing on the footpath. As they grow nearer the woman deliberately turns her back to her. The girl is taller than the man (Mary Learoyd is five foot eight), who is of medium build and wearing a dark suit and a trilby hat and carrying a raincoat under his arm. Alice hears nothing they might be saying but as she passes the woman turns again on a conscious pivot of avoidance as if she does not want to be recognized. She comes to the conclusion that the woman is Mary Learoyd. The coat is one in which she frequently sees her.

Between ten forty-five and eleven Mary Parchett, of Hildbrow, also of Sedbergh Park Road, retires for bed. Upstairs she hears her dog bark, and looking out of the staircase window sees in the moon-lit night a couple near their front gate, laughing and talking and moving over to the long grass. She knows what they are about. She draws her husband's attention to them, and he calls out, asking them to go away.

They do not go away. John Skirrow, walking his girl Alice Kairs back home from the pictures, hears a slight scream and then, imme-diately afterwards, sees a couple moving about in the long grass. Alice sees them too and she hears the woman say, 'If you will wait, I will kiss you.' When John Skirrow returns from kissing his girl goodnight the couple are still there, on the grass, but they are still now and do not make a sound.

If you will wait I will kiss you, if you wait I will.

Nellie Lister, a sister in the Belle Vue Nursing Home, over-looking the gardens and the wasteland on the other side of the railings, is on duty that night, nursing a critically ill man. It is a warm evening and her patient is restless and at around 10.45p.m. she stands by the open window, to look to breathe in a moment's cool peace from the dark land outside.

I heard a man and a woman talking as they walked up the path. They sat on a seat at the top, not thirty yards from my window, and I could hear them talking plainly. I did not actually hear the conversation but I could hear a cultured woman's voice and the voice of a well-educated Yorkshire man. The couple sat on the seat for an hour, then walked away and then came back. After some time the man became angry and excited. I left the window exactly at 1.30 to administer morphia injection, the man was still agitated and his voice raised in his excitement. The woman's voice however was not raised. A breeze sprang up and I had to close the window.

She closes the window. Her patient drifts into his morphia sleep, his thoughts neither rushed nor formed, but swirling with ghostly vacancy like Ilkley's deserted streets. The cinemas are closed now, the aisles swept clean of sweet papers and cigarette ends. In the Wheatsheaf and the Royal the beer pumps are covered by tea towels, the landlord asleep in his bed. The last bus has gone, the last train too. Otley, Skipton, Keighley, wherever, are all a long tramp home. But Mary Learoyd has not come home. At Little Gables, her parents and her aunt try to reassure themselves with the unlikely thought that she has gone to Bradford to arrange last-minute holiday details with Mrs Hemingway and missed the last bus. They do not like to call the police; they do not want to make a fuss. They will wait to see what the morning might bring. The night passes. Oh, Mary Learoyd.

At 10.30 on Sunday morning Mary Parchett goes out to walk round her garden. On reaching the bottom she glances into the shrubbery which lies about ten yards away from her garden. She sees a naked foot poking out. She calls her husband. He finds lying in the undergrowth, Mary, dead

naked below the waist. On the upper part a woollen vest, a stocking tied tightly round the neck with the knot slightly on the left side. The arms tied with another stocking behind the back, the clothing was all torn off the body. Every garment being torn. The right shoe was lying a few inches from the right foot. The face was badly bruised near the left eye. Laceration of upper lip. Cut on right cheek. Extensive bruising right hip. Bone necklace found near body. A lady's handbag (open) near right shoulder. Card and match case near. No money in bag. Two handkerchiefs one pink and one blue in bag. Purse and left glove found near right shoulder also an H T and V ring No 15472. Vest and frock torn or cut from body and turned back from breast. Right nipple smeared with soil, left clean. Blood stains on body appearance of person wiped bloodstained fingers on body. Left leg smeared with soil. The right-hand glove, part of a torn petticoat with half of a broken comb found in the Vagina, earth marks found on the iron railings 10ft 6 inches from head of body. Brown coat leather collar black and brown belt green dress split up front. Princess skirt vest and yellow scarf found under back. Wristlet watch on left wrist Metal cigarette case 3¼ inches by 2¼ inches containing one cigarette (Craven A) extracted from rectum. The wounds to the face and fractures of the facial bones were caused before death. The ligature applied to the neck when the woman was just dying or possibly just after she was dead. The comb and the cigarette case were inserted after death.

By mid-morning the police from Leeds, Bradford, Otley, Wakefield, and Harrogate have descended upon the town. They scythe the scrub land, they search garages and outhouses, clamber into empty houses and shine torches into derelict stables (the idea of insanity, a frothing lunatic hiding in a gibbering corner, clearly on their minds); they start the long investigation of the moor, its myriad paths and its smooth cracked rock, they have woods and ravines to plough, eddies of water to examine where the killer might have washed his hands. The Chief Constable of West Riding, Colonel Coke, is photographed striding through the long grass at the scene of the crime. Still beholden to Kimberley and Mafeking, the story of the scout, the romance of tracking, two bloodhounds, Mystic and Mournful, are brought over from Baildon. Given an article of her clothing and followed by an inquisitive crowd they fuss back and forth for two hours before taking off through the grounds of old Ilkley Hall, giving tongue up gravel drives, along fences and over lawns before finally coming to a halt by a gate leading out on to the Wells Road. There the trail evaporates. The dog noses are returned to their kennel.

She is buried swiftly, the funeral itself a tragedy, her mother and father too distraught, too ill to attend. Their daughter, a solitary girl who presumed a solitary future ahead of her, is buried without even those living who gave her life. They take their ghastly farewells in the pressed agony of their little house, that window looking out to the empty wooden garden seat where their loving daughter will lie no more. Already the landscape is distorted, pulled awry by the awful gravitational pull of Mary's wanton death, her black void the star into which the household will collapse.

At the funeral the crowd is huge and though respectful not silent, for the enormity of the crime is too great for silence. Many are holidaymakers and they have no funeral clothes upon them, nor an appetite for such garments. An open-necked shirt and a plain frock is the best they can do to mask their curiosity. As the service proceeds within, outside they pass her name hurriedly amongst themselves, as if in one of those decorous parlour games she might have played at Christmas, as if no one wants her name burning their hands, an uneasy chant, to tame the demon that is lurking in the town, but the name is taken up too by those who knew her, who saw her every day, who nodded to her safe presence when she passed. Mary? Mary Learoyd? They worry at those vowels, those consonants, worry at the ordinary completion of her sound, worry who they thought Mary was and who she might have been, worry too at the other one, the murderer, who he is and who he might be; a stranger or someone living amongst them, someone singing Mary's hymns, reciting Mary's prayer, bowing his head as Mary's body is lowered into the ground.

It is clear, within the week, certainly by the third, that the murder investigation is piecemeal, going nowhere. Scouts and tracking have failed to find him. The policemen couples have come back with nothing more than a clutch of old clothes and lost pocket knives in their hands. Their superiors have chased all over Britain, sending out alarms for gold-toothed hitch-hikers, dawn-crawling labourers, over-anxious salesmen with cat scratches on their guileless faces. Clairvoyants seize the opportunity and fluster around. The Reverend Tweedale, whose vicarage seems to harbour more celebrities than all the Hydros put together, makes a self-promotional appearance at the police station offering up a spiritual salesman's advice. The local mystic Mrs Newton, who lives near the scene of the crime and claims that Mary Learoyd has spoken to her twice already, is convinced that Mary will seek her out further. To maintain her purity she has avoided all newspapers (but not the press) lest auto-suggestions should cloud her vacant mind. Miss Learoyd's spirit, she insists, cannot leave the crime scene for a fortnight (an oddly exact imposition from the timeless zone of the spirit world). On the day of the funeral she takes herself down to the burial ground, and placing her small box camera on the ground stares hard at it for several hours, hoping to induce it to capture the ectoplasm, which she can see hovering by the graveside. Sadly the ectoplasm is too fast for her shutter speed.

Three weeks later comes a Liverpool spiritualist named Mr Bertram Scarff, who holds a seance in which he hopes to speak to Miss Learoyd. The beret that Mary Learoyd wore at the time of the killing is forwarded from police headquarters at Wakefield to assist his endeavour. It travels alone in a police car, sitting in a box on the back seat, wrapped up in tissue paper, Miss Learoyd's battered spirit soaked in the sweatband. It is fortunate that it is the hat he will have in his hands because the girl would have been thinking all the time of the man and the beret would be closest to her thoughts. Picking it up for the first time he immediately ejaculates, 'Oh God,' and throws it down, shouting, 'Let me go! Oh! A hand clasped over my mouth! How he glares at me! What, the man must be mad!' The seance is attended by a reporter, Mary Learoyd's brother Eric and the failed psychometric photographer. The curtains are drawn, the room fully lit, Mr Scarff standing. He is guided by two spirits, one a lady of timid voice, the other a well-educated man who speaks in commanding tones. After flitting from one to the other, being first Mary, then an observer, then Mary again, his manner changes abruptly, and with the female spirit still talking, enters into a strange soliloquy, delivered in low and trembling tones.

I must keep quiet. Someone heard me. If I go across the moors I may not be seen. Yes. But what about my hands? How am I going to wash them? No. There is someone passing. Who is that talking. (There is a very foul expression used.) I wish they would go away. Who is it at this hour of night? Yes, I know. Waiting, waiting, waiting, cursing under the breath. Then I sneak away quietly. Damn, I have scratched myself. I wonder if they heard me? There is no way out here.

(At this stage the medium turned away to his left and held up his

hands as though groping along some railings. Then he stopped with his back to his hearers.)

I wonder if there is anyone in this hut. I may be able to think of something here. I come to the hut. I am resting in the hut. Cannot stay here. Damn. I feel drunk. What have I done? How can I get out? Let me see.

(Again he moves slowly as if attempting to get out somewhere.)

I now come to a little pathway a few steps into an open road. I come to some water to wash my hands. It seems as if it is a running stream. Then I go right down this road.

(He turns as though tracing a route along the bottom of the moor, eastward.)

Ah! just got the bus. Now I jump on to the bus. Ah! they will never find out. They will never know. I go along. I feel myself travelling. I wonder if he can see anything of me. I wonder if I am drunk. Yes, I think I am drunk.

All this he reads in the newspapers, and wishing to know more about Mary Learoyd, wishing to learn why the investigation never progressed, wishing to learn why no one was charged and brought to trial, wishing to know why this most notorious of events fades quickly into Ilkley's past (a year later, for instance, on the anniversary of her murder, and the case still unsolved, no mention is made of it, the memory washed away, erased; the Ilkley Cure again). Hoping to track down the police file he rings up Ilkley police station to see how he may go about discovering its whereabouts. He imagines that if it exists at all, it will be filed away in an archive basement in Bradford or Wakefield, but, after being asked by the jovial-sounding sergeant to 'hold on a minute' he is astonished to be told that the file is 'right here', in the sergeant's very hand, and that, as long as he gets permission from above, there is no reason why he cannot do the same on his next visit.

He views it seventy years and three days to the day from its inception. It is strange to be holding it, a fat, faded thing, with tatty edges and greasy thumbprints, the loose pages in between torn and displaced. Strange too when he starts to read it, not for the bad typing or worse spelling but rather its deliberate lack of organization, its absence of purpose. There is no form to this file, no progression; there are no police notes, no diagrams, no diary of events, no summary of movements, no list of suspects, no distillation of thought. He expected to see a map of Ilkley with Mary Learoyd sightings clearly marked, to see other figures who had moved about that town that night, but there is nothing, just written statement after written statement, clay thrown upon clay at a runaway wheel, with no idea as to the shape that might result.

This is not quite true, for there is one shadow flitting in and out of the file, giving it an elusive life of its own, not the presence of the murderer, for if he appears (and it may be that he does), it is almost accidental, but rather the tantalizing figure of Mary Learoyd, this reserved woman, full grown, of sweet nature, perfectly quiet, doing nothing more than working through her days, looking after her parents, doing good at church, true to charity, and her friends, living in the shadow of her simplicity. But on occasions she steps out, into a different light. Dorothy Earnshaw is the first to voice it.

> I am a jeweller. I am very well acquainted with Miss Learoyd, I have spoken to her many times but she had never told me anything about her male friends. On Sunday August 18th I walked to Burley Woodhead. I went to Lancasters shop and purchased some lemonade. I looked around and saw Mary Learoyd a few yards behind. She looked at me and I looked at her. She dropped her head as if she did not want to recognise me. I did not speak but turned away. I looked again and Mary Learoyd had stopped where I had first seen her. She appeared to be waiting until I had got a bit away and when she saw me look back she turned her head and walked into the gateway of a house to apparently get out of my way. She gave me the impression that she was waiting for someone and did not want me to see them. I was very surprised that she did not speak to me as I have always been on very friendly terms with her. I am confident that Miss Learoyd knew me and I am absolutely sure that it was Miss Learoyd.

This sounds like a Mary Learoyd he has heard of before, the Mary Learoyd that Flora Hannah Evans saw that very night.

> On approaching the lady appeared purposely to turn her back to me. The man was facing me. The girl appeared to be somewhat taller than the man, who was of medium build, wearing a dark suit, trilby hat and had a raincoat over his arm. I heard no conversation as I passed but the lady turned her back on me as if she did not want to be recognised. I afterwards came to the conclusion that the lady was Miss Learoyd. The coat was one I frequently saw her in.

He remembers too, Mr Austin Dobson of Brook Street.

> 7.15 she came into my shop and purchased a copy of the *Radio Times*. She appeared in good health and was really more cheerful than usual. She laughed and joked for a minute. As a rule she has been very reserved.

and recalls what she told Mary Ellen, that she was meeting a friend, and what Mary Ellen said when she saw her for the last time, how she was walking slowly along Brook Street, as if 'waiting for someone'. A few more badly typewritten pages in the police file later appears Doris Baker. She lives in Lytham now, but prior to that

> I lived at 22 Tivoli Place. I have known the deceased for about 30 years. The only occasion I have seen her with a man was about a year ago, on a week night between 9.30 and 10 coming down Cowpasture Rd from the direction of the Moors. When I next teased her about it she said she had known him a bit but did not say his name, but said he came from Burley in Wharfedale. She never mentioned him again. 30, clean shaven, dark, smartly dressed.

and Richard Aldridge who admits that

> I have seen Mary Learoyd on several occasions in the latter part

of 1928 in company of a man between 11 and 12.30. In front of Mount Pleasant, the Grove, Wells Rd, Railway Rd. I do not know this man. 5ft 9. 38-45 years, medium build, turned down trilby hat, navy double breasted suit, I particularly noticed that the man walked with a slight limp with his left leg. I could not recognise the man by his face but I think I could recognise him by his walk.

Perhaps this is the reason for her good spirits, the flower in her buttonhole, her restless walking, her disappearance. Perhaps she was waiting for him, had been waiting for him all day, flushed with the thought of it, pleased and anxious to see him, see him alone with no one watching, no one knowing. Perhaps it was her own natural reserve that made her thus shy, or perhaps it was his own provenance that gave hush to their meeting, the town scandal of it all. Where had she been those two hours? Church, perhaps, where the dancing verger sweeps along. Certainly they are very close as all the town knows. Some say too close. It is what her brother Eric thinks, at any rate.

One or two of us rather resented the intimacy with the Elliotts. She was at Church a lot with Elliott alone. Several times they had sent across to Kemps Cafe for tea and they had it in the vestry. I thought she was too free with a married man. Mrs Elliott was quite aware of the friendship and used to chaff her about it at home.

Too free with a married man. Perhaps Mr Elliott is too free with a single woman. Only recently he did something which was extraordinary for a married man to do.

She had asked me to go to the house during the same week, mentioning Saturday night, she told me her father and mother were going to be out and that she would be alone. I arrived about 8.30 and left about 10. Miss Learoyd gave me a light supper, tea and biscuits etc. No intoxicants were consumed. We spent the time listening to the wireless and talking.

But whatever his foolishness Mr Elliott has his alibis, at least until 10.30 or so. Like Mary he left home some time after 7 p.m. and first called at Tomlinson's Tobacconist Brook Street, where he purchased an ounce of Ogden's Gold Flake. Then he went to the church arriving about eight. Left around eight twenty. Went to the front of the Star Inn where he met a Mr Samuel Hopkinson. Went with him to the Middleton Hotel, where he saw Ralph Mearns and John Hardwick; left about ten fifteen along with Mr Hardwick and a man called Tom, a painter. Left Tom at the top of Lister Street and left Mr Hardwick at Alexander Crescent; walked as far as the fish and chip shop in Leeds Road; saw a man called Bob Garside whom he called out to; Garside stopped and he caught up with him and walked to the bottom of Wilmot Road; remained in conversation with him for two or three minutes arriving home about ten forty.

> There was no one home when I came back except my children but my wife arrived about five minutes after I arrived, I did not go out again that night.

Movements confirmed (though ten forty is of course about the time Mary Learoyd is first seen again).

If you will wait, I will kiss you.

If you wait. Perhaps it was that promise that destroyed her, that promise she could not keep, not simply to kiss, but something else, a future, a life with him; perhaps he knew that it would never be, perhaps they both did, perhaps she kissed him once and found it altogether repellent, the embrace of man, and shied away from it at the very moment. Perhaps she had been with him all evening, listening to his entreaties, his trusting conversation, trying to batten down his storm with her strong, well-meaning placidity, talking to her man friend, her confidant, her secret. Why else take this path, at this hour, unless with someone she knew? Where she lost her life, where the struggle took place, by the stump of the tree, is the centre of this plot. They walked there together. It is rough untended space, this wasteland, fit for unlicensed acts, surely not a place for Mary Learoyd to enter quietly with a stranger. Though there are parks and river walks, the bed of the moors spread above, couples used this for something altogether more urgent, overlooked by kitchens and upstairs bedrooms but with grass and hedge enough to conceal those pressing movements, a minute from the station, where time did not diminish opportunity for those with no other place to go, live-in maids and servant girls, young men and women who lived with their own folk; where they could gain entry to the furtive game of sex, even if another might be there.

In the northern seaside towns, Blackpool, Morecambe, in Wakes fortnight, they would be laid out in rows under the piers and beyond, the working girls and the working boys, their only time like this they could take apart from front-parlour fumblings and the shared pleasures of a dog walkers' park. They would couple on the cooling shingle, their spot often claimed beforehand, like penguins do upon their breeding shelves, returning after their fish supper and evening's drink to make hurried or unhurried love as suited their young temperament, ignoring the couples on either side, possessed of each other in an enclosure as secure and private as the flowered compartments of the Orient Express, their partners touched with the same travelling eroticism.

But perhaps she did not know him, perhaps she had been walking home alone, *after* she had met someone, someone who never came forward for fear of exposure and family ruin. Perhaps two men were involved, her secret, her man from Burley, her man with the limp, the dancing verger, and another, who snatched her as she walked back, contented with her tryst, put his hand over her mouth and she, rigid and bred incapable of resistance, went with him to the centre ground, where realizing her danger fought him but briefly before he smashed her face with the rock and began his other bloody work. Perhaps it was the police's other suspect, Sam Exley.

HERBERT HORSMAN: On Saturday 23rd August 1929 I was sitting in the singing room at the Royal, sitting near the piano. Sam Exley was sitting near the steps across from me and said "Hello Herbert, will you have a drink with me?" I said "All right Sam," and he paid for a pint of beer. About five minutes later he called out "Goodnight Herbert I'm off, I have a tart to meet."

Sam Exley had been recently charged with attempted rape of a nurse but the girl had failed to identify him. Elizabeth Collins the manageress of the Royal had been on the jury that had disagreed and had seen him bailed until next Assize. On the night of the murder she had recognized him sauntering into the dance room, about nine fifteen, accompanied by a girl believed to be from Keighley.

SAM EXLEY: I landed in Ilkley about 5 to 8. I went to the Midland and had one drink. Left the Midland about 8.05 and went to the Wheatsheaf Hotel. I had a number of drinks there. While I was there a girl came across and spoke to me. I said, Don't I know your friend. She said I don't know and she called her over. I asked the girl who came over where I had met her and then I recognised that I had met her at the Brown Cow at Bingley. I treated them both to Bass and a Guinness. About nine, in company with a lame man, we left the Wheatsheaf with the girls. On the way to the Royal the girl I was with suggested I should buy her a box of chocolates and I said, what if I do? and she said, Well, we'll go on to the moors and have a bit of love, and we went into a chocolate shop on the left hand side of Brook Street and I bought the girl some chocolates and some cigarettes and then we all four went into the Royal until about a quarter past ten. We walked towards the station and the girl who was with the other man sat on a wall. At that time I said to the girl I was with, what about your promise to go up there? meaning the moors but she objected saying she could not leave her friend. We walked a bit further down and the other man and his girl went into doorway near a music shop and we went into the next one to them. We stopped there about ten minutes. I said to my girl that I want to go across to Kings Hall. I went across to Kings Hall urinal and then went across to bus driver and asked him the last bus time to Bradford and he said 11.15 from the top. I then went back to where I left the girl but she was not there. I walked up past the Royal round to the right. I had a look round but could not find the girl. I can't remember the time as I have no watch. I walked by myself through Ben Rhydding, I passed the garage near Eascroft when the bus came along. I had a pennyworth to Burley. There was an Inspector on the bus called Harold Lister from Otley. The girl I was with had a black silk coat and a small brown fur, I was told she came to the Wheatsheaf regular.

His landlady (30 Granville Road Frizinghall) said he did not come home on Saturday night until 2.15 a.m., remained in bed until dinnertime and then went out. Intercepted by the police at 11.30 p.m. the same day, on his way back home, he readily agreed to make a statement which was written down in Inspector Herbertson's pocket book. He was wearing a blue suit, (the only decent one he had) and which he wore on the night of the 24th. (Under a strong electric light, the Inspector writes, it showed no signs of roughage.) His story is born out. Elizabeth Perry Keighley, who

went to Addingham in company with my friend Annie Murray. From Addingham to Ilkley where we went to the Wheatsheaf at about 8 o'clock. Whilst there my friend Annie Murray got into conversation with a young man. I also got into a conversation with another man who only had one leg. Both of these men paid for us some drinks. The four of us left and went to the Royal. We all went to the dance room and had drinks together. We stayed until about 10pm. I myself came straight to the bus and Annie went for some fish and chips. I left the man I was with near the bus. After a few minutes Annie Murray came to the bus stand alone and together we caught the bus to Addingham. It would be about 10 past ten when I left the man at Ilkley near the bus. I do not know the man and have never seen him before. He would be about 36 years of age, 5ft 3ins, sallow complexion, black hair, dark brown eyes, stiff build, minus left leg.

And Anne Murray agrees.

At the Wheatsheaf we got into conversation with two men and then left and when straight to the Royal. We stayed together until about 10pm and all four of us came out together. The man I was with made certain suggestions to me whilst I was out in the street and I then left him and went to the Keighley Bus Stand. My friend Lizzie Perry was then in the bus. I joined her. I was with this man all the time from 8 to 10.15. The man was a complete stranger to me and I have never met him before. 30 years, thin build, pale face, long dark brown hair, supposed light cap.

He looks for more, but there is none. They go back and forth over Sam Exley and Sam Exley's night, but there is no more substance to it than Mary Learoyd's own wanderings. But reading the file there emerges more than Sam Exley, more than Mary's little secret or the verger's guilty love. As he leafs through the file the statements uncovered take on a distorted luminosity. There seems to be something grotesque about that weekend, as if the town is besieged by deformity and lust, sneaking round Ilkley's alleyways, sitting in quiet corners, drinking Ilkley's beer, watching, waiting for its moment, and thus not simply that weekend but all of Ilkley's weekends, as if in the dark, when commerce has finished, the shops have shut up, the hotels are filled with their legitimate guests, there comes out down from the hill, up from the river, on train or bus or foot, another breed of men, emerging from their dwellings, delirious with priapic fever, sniffing out heat like dogs on the prowl, scouring the bars, stalking the streets, furious and reckless, boarding-house men, lodger men, men single, men married, men with one leg or a clouded eye, men with limps or hunched shoulders, men who mutter to themselves, who drool and chase their whisky and blame Lloyd George, men who laugh crazy, men addled with bewildered pain, their talk a spittled deformity, their faces red and blurred, a race of eyes narrowing in malice, of smiles shaped by animosity, hatred in their friendly looks and their leading talk, their fingers rank with the smell of themselves, looking for the trade off, a drink and a bit of love, a drink and a bit of love, as many drinks as you want love but then a walk along the river, or up the moor, here in the doorway, on the wall, any bloody place, and later, as the fleeing clatter of her heels echoes, the five-mile walk back, sweat soaked, collars unbuttoned, tie pulled loose, pockets empty, their swollen thoughts churning leading them to the edge of their aching insanity, why she played him for a fool, denied him, their fury lighting their stumble home.

MARY ELLEN DANCE: On Friday 23rd at about 10.20pm I was in Brook St going towards my home when a man accosted me, He said Good evening, we've met before haven't we? I replied Indeed we have not, you are mistaken, He then said, No I've seen you knocking about a great deal. Can I take you home. I replied No. He then said, Have you far to go I replied That's my business not yours. I am quite capable of taking care of myself and walked away. Description of man: sallow complexion dark eyes, sharp pointed nose, high cheek bones, slavered very much when he spoke. The left shoulder appeared to be higher than the right.

On the very day of the discovery word also comes that an inmate had escaped from Scalebor Park Mental Hospital at Burley in Wharfedale the previous night. He was retaken near Otley and was back in the hospital before the discovery of the crime. This man however had a wooden leg and no such likely marks as would have been made by such a man with such a leg being found, the inquiry went no further.

CHARLES HENRY WEEKS: On Sunday I dismissed one of our conductors James Madder for dishonesty. He is an intemperate man. 5ft 7, sallow complexion, thin face, clean shaven, left shoulder lower than right, inclined to stoop, long fingers. Very well spoken, modulated voice.

man wearing a grey suit, wanted shaving badly, ginger hair called at Ben Lofthouse's house between 8am and 9, Sunday. My daughter saw him look over the wall, he just said 1911. Later he met a postman named Grace and said to him. Have you a cheque from Lloyd George for me? Lloyd George has caused me to be like this.

Hello, is that Mrs Allardyce?
Yes.
What about that promise you promised, to sleep with me and let me fuck you?
When do you say I promised you this?
Monday dinner time.
We don't have many people in, who are you and what is your name?
You know damned well you said you would. I know you are busy but I will have you at all costs and when I get you I'll tear you to pieces you bastard

John Tordoff, a brick labourer, saw a man below the Cow and Calf with his trousers front unfastened and exposing his person, waving his arms about. On the 4th of August he saw the same man following a woman up Cowpasture Road, take hold of the woman by the right sleeve, but she shook him off. He had a thin face, sallow complexion, slightly bow legged on right leg.

Herbert Pearson, 45, a labourer went into an eating house on the 26th saying that he wanted to hear no more about the Ilkley murder. "I have seen a woman lying naked in Ilkley with her mouth open."

Hello, is that Mrs Allardyce?
Yes.
What about that promise, you know you promised to let me fuck
*   you?*
What are you talking about, where are you speaking from?
You know your figure is perfect, when you walk your breasts and
*   arsehole shake. When you are coming to me I will cut you to*
*   pieces and eat you.*
I beg your pardon?
Do you know when you draw bitter I can see down your dress, but
*   when I get you I will rive your titties out.*
Who are you?

On 24th August Grace Robinson was walking along the footpath leading from the Tarn to the Cow and Calf with her two daughters when she noticed a man walking about the Moor. Walked up to the Cow and Calf rocks with her two daughters. After walking back she saw the same man again lying down in the grass. He was about 45 years of age, fairly tall, fair complexion, dressed in fawny grey raincoat. This man had all his clothing undone, he had his person in his hand and appeared to be abusing himself.

Hello, is that Mrs Allardyce?
Yes.
You know what I did this afternoon?
No.

I bought a house in Bingley and when I get you there I will strip
*   you, fuck you, tear your tits off and cut you to pieces.*
Did you say Bingley?

I am an insurance agent of the Refuge Assurance Company. I am married with two daughters 15 and 19. I was with them on August 24th. On August Bank Holiday last I went to Ilkley and went into a basement with a woman. We remained there for about half an hour. I gave her 2/-. I told her she should not be so willing with strangers and told her I would try and see her again later.

Hello, is that Mrs Allardyce?
Yes.
I am at home at Bingley. I have hold of your thighs many a time
*   and hold of your breasts. You know I have fucked you before?*
Do you know who you are speaking to?
Yes, I am speaking to Annie Allardyce, you have had hold of my
*   old man many a time and you need not say you have not.*
I have not said anything.
Do you know what I have in my hand, the biggest prick in Brad-
*   ford and I'll get you if it costs me my life. I'll strip you, rive*
*   your titties out and cut you to pieces you bastard. How long is*
*   your husband's prick?*

a commotion at the other end
caught in the telephone kiosk.

Mary Learoyd. Her name is remembered by some, that and the fact they never caught him, the man who overwhelmed her with his flood of rage, who overturned the Learoyds' life. The presumption is that he is dead now, his guilt buried or burnt with him, but he could be alive, a young man of twenty-five, in his nineties now, turning Mary Learoyd over in his mind every day and how he got away with it, perhaps the only one thinking of her at this moment as he writes. More likely he supposes that the man is dead, though there may be descendants of him here yet. Did he live long, this man, did he work in this town, buy his newspapers across the road, tend his garden, dig his allotment, tell dirty jokes in the Wheatsheaf, play cricket, hold a daughter's hand, he who raised the stone, who tore Mary Learoyd naked, strangled her dying with her own stockings, before descending into further hell; how to keep still after all that, knowing what you knew, how to keep it locked within hard and tight, even in moments of drink and abandonment. And you, you people of Ilkley, were you good neighbours to him, a friend at the dartboard, the cribbage table? And what of those other one-legged shoulder-stooped men. Have they all gone?

He stood there one night, barely moved, in the Crescent, a hotel of no great comfort, while around him swirled the tide of Ilkley's play, not one word spoken by him, save one, to a woman white-dressed, proud of the way the sun had tanned her creased breasts, cowboy tassels on her sleeve, her red lips her dangling cocktail, enjoying the singularity of her bar room age while a bevy of gap-toothed men stood around her, tipping back bottles of beer: "All right, chuck?" she said and as he squeezed to the bar, "All right?" and he nodded and mouthed the word yes as she slid off her stool and waved goodnight to her chorus (drawing a line under their glances and subtracting the sum of them). No one there for her, though she was looking for someone, he could tell, to take home or fuck on the upholstery of her car, unless he falters in respect, she would turn fast and say, "On your way, buggerlugs"; the men moved on, to this one or that, sex the battery that lit this room, on the wet of their lips and in the jingle of their change, in the crease of their jeans and the ironed check of their open-necked shirts,

on a Friday night.

later, walking back along the Skipton Road, he saw her again, coming out from the Vaults (the Middleton before it burned down), country music loud and the black hood back, her ringed hands holding the white-leathered wheel, her arms and shoulders bare to the night, while leaning against the passenger door side, hand drooping a bottle of beer, sat the gift she had awarded herself. Looking to the traffic, of which there was none, she saw him standing, waiting for her to pass, recognized his immobile ways and, putting her foot down, winked, as she turned fast and gunned the car hard, heading back into town

Coming Soon
Nov. 8. Kings Hall
Folks You Ain't Seen Nothing Yet.
Do Not Miss
THE TALKIE OF TALKIES

THE SINGING FOOL
The Most Wonderful TALKING and SINGING Film
OF ALL TIME

ILKLEY (12)

BRAVO ILKLEY!

[Saturday 15 March 1930]   I went down and joined up and joined up in the rugger club and I was put in the A team and it was only a couple of games later when the captain got a new job and was sent over to the Midlands and so I was given his place in the first team and I played left flanker, and as it happened on this day we met Otley the cup holder. I had two cauliflower ears at the same time. I went into Leeds, there was a shop there that made fittings for all sorts of broken bones, or anything to do with legs, and so I got a leather scrum cap and I went to this place and I said I want big ear flaps put on and I want you to make two metal plates to go right over my ears to keep the pressure off the ear itself and then you can line the inside of it with wash leather, and so my scrum cap was banded all the way round so it was a little bit like an American rugger player and with these things on I felt I could tackle anybody and if I caught a heel no longer did it damage the ear I just heard it making a "pong" so I'd go for anybody, I loved it . . .

It was going to be a tough game, the third round of the Yorkshire Challenge Cup, Ilkley against Otley. Though Otley were without their two internationals, Malir and Bateson, Ilkley had men missing too, their regular right wing pair Chapell and Davison; the pitch was Otley's, their pack heavier, more experienced, the crowd expecting Otley to win. The mid-March weather was more akin to deepest winter than the coming of spring, the pitch covered in snow, the wind strong and bitter, and as they came out, their hundred or so supporters flapping their arms and stamping their feet on the frozen ground, the snow came once again, not lightly, but a furious blinding blizzard, its sudden flurries tugging them this way and that, the ball as slippery and evasive as the ground beneath their feet.

Otley started in, playing a confident passing game, Ilkley, less sure of their abilities, confining their attack to their forwards. Fifteen minutes after the start, disaster struck Ilkley.

Our captain who was the fastest man on the field, he was left wing, he was carted off to hospital very early on with concussion, and then Tommy Kay, fly half, he got a leg broken and when they lifted him up he put his weight on and said Nay it's broken. I think I shall have to go off. Then Douglas Todd he was a back row forward, he had five stitches in his eyebrow and he had to go off, so that left us three men short and no replacements in those days and it was just getting sludgier and sludgier with the sleet and the churned up mud underneath. We scored a try, right at the end of the first half, so when all this snow came down, three men were taken off then, we just had to play a game of defence and we didn't try any attacking, we got the score and so we had to keep what we got and not risk anything by giving it away, and we just hung on and hung on and hung on, holding them for forty minutes and when they got the ball and came on dribbling I just used to fling myself down on top of the ball as you were able to in those days and so mud used to go down the back of my neck and come out of my trouser bottom. On and on it went and I said to the ref., when I was just about the end of my tether, How much longer? and he looked at his watch and he said two and a half minutes and I said I think I can just about last out, and when the whistle blew and we went to the changing room there wasn't a single person who could take their boots off, they all had to be cut off, just covered with slime and mud. This was a famous game and we knocked them out.

Talking to those who played that day, those who stood on that freezing pitch and cheered themselves hoarse, it is as if it had been but last week when the town whooped and carried their muddy heroes on their shoulders round the streets, only yesterday when a small boy held out his exercise book, asking one of them for their autograph, yesterday because it is particularly theirs, not muddied by intrusive fame or excessive expectation, seen by them alone, accounted by them alone, its play and its skill known only to their hearts, its foolhardy bravery needing no other adornment than the spirit of that captured moment, and because it is theirs and theirs alone to uncork and sniff, he can drink it down in no other way but in this bare recollection.

And here's another thing: in this roughness, in the snapping of the bone, the twisting of the muscle, the cut on the eyebrow, there appears no malice, no spite, just determined endeavour: listen to the men who play

another rugger match and I think this was against Kendal on our home ground, they had some manoeuvre they were working and they kicked the ball from the east side to the west side where the stand was and all their men came shooting over towards the ball: I was right flanking and I came down and I gathered the ball and stopped it going into touch and all these people were streaming against me and I went straight across them – it wrong footed the lot and I got right down to the centre and there was only the full back. My friend Dudley Turner, I did all my training with him, we knew each other's speeds, he came out of the three quarters and up to me and so I just waved him carefully to keep behind because we'd left all of them behind and there was only a full back and I wanted to draw him right away, he had to go with the man with the ball, and I was running straight for the posts and before he could tackle me I passed to Dudley and he went straight round and we met together underneath the goal posts and together we planted it down.

13 November 1930

A letter dated 17 October 1930 was read from HM Office of Works stating that:

The Ancient Monuments Board of England scheduled certain rocks etc., the property of the Council, as ancient Monuments, the Schedule being as follows;

Cup and Ring marked Rocks on Ilkley Moor (including Green Crag; Pancake Rock, near Barnishaw Well; Grainings Head; Badger Stone; Weary Hill; Hanging Stones; Intake Heads, West of Woodhouse Crag): Green Bank Earthworks.

Resolved
    That the Schedule be approved.
    and some marking disapproved

14 January 1931

Resolved
    That this Committee view with disfavour the practice of monumental masons in placing their names in conspicuous positions upon headstones and caulstones erected in the Cemetery and suggest that when grave spaces are reserved the Cemetery Registrar call the applicant's attention to this resolution.

DEATH OF DELIUS

WESTON VILLAGE FORECAST
REMARKABLE MANIFESTATIONS

by the Rev Charles Tweedale
Vicar of Weston

In the night of January 30th '34 about midnight I was just composing myself for sleep, my wife fast asleep by my side, when I heard her uttering little incoherent sounds in her sleep. Then suddenly she began to sing in a loud strong man's voice

> When the winds sing low low low
> When soft breezes blow blow blow
> Then I come for Delius to go

The last line was absolutely shouted in a most astonishing and impressive manner.

At breakfast I waited to see if my daughter Dorothy had heard any of this, as she sleeps in the room above. During breakfast Dorothy asked, "Was mother entranced during the night? I heard another voice, not yours, shortly after you came to bed – I then saw a brownish red light which flamed out against the wardrobe like a big moon."

Before I could answer my daughter Marjorie chimed in saying, "In the night I heard the small piano in my bedroom sounding two notes loudly and it frightened me."

Astonished at this recital I said we would sit after breakfast and we did so. Our wonderful spirit communicator C—, who departed this life eighty-five years ago, came and said it was he who had entranced my wife and sung the verse. He said that I had not got it quite right and this is what he was trying to make her sing

> When the winds sing low low low
> When soft breezes blow blow blow
> Then we come for Delius too
> Who has other work to do.

C— said that this portended Delius' passing, and that the brown light seen by Dorothy in her bedroom was Delius' aura, and that he C— had also sounded the notes in Marjorie's bedroom. I said should I tell Delius's sister? C— said, "Yes, for evidence."

Here is what has been often asked by unbelievers, a perfectly clear forecast four months ahead of a coming event, witnessed and evidenced beyond the possibility of denial, clearly providing the incursion of the spirit world into our mundane affairs and announcing the passing of a famous man from this world to the next.

House of Commons Standing Committee, Licensing Bill

[23 February 1934]

Mr Lockwood (Conservative candidate for Hackney Central): I have received a telegram from the Chief Constable of Yorkshire, which states that where extra hours had been granted, public houses were now better conducted.

Several members rise to ask from where the telegram had come.

Mr Rhys Davies (Lab): There is no Chief Constable of Yorkshire. (Laughter)

Mr Lockwood (consulting the document): It is from the Police Superintendent of a town in Yorkshire called Ilkley. (More laughter)

Mr Holdsworth (Lib: Bradford South): Leave Yorkshire to me. There is no police superintendent at Ilkley either. He is in Otley.

A voice: Does Ilkley exist?

Mr Rhys Davies: Ilkley is a seaside resort in the heart of Yorkshire.

[Jan 19th] Battery Quarter Master Sergeant Jon McRink dies aged 42. Took part in the retreat at Mons and though fought through the war came out without a scratch. Gassed on one occasion and buried when a shell exploded nearby. McRink was one of the first British soldiers to enter Germany at cessation of hostilities and the first Active Service Postcard was sent by him.

died aged forty-two
had come through
without a scratch

[21 September 1934]   Ilkley Tradesmen's annual cricket match appears to have entered fully into an era of renewed prosperity and popularity. It moves from success to success.

It has evolved now from its old beginnings, the first match taking place in September 1880, a tradesmen's cricket match, W. Lister and Ellis Beanlands the organizers, raising money to pay off Ilkley Cricket Club's debt, but quickly became more than that. It took two years for the top hats to come out, the white hats and the black hats, every man a moustache, some in striped blazers, some riding up to the pitch astride donkeys poached from Mr Butterfield and Mr Jack.

(In 1883 the weather was so bad darkness overtook the match. Batsmen trying to run between the wickets lost their way, so to light them they laid sawdust between wickets, and they ran on that. Fielders fared no better, only able to tell if the ball had been hit by the sound of it smacking the bat, holding their hands out hoping for the catch as if they were Zen masters.

A little later, in the same match, half a dozen runs were added to the score before the ball was discovered two yards from the wicket

It has evolved further now, the colour of the hats now denoting the delineation of sex, women allowed on their hallowed field, white. The town came out to watch as they did every year, even though the clouds were heavy and the light bad, the promise of rain hanging low over the town. It was still though a tradesman's event, the greengrocer and tobacconist, their pencils idle upon the counter, their overalls hung up, their premises locked up, marching out on to the playing field arena, their black hats bobbing tall against the green, setting out their stall to the surround of their assistant ladies, now decked out in fancy dress, a cowboy and cowgirl pulling a wooden horse, an onion-toting Breton, Dutch boys and Dutch girls, Joan Marshall dressed up as the Ilkley herself, set like a precious stone on a bed of heather, the men with the usual handicap strapped to their legs, not simply in the left-handed bat they had to hold, or the compulsory walk back to the pavilion once they had reached the full score of ten, but playing straight in the sight of these shopgirls in their audacious costumes, every frill daring them to throw off their rigorous shop-worn dignity and act sufficient fools themselves, propelled by that uneasy good humour that comes with rigid demarcation between shop owner and shop girl, that and a snifter perhaps courtesy of Mr Dinsdale's closed counter.

that's when I used to work at Dinsdales on the Grove, we all used to just dress up. I used to dress up as a little girl with a big bow, it was very good fun, all trade people. He was always very smartly dressed, Mr Dinsdale, very smartly, he had thin tache, very thin, twirled, immaculate, he was, a perfect gentlemen; he taught you, you were trained to say good morning to the customers when they came in, good morning when they went out, and you had to wear something brown. Eight in the morning till eight at night, nine on Saturday, on your feet, not much pay, used to have to polish his floor every day on my hands and knees, used to have to polish the brass scales, used to have to polish everywhere regularly, mahogany all around; there was a lot to do, a lot to do; pipes and cigarettes, behind the counter where we had mirrors there was a very narrow cupboard where we used to have to stack the big packs of matches; you all had to do your orders, roll the cigarettes; I used to love rubbing the tobacco, it smelt lovely, I used to have to rub it up for them, even when they smoked pipes. I was a good saleswoman. Somebody once told me I should have had my own business; they'd come in for a five shilling pipe and go out with a twenty five

shilling one. Men brought their little snuff boxes to weigh
out for them, whether they had the money or they hadn't
I don't know, they lived in these houses but they didn't
always pay, you'd get so much paid off and that was it.

It was a good shop was Dinsdales, it was a nice trade;
the chemist was a good trade too. I used to help the
chemist with the dispensing. I wasn't qualified but I could
fill the bottles with the stock mixtures; they used to go to
the doctors and they all came in with the same prescription and they all thought they were getting better and I
used to have a lick of all these bottles and I think they kept
me well, these mixtures: When you've worked in shops it's
marvellous what knowledge you glean isn't it? I've worked
in dress shops, sweetshops, papershops, I've done them all.
I love trade, right keen on it

The game was in full swing when the downpour came,
driving spectators off the field, and though the umpires were
quite willing to pull up the stumps, they banged down their
hats, wrapped their fancy clothes in mackintoshes and coats and
carried on to the end, drenched and soaked as is the require-
ment of people in this town. The women won by a margin of
14 runs. Women 133 Men 119

When I worked at Dinsdales we
used to have a dance club on a Saturday night at the
    Winter Garden,
I used to go and serve drinks,
I was a great dancer, we
used to enjoy it, enjoy anything like that, ballroom
    dancing,
waltzes, quicksteps, I mean you made your own pleasures,
when I was younger

used to have the Pierrots down by the river,

used to have a pavilion there,
used to go down there and see them on the matinee,
used to be lovely, I
used to go pictures, matinees, my father built the Grove
used to love the matinee pictures.

used to go the Fairground where the Wheatsheaf was.
used to be always a parade, the Whitsun-tide Walk,
used to come up on the main road
used to make a point of going to see that
used to work in the New Cinema as an usherette
used to wear a blue uniform and brass buttons. I'd be
      about
sixteen then. For the first few days I thought it was very
      good
but after a day or two I
used to pick all the faults out in it, funny in't it
how you can do it.

used to like that job. I remember the orchestra there,
      Mr Collins
used to come in the season
used to get all the ladies going in for coffee
used to play on a Sunday evenings, during the war we
used to have the soldiers come from Otley
used to have some riots

used to play my piano and I let that go to somewhere I
used to baby-sit, and then you miss it,
used to have a chair in shops, they don't now
used to work part time in a men's shop in Leeds Road,
      Easbie's
used to work in the morning and when I washed Tom's
      shirts I
used to fold them up like they did, in the shops

When the army was around we
used to entertain quite a lot of the fellas, my mother she
used to bake a lot, she

used to have them in here, she
used to have them all in, they
used to call round, call her, lady, I
used to get some very nice letters from them when they
    went
but I only ever heard from one who lost his life
his mother wrote to me from Wales and said
that he died. I met a French Canadian when they were at
    Burley
he got struck and he thought I ought to go over there to
    Canada,
turn Catholic, he said. I always imagined
living in a wig-wam, so I said no,
funny life in't it,
all the things that happen.

You remember Mr Hampshire, the greengrocer in Brook
Street. He used to raise his bowler hat to answer the telephone, he did, to customers. Good morning, madam!

Procession awards.

LADIES' COMIC DRESS
1. Miss Moisley (Charley's Aunt)
2. Miss Mennel (Little Girl)
3. Miss Dingle (Smutty)

LADIES' HISTORICAL DRESS
1. Miss P Whelan (Crinoline)
2. Miss McGillway (Cowgirl)
3. Miss Hodgson (Cowgirl)

that's all of us got together, that's me with me check dress
on, that was Phyllis Whelan, she worked in the shoe
shop on the Grove, (she's died), the Dutch girl is Margaret

Dickinson, she married a man from Menston, (she's died), the cowgirl Gwen McGillway she married a smith from Otley and went to live in Skipton, that one they called her Armstrong, now she was a Hodgson, she lived in Nile Road, her father used to work in Dinsdale's, in the wine shop, and the woman with the pipe that was Claris Bedford, they lived in Dean Street (and she's gone). When a lot of the business men died off it kind of fizzled out, nothing goes on that's the same. We did enjoy it, it were good, 1934.

ILKLEY (13)

THE POOL

14 February 1924

Mr Dobson said that the paucity of bathing facilities was a disgrace to the town. Members would know that the baths had previously been heated by water from the Brewery but the Brewery had now been disposed of to a Bradford firm. There was some doubt as to whether the supply of hot water would be continued. Unless another system of heating the water were found the baths were bound to close. During four or five days of the week something like 150 children had taken instruction. If no provision was to be made for them it was a very serious blot upon Ilkley. Could not water be laid on to the baths from somewhere? A small amount of water used to be obtained from the laundry, but not a satisfactory amount for the children bathing. If the baths were closed there would be nowhere except Ilkley Grammar School. The Grammar School Managers had been very kind in the past but they could not be expected to allow the use of their baths indefinitely. He thought it disgraceful that a place like Ilkley, which boasted of being a health resort, had no baths. When they remembered that they had something like 630 children attending school in one alone and no provision for swimming instruction, it was a very serious matter.

27 May 1925

The Chairman submitted a Report with regard to the provision of Lawn Tennis Courts, a miniature golf Course and Putting green and stated that the subcommittee appointed to consider various sites viz. 1) The Recreation Ground 2) the land on the east side of Keighley Road (near the bandstand) and 3) the land adjoining the Rugby Football Field acquired by the council as a site for an Open Air Swimming Bath. The Committee were in favour of providing tennis courts on the last mentioned site whereupon it was Resolved

That application to be made to the Minister of Health for sanction to utilise the land forming part of the Holmes, acquired by the Council as a site for an Open Air Swimming Bath and Resolved

That a golf putting green be laid out on the land immediately above the bandstand, West View Park, that the necessary apparatus be purchased and that a charge of 3d per game be made for the use of a putter and golf ball.

URBAN DISTRICT COUNCIL

7 October 1927

Mr Dobson: One wonders that the time has gone so far without a very strong protest being made. There are 700 school children attending the elementary schools and over 500 houses in the town which are not provided with a bath. To think we do not possess a swimming bath is truly disgraceful.

VOTE FOR DINSDALE

AMALGAMATION

This is the paramount question before us at the present time and if I am returned as your representative I shall continue to use all my efforts to fight any linking up of Otley and Ilkley

Bathing Pool

I am Chairman of the Committee dealing with this question and I am proud to say that after consideration of various schemes, we have evolved and are proceeding with a scheme for building of a large bathing pool at Middleton which we anticipate will be a paying proposition and will NOT be a charge on the rates.

Beautiful Ilkley

Contrary to any statements you may have heard I am NOT in favour of any scheme against the removal of trees except when they have been a danger to the public. It was never the intention of the Council to sell a large proportion of Middleton Wood or to interfere with the rights of the public or their walks.

Ilkley Gazette

[22 June 1934]   Glorious summer last weekend saw bathing crowds on the river bank – in the Wharfe rivalling those of last summer. Many were asking, Where is that bathing pool they talked about a year ago?

They looked about, these municipal men, aware of their forebears, some of the same names still carrying the flame of the municipal torch in their ageing hand: they have the roads built and the river breached, laid the railway to the twin cities that motor Ilkley's trade; concert hall and library the bread and butter wrapped around the meat of the town's official business; commerce, car parks and the great gift of the moor all accounted for, and yet in that liquid valley, where infinite distance lingers, they resolve to build one final thing – at long last aye to build a pool – and to apportion it so in that formal document as an out-of-doors pool for bathers, not for swimmers (the difference being in the absence of lanes and the desire to play about, skipping like on the stepping stones, jumping like from the bridge or feeling the spray like the gushing of the Strid). So, it was,

Resolved:

that the diving stage be fixed in the centre of the northern side, that a double chute be fixed some distance to the east thereof and a small diving board some distance to the west; that a chute for small children be fixed on the edge of the shallow portion of the pool. Surveyor Report dated 9th October be approved and adopted: that four standards equipped with floodlight lanterns be erected for the purpose of lighting the pool, and that Electrical Engineers be requested to prepare a scheme of lighting the diving stage as to obviate the need for a lamp standard adjacent thereto.

9 January 1935

The Surveyor submitted a report upon various matters in connection with the Swimming Pool and it was

Resolved
     That it be Recommended to the Finance Committee
1) that a cafe be erected in accordance with the Surveyor's suggestion, at an estimated cost of £1,487: 0: 0: and
2) that heating apparatus be installed at the Swimming Pool at an estimated cost of £160.

Mr Skinner's design is very different from other open air swimming pools, 1,675 square yards in area a portion 75ft by 30ft which varied from 6ft 6in to 7ft 6in provided a full area for water polo, and a wide area shelving from 43ft to the edge which is absolutely safe for children, heated by the sun's rays.

Application be initiated by advertisement for two female box office attendants at wage of 25s; for a man and wife to act as

attendants in the dressing cubicles at a joint wage of £3 5s 0.:
for a swimming pool instructor and general grounds man at
a wage of £2 10s. 0d. per week and a youth to assist the last
mentioned employee at a wage of £1 0s. 0d. a week.

Bathers. Adult 6d. Junior 4d.
Spectators 3d. Transfer ticket 3d.
Costume or towel 2d. No charge for motor cars.
Season ticket 7s. 6d.
For bathers, books of tickets in multiples of 12
to be issued at a price equal to 25% reduction.

And that the Pool be named The Ilkley Open Air Bathing
Pool and that it be officially opened by the Chairman of the
Council (for the year 1935/36) on Saturday the 4th May next.

They had forty hours of sunshine over those four Jubilee days,
Saturday through to the Tuesday. Thousands poured in from Leeds
and Bradford, 3,000 by train alone, most come not to celebrate
the King, but to celebrate the moor and its high paths and their
freedom upon it, like Joad had demanded, to capture the moor in
their heart and take it back apiece, have it unwrapped in the snug
of their hearth, go to bed with its ache on the back of their legs,
make love with the scent of it in their hair, feeling free, like a body
jumping off the bridge, or flickering like a torch, bright and illuminating the landscape by its presence.

For it was an event, this day, and would have meals and speeches
devolved upon it, processions and competitions. Up on Beamsley
Beacon stood a great bonfire, a tumbling statue, made giant by the
work of Colonel Muller's scouts, carrying its great lumbering body
piece by piece up the long climb. It had been weeks in the building
and for the last few nights huddles of scouts have kept vigil over it,
lest some artful Bradford lad should steal up there and put a match
to it before time. It is one of many bonfires on these heights,
bonfires to the east, bonfires to the west, up over Keighley on Otley
Chevin, down Rawdon way, a chain waiting for the dark and the

witness of the royal linking time. But that is for the evening; they have a day of themselves before that spectacle, a day in the seat of the town, in that great space that they have maintained by the river, where at long last they have built this thing, this pool their last great building.

It is good that it has no roof, that it is open and bright, set in green and sparkling blue, that when you come over from over the moor it glitters sparkling blue, like when you catch sight of the distant sea, and he remembers driving into Lulworth after the long journey, cramped and impatient, and at the top of the hill, by the army range and the tank tilted on a plinth, he would see that triangle of water between Bindon Hill and the Purbeck Hills, the water beyond the Cove, and the exhilaration in knowing that its sound and its touch was but a walk and a rubber ring away.

There is a procession first, with stands erected for it. The weather is what it should be, the war is long gone. It does not seem possible to get any better in this modern town. There are the usual matters obtaining to an event, fancy dresses, a Silent Night, a Zulu warrior, the Bisto Kid, Dresden Shepherdess (how she will be broken in the coming years), Miss Muffet, Fyffes bananas and the orange blob of a new thing, a Belisha beacon. Behind them come, decorated with bunting and flags, the heavy horses of the council and the lighter animals of the Victoria laundry, the polished fire engine, then the stuff of Ilkley's trade, its vans and cycles, and its sparsely decorated lorries, with waving tableaux loaded up at the back, 'Peace Be unto all Nations' (Mrs Brown's party), 'Blossom Time' (Mr Mennell). From the Town Hall up Chantry Drive, along Whitton Croft Road, up Wells Street, 400 entries, 250 in costume, so many children that they have to fall in four deep, along the Grove, up Cunliffe Road and Church Street, Leeds Road, Nelson Road, Brook Street by way of Railway Road.

There are races run, egg and spoon and sack races and three-legged ones (won it is written by Peter Titchmarch, though he always thought that the three-legged race required the participation of two), and in the afternoon comes the time to open the gates and let the flood in. They had opened gates before, held ceremonial keys and given speeches, but this is the bloom of Ilkley's flowering past, as if all its history and all its present have been brought to bear on this plain plot of land. They move and gather at the gates, the Ilkley band playing, some children so eager to jump in the pool that they are already changed, their bathing costumes covered by bathing wraps and mackintoshes (they had been waiting all their lives for this water, all their fathers' and mothers' lives, and now they would be jumping and splashing for all of them). It is a magical time, a fairy-tale setting, the blue of the water reflected in the sky, the good King on his throne, the wooden giant standing guard on Beamsley Beacon, while on the backdrop, through Middleton wood, comes the shimmer of a hundred thousand bluebells, soaking up the dappled heat, lending their own glow to the day's royal colour.

Mr G. Mennell unlocks the gates, with Dobson at his side, Dobson who has banged upon the table for the need for this thing, and here he is, Chairman of Ilkley Council, presiding over the King's Silver Jubilee and two girls anxious to run in and take the first plunge. For today and tomorrow and the day after that, the pool is free, and then on it is pocket money, afternoon treats, and school trips. But before that, Dobson speaks, bringing it back, as all things Ilkley, to the river.

If you wish to keep fit and well, there are three exercises I should recommend. They are swimming, walking and riding. In Ilkley you have every facility for walking and climbing the moors, you have every facility for horse riding but you have not had the facility for swimming. When I was a boy and wanted to bathe we went to the river, but the Wharfe is a dangerous river especially for beginners.

In the swimming pool they run, but are quickly hauled out, for the display of swimming to be given by Yorkshire's chlorinated celebrities, people standing three deep on the pebble surround: Tom Barry,

Yorkshire Diving Champion 1931–33, Lily Cullingford, Yorkshire Ladies' Senior and Junior Champion, Mary Rigby, Yorkshire Schoolgirl Diving Champion, followed by a competition for the neatest and smartest modern bathing costume, the modest requirements of the age. 1st Kathleen Hawson, 2nd Kathleen Denby, 3rd Mary Mennell.

Then the real fun starts, the rush for cubicles so great the attendants are overwhelmed, unable to cope with the demand. They swim all the afternoon, swim and splash, run in and out of the shallow end, jump shrieking into the deep, the lower divers watching with envy the arms of their braver brethren flashing down, and when the dark comes stealing over they light their lights and swim some more. But as the dark settles, they leave the pool for the first time, their wet footprints drying for the first time, the filtered water settling back after its first thorough disturbance, rub dry their hair, hoick their clothes over reluctant skin and hurry out, for now it is time to make their long way up Beamsley Beacon, to climb that long road up to where the bonfire stood, or more easily to the tarn and the Cow and Calf, where they might see the flourish to this night. A slight breeze has blown in from the west, a haze settling over the town but not strong enough to obscure the view. Signal for lighting was to be given by chain of rockets from the pool to the beacon itself. As the Town Hall clock strikes ten o'clock Councillor Dobson strikes his match and lights the first set of rockets, the chain climbing from the football ground, through Paw Pots and Windsover Farm, from Moorgate and Mr Pullar's farm, bursting ever higher in red and green stars until finally acknowledged by the two from the beacon itself. Rawdon is already aglow and with a cry of 'There she goes!' they see Otley Chevin afire too. They drive in the torches then, Colonel Muller's boys, plunge them deep into the great body of the jumbled Rombald, into his stomach of fallen trees and broken furniture, his rings of old tyres, and watch him come to life again as the flames leap and once more the moor falls under his jumping shadow.

ILKLEY BATHING POOL
OPEN DAILY 10 AM TO 9 PM
WATER HEATED AND FILTERED
CAR PARK   CAFE

It is the sum of all Ilkley, this water, this space, their municipal owner-ship. They have had their water, water from the river, water from the moor, water rushing down becks and poured in sitz baths, cold water tamed on the tarn, cold water held in reservoir basins, water to drown in, water to bathe in, water to carry their livelihood away. Now they have it served up on a plate, not enclosed, for that would not be Ilkley, they could not deny the White Wells heritage (the difference between an open air pool and an enclosed one is one of pretence, the latter motorway swimming, cruising in the motorway lanes, pausing for breath of the wet shoulder while great intestinal tunnels defecate into the soiled water and mechanical waves slosh from side to side, to make water more fun (as if it need that) – but here laid out like a picnic on the grass in sight of a bluebell wood, Ilkley's open-air church, the cubicle where one changes into the clothes of the ritual of worship, the water the baptism and the wedding-cake fountain the altar where vows are taken, promises made). This is how it was then when he was young, how it is seen now, and it was when the first clink of the turnstile was heard and the crowd clapped as Tom Barry ruffled it calm with the break of his slick combed head.

Report of the Meteorological Observations taken at Spence's Garden and Silverwell Cottage during the Month of May

Spence's Garden		Silverwell Cottage
1.40	Rainfall During the Month	1.01
5	No. of days on which rain fell	6
73	Maximum Temperature	71
28	Minimum Temperature	30
48.9	Mean Temperature for month	46.46
253	Hours of Sunshine	[—]

is what they had for their first month of swimming pool

For the Jubilee each man received five shillings when he went to the Employment Exchange

BURIAL BOARD, MOOR AND PARKS COMMITTEE.

8 April 1936

Resolved

   that schoolchildren in all the local schools be invited to subscribe to the cost of purchasing young oak trees to be planted
in Middleton Woods; that such trees be planted by children rep-
resenting the various schools on the occasion of the Coronation
of King Edward VIII, and that 60 trees be planted 8 July 1936

THE CORONATION MENU
12 May 1937

Grape Fruit
Clear Oxtail Soup, Green Pea Soup

—

Boiled Scotch Salmon, Cucumber, Parsley Sauce
Saddle of Lamb, Red Currant Jelly or Mint Sauce
French Beans Cauliflower New Potatoes

—

Sorbet

—

Roast Spring Chicken
Salad

—

Asparagus, Melted Butter

—

Meringue
Charlotte Russe
Wine Jelly
Green Figs

—

Peach Melba

—

Sardines on Toast

—

Dessert

—

Coffee

Burial Board, Moor and Parks Committee

8 September 1937

a letter from Messrs Fred Lister and Son of Otley making application for permission to hold the annual Sheep Sales on the Bridge Field Ilkley on Sept. 21st and October 19th next

Resolved

That permission be given, Messrs Lister and Son to pay the sum of £2 10s. 0. for the privilege and to remove all hurdles and huts belonging to them immediately after the sale.

Ilkley Feast is now little more than a memory. Even the paraphernalia of roundabout and coconut shies have failed to appear this year. Many old memories of the Ilkley Sheep Fair were awakened by a sale of sheep conducted by Mr F. M. Lister in the Bridge Field on Tuesday. The Ilkley Sheep Fair was formerly one of great importance to farmers of Wharfedale but it was a dying institution before the war came, and that disaster finally brought it to a close.

Burial Board, Moor and Parks Committee

8 March 1939

The Clerk reported a letter received from the Ministry of Health with respect to special arrangements to be made, in the event of war, in regard to persons killed in consequence of war operations in this country. The Minister suggested that the following matters should receive immediate attention

a) a review of existing mortuary accommodation and buildings which might, in case of need, be used to supplement it
b) a similar review of existing and potential burial accommodation

c) a similar review of transport facilities, and likely to be needed
d) a provisional selection of the personnel required

AIR RAID PRECAUTIONS SUB-COMMITTEE MINUTES

Mr Slater, Chief Sanitary and Building Inspector, had recently completed a course of training at the Civilian Anti-Gas School and had been successful in obtaining a First Class Instructor's Civilian Anti-Gas School Certificate.

15 March 1939

Whitfield Beanley, Hargreave, Hartley, Mennell and Pyett

Resolved
a) That advertisements be inserted in the local newspapers inviting applications from suitable persons as volunteers for the work in connection with air raid precautions and the training of such volunteers by the Chief Sanitary Inspector as soon as possible.
b) That the Chief SI make arrangements in co-ordination with the Chief's or various departments concerned for the training during normal working hours of the Council's staff and employees

20 July 1939

Chief Sanitary Inspector reported inter alia upon the progress of anti-gas training and that out of a total of 70 persons who had taken an examination, 64 persons had been successful in attaining the required proficiency. It was

Resolved
that those successful candidates whose names appear on the Register as having volunteered for the Council's Air Raid Precautions Scheme be recommended for the Home Office badge.

13 August 1939

Resolved

That an appeal be made to members of the public who have house cellars suitable for use as air raid shelters asking them to place such cellars at the disposal of other persons who have no such facilities in their own home.

There was a manager of Lloyds Bank called Milner, should have retired 1939 but they kept him on for the duration of the war. Colonel Seebag Montifiore, related to the Seebags of the City of London and who was in charge of Officers' Training School which had taken over the Middleton Hotel, went into Lloyds to cash a cheque, went in with his uniform and his adjutant two paces behind him, and the clerk behind the counter said as you have no arrangement here I'll have to call the manager through, and they called Milner through. Milner, who wore a monocle, came up to the counter, screwed his monocle in his eye, looked up at the Colonel with all his First World War ribbons, his DSO and MC and his red tab, he said, Well this is most irregular. Do you have any identification?

18 November 1939

Resolved

That the clerk be instructed to communicate with the sub-controller for the Skyrack area asking him to use his good offices to obtain an issue of water-proof coats for members of the Warden Service

During the war Ilkley had a tremendous record in national saving schemes, bought more Spitfires every year, more than any other per head of population. There were really two people behind that, one was Percy Dalton who was in the butchers, spice trade, additives, very prosperous, very outgoing. He used to put all his own money into these national savings weeks and when it was all over and got the credit for buying, he used to pull it all out again.

BURIAL BOARD, MOOR AND PARKS COMMITTEE

3 November 1940

Resolved

that a letter be sent to the West Riding Education Committee referring to the County Agricultural Committee's circular letter asking the Council to implement the Government's Grow More Food and Dig for Victory campaign and pointing out that if the Education Committee will hand over the site of the proposed Girls Modern School at Ben Rhydding for the duration of the war, the Ilkley Urban District Council will be prepared to cultivate the land for food production purposes.

During the war you couldn't get Kellogg's cornflakes so the government switched Percy into manufacturing cornflakes, the biggest in England, Dalton's cornflakes, the Rombalds sunshine breakfast.

3 January 1941

It was decided to provide forthwith sand bags to be stored at the foot of street lamp standards in the more built up areas for use in dealing with incendiary bombs. The c. decided that the bags should first be put through a suitable proofing process and in view of the fact that such proofing is known to extend very considerably the life of the bags, it was decided that the county council be asked to reimburse the Council in this respect.

An inspection had been made of certain lands owned by the Council.

Resolved

That the following land be cultivated

The Holmes from the New Bridge to the Wheel

A field on the north side of Denton Road near the Bathing Pool

The greater part of Leeds Road Recreation Ground

Land adjoining New Nurseries, Little Land, Ilkley

Part of the Ben Rhydding Sports Club's land

BURIAL BOARD, MOOR AND PARKS COMMITTEE

10 May 1944

The Clerk was instructed to have posters painted and exhibited in Middleton Woods warning members of the public that legal proceedings will be initiated against persons who pluck blue-bells or other flowers and plants in the woods.

They were all in the Young Conservatives and it was incest, a young Conservative married a young Conservative and then when the war came everybody expected air raids and nothing happened and servants went home and the OTU came and commandeered all the halls, all the empty houses and all the girls thought they'd gone to heaven, all those young officer cadets walking about. The young girls in the big houses had first choice of course, their mothers invited the cream home for lunch and the local girls chased what remained and it was astonishing the number of girls you knew and went to school with and used to talk like that suddenly started posh and started saying oh rather! It was funny to watch them. The officer cadets had a dance every fortnight or so and the local girls would die for a ticket to one of those. After the war it changed completely, nobody was going to be a servant, very few people wanted to work in shops, everybody had ambition, they wanted a good well-paid job and as the big houses became flats and the hoy palloi disappeared

and the old Ilkley time resumed, old stories, old habits, old peculiarities running up and down the street.

Mr Dell, the Ilkley boatman, wrote to Leeds University Medical Officer for Health. He has often walked by the river conscious of the fine quality of air in that area. However when he moves away from the river bank, the quality of air appears to fade. Is there any scientific evidence to advance the theory that the fast running fresh water had health-giving effects on the air above. Dr Proctor, a doctor, says there is no evidence.

Jack Brumfitt lived on Denton Road and it always used to flood very badly. He always used to go in to Beanlands to get himself a sandwich and he'd take it in the Constitutional Club and eat his sandwich and have a pint which was not allowed. One day, when the river was in full spate, as he was about to go someone said, Look you better be careful, Mr Brumfitt, on the way home, it's flooded. It'll be right, said Jack. He went across the Old Bridge and there it was, flooded. The postman was coming down and he said Are you all right, Mr Brumfitt? and Jack said I don't know how I'm going to get across this! So this postman, and he was a big man, said, Well, get on my back. So this postman is going through water up to his waist, carrying Jack across and he takes him and puts him on his front door step absolutely dry. Thank you, Jack says.

Postman turns round, goes back out on to Denton Rd and Jack shouts EH! very sharp. Postman looks up and says, What you want?

Shut bloody gate

Sam Tipping used to stand outside waiting for business and he'd see this lady walking up the street carrying a big bag of shopping. You can't carry that home, he'd say, I'm going to run you home. No it's all right I'm just waiting for the bus. No you're not, I'm going to take you. He had this big Jag, so he gets this lady and her two shopping bags, and drives her up to her house. They'd get to the door and he'd say, A very nice house is this, are you thinking of moving? No, not really. Well, tell you what, if you just let me have a look round inside I'll tell you what you'd get if you were. He sold hundreds and hundreds that way.

He lived in a coal yard in Little Lane that had a piano with a huge treacle tin on top. Used to have a poster outside his shop listing the properties he'd sold and every so often it would say something like, No 45, Tivoli Place. TWICE! There was a little plot of land on Leeds Road near the school there, with a little wooden shack on which for some reason a rival firm administered, but he rented and he had a sign up there saying

TIPPING for all available properties in Ilkley District

Douglas Hartley took him aside one day and said, in the nicest way he could, Sam the next time you paint that sign don't put *all* available properties. It's not right. Sam immediately had it repainted

TIPPING for ALL available properties in Ilkley District

(His son, Jack, delivering coal for his father, used to stop the coal wagon on the New Bridge and dive into the river to wash all the coal dust off

Tariff Coffee 6d. Soup 6d. Horlicks 9d. Bovril 8d. Tea per cup 4d. per pot 7d. Fruit Melbas 1/3 Cream Trifle 9d. Fruit Jellies 6d. Cream Meringues 6d. Ice Cream assorted flavours 4d. chocolate 6d. Cakes and pastries 4d. 5d. 6d. Tarts jam etc. 3d. Biscuits per portion 3d. Biscuits chocolate 4d. Potato Crisps per packet 4d. bread and butter 3d. Jam assorted 3d. Sandwiches boiled ham or meat per round ¼d. lettuce and tomato 10d. lettuce and cheese 10d. set High tea per head 3/6 Cold Boiled Ham Assorted Cold Meats Salads Various Bread and Butter, Two Cakes or Sweet, Tea.

Geoffrey Clough was left £3 million in 1953. Survived on £35 a day. He always, always bought someone a drink. Anybody. If you were at the bar and it was his turn he bought you a drink, whether he knew you or not. Drove with a friend one day to the Compleat Angler in Marlow and Cliff walks in. Geoffrey had never watched television in his life. Geoffrey comes to the bar and says to the barman, "Could I have a m m m," he licked his lips all the time, did Geoffrey, "could I have a a a whiskey please," and the barman said "Certainly, sir. A large one or a small one?" and Geoffrey said, "A m m m large one." The Barman said, "Would you like Whites or Black Horse?" and Geoffrey said, "B . . b . . b . . . Bells please." "Would you like ginger, or soda or water?" Geoffrey answered, "For Christ"s sake, Rombalds." The barman was still lingering over what Geoffrey might have meant when in walks Cliff Michelmore. Geoffrey says "Good evening." Cliff Michelmore replies, "Good evening". Geoffrey says, "What are you having?" and Cliff Michelmore, thinking he was trying to become familiar says, "No, I'm all right, thank you." Geoffrey says, "What you doing here then if you're all right?" Michelmore says, "No honestly, I'm quite all right, I'm just going to have a Scotch." "I'll get you that," says Geoffrey. "No, please," says Michelmore, quite firmly now, "please don't bother. I'm all right." So Cliff Michelmore takes himself to a table and sits down. Has a quiet drink. About twenty minutes later Geoffrey goes up to the bar once more and he turns to Cliff Michelmore. "Same again?" Cliff Michelmore looks up. He's getting a bit fed up with this. "I said no," he says. "I'm all right." Clough looks at him between the eyes and says, 'Excuse me, don't I know you." Cliff Michelmore sighs and says, "Probably." Clough says, "I thought I did. Are you a comber or a spinner?"

April

Resolved that the Bathing Pool be offered free of charge to the Australian Rugby Touring Team. Likewise a contingent of Dutch scouts shortly visiting.

Dear Sir,
    I am taking the liberty of writing to you to make my application for situation as an attendant at either the Bathing Pool or Sports Ground. I was employed by the council as park attendant last year which duties I carried out to the Council's satisfaction, at the end of the season I went back to my old employment I. E. Gardening but had to give it up on account of Health reasons. I hasten to add, that I do not think that those reasons will be any detriment to my carrying out the Duties satisfactory,
    I beg to be yours obediently F.J.B.

From the Engineer and Surveyor: I am afraid that Mr B. would not be suitable owing to his disability: also he is suffering from foot trouble which is not yet cured.

His leg let him down, Mr B. with his feet of clay, not suitable for the slippery wet of an open-air pool, to chase the squealing boys, the jumping girls, scold the ducking bully or at night, in these modern times, bring skinny-dipping swimmers of Bradford to book, bringing their wayward city manners to this healthy spa

PC Swift Tuesday 17 May 1960

I respectfully report that at 12-10 am on Tuesday 17th May I was on duty in Denton Road Ilkley, near the junction with Middleton Avenue, when I heard sounds of shouting and laughter coming from the direction of the Swimming Pool and Denton Road. I went to the pool and saw four motor vehicles, Austin Saloon motor car Reg. TLE 92: MG sports car Reg. XDV345 Austin sports car SAK 340 and a Bond Mini car reg. 374 9UA parked outside the main entrance. The shouting and laughing continued from the direction of the pool and I could hear also the sound of persons splashing and jumping into the water. There was a pair of wooden steps leaning against the wire fence at the side of the main entrance and the persons in the pool had apparently climbed over the fence which has barbed wire at the top. I shone my torch and could see persons running about but could not see what they were wearing. I shouted to them to come out and after a few minutes they stopped running and jumping into the water and shortly after a number of men and women came to the fence and climbed over. There were six women and five men and all admitted not having any authority to be in the pool. I asked them how they got into the pool and they stated by climbing over the wire fence with the help of the wooden steps.

Sydney T. 40 years Woolsorter Shipley
John D. 20 years Hotelier Bradford
Keith D. 24 years Self-employed Shipley
Tom H. 24 years Free Lance Journalist Bradford
Dave S. 21 years Journalist Bradford
Rita D. 19 years Self-employed Shipley
Maureen D. 21 years TV Tester Bradford
Jacqueline S. 19 years Clerk Bradford

Joan H. 19 years Shorthand Typist Bradford
Sandra W. 19 years Model Bradford
Rosemary D. 22 years Bradford
Maureen D. and Jacqueline S. are not known at the addresses
    given

Dear Sir
    I should like to apologise and convey the sincere
regrets of myself and others who were found inside Ilkley
open air swimming pool on the evening of Monday May
16th. Although explanations are difficult to express and
excuses hardly justified I would like to say that none of the
people involved have ever done such a thing before nor
are they likely to do so again.
    The outing was purely the result of high spirits
without there being any intention of causing damage or
committing acts of hooliganism. If however any harm was
inadvertently caused or much inconvenience resulted then
I should like to sincerely apologise on behalf of everyone
and help rectify the position by offering payment of cost.
    Trusting that my offer will meet with your approval
and save you further inconvenience I humbly apologise
again and give you all our assurances that such a thing will
never occur again.
    Yours faithfully David S.

The damage they had done to the turnstile was £5 10s. 0d.

He can almost hear the youth coming, the beered driving of the
car and the squealing of the dare, clothed or unclothed it does not
say, but some fun in the changing no doubt, and a hasty wet retreat
behind bushes, pulling on whatever came to hand when the torch
was shone and the whistle was blown. They're not quite there yet.

ILKLEY (14)

1967

The membership card is pink, and across, from top left to bottom right, an invitation to Swinging Yorkshire, via the admission to the Sunday Scene at the GYRO CLUB. It sounds as if it ought to be a dive, a place of dank descent, ducking your head down the Day-Glo stairs and the bulging black walls, the boom of the bass beating up the narrow stairs as you discard the parental day and plunge into the pubescent pool of night. But not here. The Gyro Club has its headquarters and holds its weekly meetings in a function room on the edge of Ilkley Moor under the roof of a small hotel.

You have to visit the place to understand just how incongruous the event must have been. It is not the fact that it is now a rest home for the wealthy, that a portable tape recorder plays Jack Hilton and Ambrose in the foyer, while implacable spinsters guard the entrance, their teeth stained with suspicion; nor is it the green and solitary parrot that broods impatiently inside his cage, waiting to bite the hand that does not feed it. The soporific weight of the heavy curtains has not muffled this story, nor has the flotilla of carpets that run deep along its silent corridors sunk it. The improbability of this tale does not reside in the hotel's present nor in its distant past, but in the hotel's very position, not near the hub of the town, in quarters that invite a certain amount of squashed and hurried activity, round the back of the station or somewhere out along the Leeds road, locations both of which acknowledge the sound of the city, but in the town's barren upper reaches, on Crossbeck Road, the last civilized road the town possesses before the moor takes hold. Here, as that dark and restless sea washes against the final reaches of the town, stands this solid but minor hotel, in its day a hydropathic establishment, part of Ilkley's early fame, but by the time of this particular visit something of a backwater. Its facade, which you see first, stands back from the road, high and raised. But this is not the front. The front, like many a cliff-side dwelling, has been turned about face, to be witness to the moor, protected by a low stone wall which marks out the reclaimed land on which you might park your car. To the left of the main building is a rectangular addition, with what looks like a pagoda for a roof; a ballroom no less with a maple-wood floor and a small, triangular stage wedged into the near left-hand corner, room for two hundred, two hundred and fifty persons. High above the hotel entrance between the first and second storey hangs a name in unadorned iron. No definite article, just the bald name. TROUTBECK.

Why the Troutbeck? Why here along this submerged residential road with its collection of large implacable houses set back on gravel drives, granite names chiselled on to granite walls, squat pillars guarding the gates like half-dormant dogs; Crossbeck Road speaking only of grandiose quiet and the desire for well-brought-up property to be left alone? Further along, as the road opens up again, they could have booked into Craiglands, which, though haughty and formal, at least boasts an eighty-two-foot ballroom, enough to contain the event twice over. Down on the Skipton Road, overlooking the river (and owned by the same outfit), stands the Ilkley Moor Hotel (formerly the Middleton), the annual billet of the visiting Australian rugby team, and therefore conversant with rowdy and indecorous behaviour (and which, when it flamed to destruction over a year later, could have pointed to this earlier incendiary occurrence as the slow-burning cause of its subsequent conflagration). But neither has been chosen, nor has the Crescent nor the Kings Hall on the right wing of the Town Hall, scene of so much of Ilkley's communal life. These are too safe, too predicated upon Ilkley's paternal municipality. Perhaps it is right that the Gyro Club is held next to Ilkley's wild unruly heart, where the wind cries any name you wish to hear and where, at any moment, the ever-falling mist might make it so hard for you to see.

The licensee of the hotel is one Bertram Douglas Edwards in respect of which he holds a full Justices licence, a supper hours certificate, and a public, music, singing and dancing licence Monday to

Saturday, 11 a.m. to 3 p.m. and 5.30 to 10.30 p.m. and a public music and singing *only* licence on Sundays, 12 noon to 2 p.m. and 7.30 p.m. to 10.30 p.m. The hotel is owned by Splendour Properties Investments Ltd. in which Mr Edwards has an interest, with registered offices at 4 Lloyds Avenue, London. The Gyro Club is managed by his entrepreneurial son, young Philip Nigel Edwards, who hires this Victor Silvestered space on Sunday evenings for the purposes of holding the weekly club functions.

On the evening of Sunday 12 March 1967, at around five thirty, a dirty Commer van grinds cautiously up the steep and semicircular drive. It has not travelled far. The night before, the van stood outside the International Club, Leeds and the night before that, the Friday, it was parked alongside the Club-a-Go-Go in Newcastle. Inside the van are four men, three of them white and British, one black and American. One of the three white men, Jerry, is what is known as a roadie, the other two are musicians, one a guitarist, the other a drummer. The white guitarist used to play lead guitar or rhythm. Now he plays bass. He's easy with that. When they started out together the group held auditions for another guitarist to join them, to play rhythm to the American's lead, but the truth is, thanks to the length of his right thumb, the American can play both rhythm guitar and lead guitar at the same time, which is in itself an unusual accomplishment. But then he is an unusual guitarist. At the back of the van rattles their equipment; speaker stacks, a Fender jazz bass, Ludwig drums, and a Stratocaster guitar, with a vibrato arm that when yanked all the way back will propel the guitar and its pilot somewhere close to the orbit of Gemini XI, the last in the series before the Apollo space programme to put a man on the moon takes hold. The switch for the guitar's three pickups is wedged between settings so that when the American runs his fingers up and down the fret the notes seem to accelerate and slow down at the same time, like a rocket lifting slowly from its launchpad. Rhythm and lead, fast and slow, a sea of contradictions. There are two additional pieces of equipment this man requires for his flight. The first is an Arbiter Fuzz Face pedal which distorts (or rather clarifies) his intentions; the second is the Octavia pedal, which adds a note one octave higher to that which is being played, the floating butterfly to his knockout punch. The black American has been in England for one hundred and seventeen days.

His two forenames are the same as the name of the designer of the speakers he favours, James Marshall, but he is better known as Jimi.

They climb the drive and park by the low wall. They slide open the van doors and step out. A dark wind pulls at their thin-trousered legs. In the dim distance they can hear the moor prowling about the coming night. Opposite shine the beacon lights of the Troutbeck and framed in the doorway stands the outline of the club manager, waiting. They pull on their cigarettes, stub them with the scuff of boot, move across and introduce themselves. The manager is not particularly impressed. He has seen any number of them, cocky young lads hoping for the big break. It could be all right, though. This lot have a following, he has heard. He just hopes he will cover his costs. Dad doesn't like it when he doesn't cover his costs.

While the roadie sets up the equipment, the three members of the band take up temporary residence in the small room at the back of the ballroom. This is the waiting time, and to pass it as best they can they play a hand of cards or set out one of their preferred board games. They have brought a number with them, as usual. Scrabble, Monopoly, Risk; Risk is their favourite. It is quiet up here, but elsewhere, along Ilkley's quiet approach roads, things are beginning to stir. A trickle first, cars coming making their way up the empty highways of Brook Street and the Grove, then, unusually for these days of rest and the time of night a thicker, more congested stream, cars over from Bingley, cars over from Harrogate, Keighley and Skipton, cars from Otley beetling out from Leeds suburbs and Bradford back-to-backs; the traffic is beginning to fill the roads, snakes of black bonnets squirming their way into Ilkley's sleeping centre. The Gyro Club has advertised other functions, hired other bands, attracting any number of youths, but tonight it is as if a piper has gambolled over hill and dale, town and city, blowing his horn, and they have all heard his call. There is no need for any of them to ask the way, for momentum carries one car after another, couples in the front, couples in the back, girls perched on boys' knees, heads and hairdos pressed up against the roof, hands on black-tighted knees and girdled waists, vans full of mates and beer bottles, legs and arms and empty fag packets tumbling out of the doors, a sudden flood surging the wrong way this time, charging up Wells Road towards the Moor, running like leaping salmon running to lay their adolescent eggs. And it is true. That is what they have come here to do, in their battered and borrowed cars, to jump and frolic and spawn in this their breeding ground. They swarm up the drive and into the hotel, past the gloomy foyer and the narrow hotel bar, past the empty television room and the forsaken residents' lounge, along the worn carpeted corridor, past the gold-framed hunting prints and the rack where the morning papers and back numbers of *Country Life* are held, towards the end of the passage where to the right lies the gloom of the empty dining room with its clanking cutlery and its cabbage smells, and to the left, guiding its souls like a lighthouse, shines the incandescent light of the ballroom. At the edge of its circumference Philip Nigel Edwards is seated by a table. A young woman with long fair hair is standing next to him. There is no till upon the table, no pen, no papers, no membership book, simply a bare metal cash box in which a jumble of half crowns and florins fight space with a pile of scruffy one pound and ten shilling notes. Beside it lies a bundle of unused and unnumbered pink cards. The Gyro Club. As they each reach the table Philip looks up and says, 'Ten shillings.' They give him the money and the young woman hands them a blue ticket torn from a roll, while Philip takes hold of their right hand and stamps it with an ink stamp which reads TROUTBECK HOTEL RECEIVED WITH THANKS, PAID. He does not ask for their names, nor their address, nor if they are members of the club. He merely nods them through and turns his attention to the next supplicant. Now they can move into the ballroom, now they clean themselves of the detritus they have brought with them, plunge into the thrashing water, baptize themselves, take another Ilkley cure.

A few doors down Mr Harvey peels back his curtains and looks out again. The road is chock-a-block with strange vehicles, scraping walls, climbing on to verges, planting their tasteless bumpers on to moss-plucked drives without so much as a by-your-leave. He can see dark shapes swirling up and down his road, hear the tramp of Chelsea boot and the totter of high heel, slammed doors and rude laughter puncture the air. He has had to put up with a certain amount of aggravation ever since this wretched club opened in November, but nothing on this scale. This takes the biscuit. He lifts up the phone.

I am a Police Sergeant in the West Riding Constabulary stationed at Ilkley Section of the Otley Division. At 8.45 Sunday 12 March 1967 I was on duty at Ilkley Police Station when a complaint was received from Mr Harvey of 33 Crossbeck Road to the effect that cars were parked on both sides of Crossbeck Road and that there was only enough room for single line traffic. I visited Crossbeck Road. I met Mr Whitman who lives at No. 31 and he made a similar complaint. I was informed that the drivers of the vehicles parked were attending a function at the Troutbeck Hotel. I went to the Troutbeck Hotel and on arrival I found 100 cars parked on both sides of the road in Crossbeck Road outside the hotel causing an obstruction and many were parked without lights.

On entering the Hotel I immediately noticed that the foyer of the hotel was crowded with young persons, the corridor from the foyer to the ballroom was also crowded as was the lounge bar off the corridor, the persons were standing in the corridor drinking. I made my way through the crowded corridor to the small lobby at the entrance to the ballroom, the Manager of the Hotel, Mr Wilks, was standing at the table with a Miss Beattie and they were taking money and admitting persons into the ballroom. I pushed my way into the ballroom and saw that it was packed to capacity with persons standing, there was very subdued lighting as for discotheques, there was no room for any person to dance as the floor was so crowded with people, and in my opinion there was more than 600 persons in the hall. I pointed out to Mr Wilks that when I had paid a visit to the premises on Friday March 10 1967 I reminded him that the maximum persons allowed on the premises with normal lighting was 250 and he agreed that I had done this. I then told him to stop admitting persons into the Hall, the persons trying to enter the ballroom became agitated, as some had been queuing for a while, others had pass-out (rubber stamps) and wanted to re-enter and it looked as if the situation would get out of hand.

Six hundred youths standing on windowsills and tables, pressed up against each other in the enforced intimacy of expectation. The discs that are being played are ones taken from the current charts, but in truth this crowd can hear not a note. Even if they could they cannot dance, so great is the crush, indeed they can barely move at all, whether it be to the bar or to one of the hardboard cubicles where expressions of romance and desire are traditionally given form. That is of no concern to them either. They have come here for another, more pressing matter and they are tired of waiting. As Sergeant Chapman urges Mr Wilks into action they begin to move in the only direction they can, jumping up and down, up and down, a generation of pogo-trained children come of age. In the little serving alcove the beer bottles rattle, the glasses shake. They are sending out earth tremors, radio pulses, morse code, the ripples running out along the moor's floor to where the Apostle Stone stands, pulsating out over Blubberhouses to the spiked puffballs of Menwith Hills. The floor creaks, the walls tremble. The crowd rises and the crowd falls. They hear their train a-coming.

In view of this I told the manager to close all entertainment, shut off the music which at this time was records on a record player; also to tell the persons who had vehicles on the Cross-beck Road to remove them as soon as possible and so clear the obstruction on the road. This did not have any success in getting people to leave the ballroom so I went on stage and addressed the persons in the ballroom, told them the position and asked them to leave but everybody was demanding their money back.

I went to the Hotel foyer and telephoned PC Taylor who was on duty, and instructed him to inform Inspector Millar of the situation, also to send PCs Rushworth and Coles to attend and assist me in the hotel and for the 999 car to attend and assist with the traffic problem. While the manager Mr Wilks was trying to re-arrange payment of admission, I returned to the ballroom and found that the beat group booked for that night had gone on stage and had commenced the performance.

James Marshall steps out. Like a fairy-tale soldier he wears a military jacket purloined from the Crimean War; blue and red with gold brocade ejaculate spilling down the unbuttoned front, set off by a pair of velvet-tight crimson trousers pulled hastily over his errant crotch. He stands before them in a parody of a military parade, flaunting his own discipline, ready to order his arms. He picks up his white guitar, which, like the musketeer and his cartridge pouch, he will service with his mouth in moments of extremis. There is no sound check, no tuning of instruments, and no order of play has been decided. Give me an A he says, and the bass guitarist, ever obliging, gives him an A. Thank you very much, says James Marshall, and sets off.

They start with 'Killing Floor'. They always start with 'Killing Floor'. It is not an easy number to start from cold, but that is the way he is, staking his ground, establishing his power and pace and the speed of his machine as it levels the room, no prisoners taken. The effect is furious. There is a suck of air, a collective intake of breath as the audience burst into flames. This man is an incendiarist. He strikes his tinderbox and they burn swiftly. He is heat and energy and they are consumed by his strange and compulsive beauty. But as the number gathers momentum another figure appears upon the platform.

I went on to the stage, spoke to the leader of the group, whom I now know to be a man called Hendrix, I told him the position and the action that had previously been taken and he stopped the music, he tried to persuade the persons to leave the hall, but they would not do so and commenced shouting, stamping and chanting that they wanted their money back.

James Marshall backs into his speaker stack, drowning the noise with feedback. Rendered temporarily deaf Sergeant Chapman retreats to the rear of the stage where, ears burning, he stumbles across a bank of switches. Determined to shut the music off at all costs he pulls at them swiftly, one, two, three sockets, flashes of electric blue arcing over his constabularic hands. But he has not silenced James Marshall, nor his crew. The feedback is still howling, the crowd is still alight. All he has managed to achieve is to turn off the ballroom lights.

It takes them two hours to clear the place, as the hydra of Yorkshire youths circle the Troutbeck trying to re-enter through door or ground-floor windows. But finally they leave, disgruntled at the police, disgruntled at the Gyro Club, disgruntled at Ilkley, disgruntled most likely at themselves for not overcoming this all too adult obstacle. Though they know it not, they have all entered the record books, witness to James Marshall's shortest ever performance. In the abandoned ballroom, young Peter surveys the damage. In their frustration the tormented youths have taken up all the tables and chairs and flung them in an unruly pile up by the ballroom entrance, hoping no doubt to place Sergeant Chapman, Inspector Millar or even young Peter himself upon the peak, haul it to Beamsley Beacon and drive back home under its vengeful glow. Peter starts to dismantle the structure. He is in a bit of a mood. The Gyro Club is out of pocket. Dad will not be happy.

Down the road, James Marshall and his three companions finish their beer and turn into bed. Tomorrow they fly to Amsterdam. Down at the station the police are reviewing the situation. It is not the crowd as such. They are used to crowds, to clogged roads and charabancs. At some Whit weekends the excursion trains have been so laden that the wheels have slipped to a standstill on the steep incline at Menston Junction; walkers, swimmers, day-trippers, Ilkley can teem with the best of them. Ilkley craves a crowd, crowd is trade; the crush of bodies gives it heart; shopkeepers, assistants, hoteliers, railway porters, taxi drivers, cooks, waiters, they love it one and all. Except this one. This crowd is not trade and this crowd they do not love. This one is made up of thee and thine, and is propelled by another influence altogether. The time has come to put a stop to this sort of nonsense. And so, under cover and on following Sundays, unobtrusive observations are made.

I am a Detective Officer in the West Riding of Yorkshire Constabulary, stationed at Horsforth.

On going into the ballroom the room was in absolute darkness except for the stage lights, a spot light attached to the ceiling with a red filter over it, and two candles stuck into the tops of empty beer bottles one on each side of the room. After about ten minutes these candles had been blown out by persons in the ballroom. On the stage there was an all male seven piece beat group with their instruments attached to amplifiers, playing modern beat music, one of the group was singing into a microphone. At this time 8.40pm there was about 120 members of the public in the room, about 80 of these youths whose ages would range from 15 to 25 years, and the rest girls of which three quarters of them would be under 18 years of age, in fact some of them looked like schoolgirls.

In the middle of the floor about twenty to thirty people, mostly male youths, were engaged in modern beat group dancing with about twelve young girls. At the rear of the dance hall in a small alcove which was in complete darkness I saw four teenage couples. The girls were lying stretched out on canvas chairs which had been placed together, the boys sitting down on the end chairs and they were kissing and fondling each other, oblivious of anything that was going on around them. During the evening the bar was open in the ballroom and drinks were being served by a young lady and a youth. Before the interval I bought one pint of Worthington 'E' beer and was charged 2s 9d. Dancing continued until 9.30pm.

At 9.30 the beat group left the stage and music continued on records. During the interval I again went to the bar. I stood at the side of the bar and saw two girl couples served by a lady behind the bar. These girls were obviously under 18 years of age, one of the girls was served with two bottles of Barley Wine, and the other two bottles of light ale. I then went along the passage to the Gent's toilet which is near the hotel reception desk. Near to these toilets are some carpeted stairs. Sitting on the stairs I saw two young girls, again under 18 years of age kissing and cuddling, taking no heed of other customers who were passing the stairs.

At 10pm the beat group came back on stage and started to play modern beat group music, and one of the group was singing into a microphone. It was apparent that the sound on the amplifiers had been increased in volume. At 10.25 the beat music got faster the spotlight on the red filter started to go in and out with the beat of the music. At 10.30 the same thing was happening, but in addition, blue tubular lighting on the ceiling came on, flashing in time with the music. This gave the effect of making the dancers more enthusiastic. They started to shout and scream and this continued until 10.45 when the group finished playing.

At no time did I see anyone supervising the dance. There were no books on the table at the entrance, nor was there any list of persons who were members of the club. It was obvious that the ballroom was being used for dancing and was open to anyone regardless of age, within reason, who was willing to pay the 10s. entrance fee

Time to spring into action. On April 2nd, they reappear, in uniform. This time they mean business. They take names and addresses and statements; a ladies' hairdresser (apparent age 16), a secretary (apparent age 21) and a schoolgirl (apparent age 15 years).

I am a schoolgirl attending Skipton High School for girls. Towards the latter end of Feb. 1967 I started visiting the Troutbeck Hotel, as I heard that "Beat Groups" visited there and it was possible to dance. I visited this Hotel every Sunday night from the beginning of March 1967. I was not a member of the Gyro Club, I was never asked if I was a member when entering the ballroom, and never asked to produce a membership card. Altogether I attended about six times, and dancing took place on every occasion except the night when Jimi Hendrix should have been on, then it was too crowded to move let alone dance.

They tuck their statements in their pockets. Inspector Millar cautions Mr Philip and promises to return on Tuesday to question him further about the Gyro Club and its members and the manner in which it is run. Philip Nigel Douglas Edwards has two days to get his story right.

Inspector Millar

At 4.25 Tuesday 4th April 1967 I interviewed Philip Nigel Douglas Edwards.

What is your connection with the Club?
I'm the Manager.
As manager do you attend all the club functions?
Oh yes.
Can you explain why a large number of persons attending the function were not club members?
That was entirely due to Harrison who is new to the job. They either have membership cards or they don't. We don't even allow visitors in.
Does the club have a list of members?
Yes.
Is there a Club Committee?
Yes there is.
Who is on that committee?
Myself, Joan Beattie, Stuart Frais, Daniel Pollock, David Bullock.
Are there any club rules?
Yes there are.
How many different types of membership cards are there?

Two. Some blue and white, which were the original, and pink ones which are now in use. They are not numbered until they join and then they are numbered in ink.

Who completes the membership card with the number etc.?

June Beattie.

Who is the club secretary?

June.

Who is the club treasurer?

She is also the treasurer.

Has she anything to do with the booking and organising of these club functions?

No, that's all my department.

Is any member of the committee involved in the booking and organising of the functions?

Apart from discussion, no, I do it all.

Would it be possible for a person to become a club member and the club not have their name and address?

No.

Can I see a list of members, the club rules and any other documents relating to the constitution of the club?

Yes, you can. You can't see the club rules because they are at the printers being re-printed. They have been there for three weeks.

Can I see a copy of the old club rules?

They are the old club rules being reprinted at Nottingham or you could have had them before.

When a person joins the club are they always given a copy of the club rules?

Yes, that's why we've run out, because we now have approximately 1,700 members.

How long has the club been in existence?

It started on Sunday, November 13th 1966.

Since that time has the club held any meetings for members?

Yes, we meet every two months.

Do members attend these meetings?

Yes, they do.

Where are the lists of members?

There is one at the Troutbeck at the moment and a larger one which is at the accountants at the moment with the accounts and things.

At this stage he leaves to make arrangements to have the book at the Troutbeck sent down to the Ilkley Moor Hotel, but returns shortly afterwards.

No one at the Troutbeck at the moment knows where it is. Only the Chef and Mr Wilks know and they are both out. I'll bring the book to Ilkley Police Station this evening.

This he never did.

If there is a list at the Troutbeck why have you not produced them to me at the hotel when I have been there and asked to see it?

There is a list on the board and all members are not on it. The board isn't large enough to show all the members.

When I asked you in the past to see a list why didn't you draw my attention to the list?

You remember the night of Jimmy Hendrix. I thought you saw it that night.

Apart from the members lists and the club rules are there any other documents dealing with the constitution of the Gyro Club?

No.

To whom does the proceeds of the club functions go?

They go to the club.

Several times in the past I have told you I would like to see the list of Gyro members, the membership cards issued to them, a copy of the club rules, and who is on the club committee, and advised you to send a copy to the Magistrates Clerk and the Police Superintendent at Otley and it appears that you have not done so. A few weeks ago the Police had occasion to clear the Gyro from these hotel premises due to gross overcrowding. I told you then I would like to see these documents but you never have produced them. Can I see these records?

No answer

Are there any records of club membership, etc.?

No answer

Ilkley UDC To Clerk of the Council

Public Dancing on Sundays
Public Health Acts Amendment Act 1890

Please find enclosed a file together with the evidence of a number of persons who were present at the dance on the 2nd April 1967 for any action you may deem necessary. It would appear that public dancing is still being continued at these premises as indicated in the statement of Michael B and Margaret O'H. There appears to be no club rules, no fixed membership, no committee of members, no proper register and no club records. Indeed the only record of the existence of this club produced to the police only after several requests over a period of months, was a cheap memorandum book reputed to be a record of club membership.

Dear Sir,
I am in receipt of your letter of 13 June Ref. GMS/MEG

As you were informed in our recent telephone conversation, I am not prepared to give evidence on your behalf against someone who was providing entertainment which I enjoyed. It would show a great lack of integrity on my behalf for me now to state that what went on that night was against the public good when I do not believe this to be so.

Whereas the information given in my statement to the police was correct, I do not wish to be associated with a prosecution based on laws which I feel most strongly should be amended.

If in fact serious offence was given to persons attending this function by what went on then surely there will be those amongst the offended who will be only too pleased to come forward and support your case. If such persons cannot be found then it would be presumptuous to spend public money on a prosecution without a mandate from the allegedly wronged public.

Yours faithfully

Miss O'H

After hearing evidence of Sunday dancing at the Troutbeck Hotel, where it was stated that a licence permitted only music and singing Otley Magistrates yesterday ordered that the dancing licence for the hotel for other days in the week should be revoked. Three men were fined on summonses in connection with the dances, Bertram Edwards Company Director of Ilkley Moor Hotel fined £67. His son Philip 27, manager, of Tivoli Place £155, and Desmond Wilks 39 Manager of Troutbeck Hotel £23.

THE RED TRICYCLE

(1)

It is 30 March 1999, forty-five years ago to the day that Michael Airey was drowned. It is a bright morning and upon waking he resolves to do what he has promised himself the past week, which is at the appropriate hour to take himself down to the bank where Michael and his tricycle fell, and to follow their journey for the last time. An anniversary of sorts, a reunion between a fifty-two-year-old boy and a six-year-old man, to relive a meeting which never took place, to stretch out a hand which was never grasped, to save a life which was never lost. It is a long time in the waiting, that morning, barely moving out his room, reading that bare report once again, walking twice down the garden to watch the waters that had preceded that time, how sweet the dance of its voice, how soothing, how sad, its perpetual murmuring history, before returning to sit on the edge of his bed, waiting for the clock to strike. When the hour comes, the walk itself is not what he expected, seemingly without cause or hurry. He does not notice steps or feet or the rise and fall of the ground beneath. There is only the river, first along the towpath, then beside little market garden before stretching out alongside the length of the municipal park. It is difficult to be alone here, with the ducks feeding and the children playing and Michael Airey boys throwing Michael Airey stones. Crossing over, he leaves the town, keeping the river close, first by the footpath which takes him up to the sharp bend and the darkened cemetery opposite and then on to Denton Road itself, where, half a mile ahead, on the broad pavement, Michael Airey is racing towards him. He quickens his pace now, the distant call of a town boy urging him on. It is but five minutes to reach Nell Bank, five minutes to the cluster of trees and the steep bank, but though he hurries, though he can hear his breath panting, his feet pedalling, that bright and bouncing tricycle ringing its bell, when he reaches it, the road and the river are empty. Michael Airey is gone.

He walks on. He reaches the bridge under which Michael Airey passed, where the off-duty policeman stood looking at the half-submerged body. In his hand rests a self-consciously picked roadside flower. It is what one does for the dead, pick flowers and throw them on the water, pointless in ordained symbolism, but a gesture nevertheless, and also granting him the ability to see at least one flowering thing carried away on the mercy of the river. There is another man on the bridge, looking downstream towards Burley, as he wants to, and for a moment he imagines that he too might have come to witness Michael Airey's passing, to think of that small boy and what he might have been. Coming slowly to the centre and leaning on the ironwork nearby he is driven by the desire to talk to this man, to explain the yellow flower in his hand, though in truth he cannot explain anything. Why is he here, why is Michael Airey so important to him? Can he recall his voice, the dance in his eyes? Can he remember his laugh, the curl of his hair, or anything in particular that he did?

He throws the flower upon the water and, speaking Michael's full name, watches it as it floats away, hesitantly at first and then, as its stem meets the current below, with greater purpose. He follows its zigzag progress, over ripple, under snagging branch, until he can no longer see it, until the colour fades, until it sinks, until his eyesight fails him, and then, vision denied, redirects his gaze to the water below. He is struck by the thought that the water rushing past him now could be the same water from all those years ago, completing its long pilgrimage round the earth from the moor to sea and back again, mixing with waves and current, visited by darting shoals, cleft in two by tankers, rising again under another sun to billow up in cloud, blown across the world to fall again on Cam Fell or any other of the eager gulleys that feed this body; here again, surging past him, as it did then; and more than that, that in taking Michael's body so thoroughly, taking him and his tricycle so swiftly, atoms of Michael and atoms of the tricycle would have been taken out to sea too, swum in those currents, floating up, riding, as he did, above the earth, travelling back on cloud and wind to his old home, and that this water that he sees so close has small grains of Michael Airey within its mix, that he has been right all along, Michael Airey *is* always here, *is* always on his tricycle, always falling, always tumbling.

Ah, memory! Wishful thought! It is restoration he craves, restoration of life, life denied, life stolen, life smothered. So many lives, so many suffocations, living and dead. The hope of our beginnings and the sadness of its passing, the sentence that childhood can sometimes pass; to fall off the red tricycle, never to return (or climb back on with twisted limb), or to pedal through, bell ringing, boot filled with covered memory.

Some months ago, at an agricultural sale near his home, he saw, in the line of rusty machinery, old threshing machines, tractors, handcarts, a small red tricycle with a boot, similar, if not identical, to the one he used to ride. It stood there, like all the other equipment, oxidized red and seized up, unable to move without squirts of oil and greasings of cable, and a strong arm to break free the lock of rust. The boot was dented and the tarnished handlebars were encrusted with rotting rubber but its pedals were black and its spokes were straight, its saddle and spirit were true. It stood there silent, unadorned, once the apple of a small boy's eye, now abandoned. As the auctioneer moved along the line, selling off mole traps, mangles, rolls of netting, drawing ever closer to the small thing, he stood next to it, patriarchal, as a father might a sleeping child. It needed only a soft word to have it woken. He wanted to buy it for himself, not to use it or to restore it, but to take it home and have it just so, silent, forlorn, so that it might stand with its back to him in the shed, so that he might pass it by daily, aware of its presence, a messenger of the past, a rusted means of going forward, of leaving it all behind and keeping it all alive.

He has a red tricycle and he rides it still, though his knees stick out awkwardly, his feet ridiculously small, describing absurd and clumsy circles. He rides it past Fletcher the greengrocer who stands in the doorway, shaking his head. He bumps along streets no longer cobbled, past wine bars that fade into the future before his eyes; the young drinkers have not been born yet, or if they have they suck on rubbery teats and yawn milk-sweet breath. All has vanished, past and present, he cannot see them, cannot bear witness to the change. At every turn of the pedal, every clank of the chain, he leaves himself behind. Years drain him away. His appetite are not those of a man: he is lost, though he knows where he is and where he is going. He is no longer quite himself.

He rides down to the graveyard, searching for Michael Airey's earthly plot. He is tired of water, fluidity. He wants to stand over something solid. He reads inscription after inscription, some on headstones, some laid out on the rim of the oblong, but none bearing Michael's name. Phillipa Joan, beloved little daughter of Philip and Angela Fawcett, died 3½ August 25th 1835, John Shuttleworth 1909, Hilda Mary Stones, May 7th 1915, who lost her life on the *Lusitania*, George Mott, died July 9th 1937 and his wife exactly twenty-nine years later, July 9th 1966. Ah, they are all here, the skippers and strollers of this town, even if he cannot find them, it is somewhere here they lie. Suddenly around the bend he spies a bunch of blood crimson flowers, wrapped in cellophane with a note, not a note, a letter, to a young woman who has died a year ago today. He cannot forbear but to draw close, not to invade, not to read, but to look; tears are in his eyes for their love and their loss and their need to talk to her still, their dear daughter, their dear sister and friend. She lies, as do they all, by the Wharfe, as will we all lie by shifting waters of time, and as he looks upon the crimson cellophane and the handwritten note he is reminded almost wilfully of his red tricycle and the crackling brown wrapping around the handle and how inviting it had first been when he had first trundled it around the carpeted room and then, later, alongside his mother's footsteps, straining like an untrained puppy and then, growing bolder, breaking the unseen leash, racing ahead, head down, crashing into obstacles, barging into shoppers' wicker baskets, frame-juddering between pavement and gutter: and so he pedals faster, generating his own electricity, lighting the ground beneath his feet, travelling in time, sparks in his hair and electricity arcing from his fingertips. He is H. G. Wells' child, he belongs in the past and in the future. But the present. What to make of that? He is alive, bending his spokes with the power of it, faster and faster his feet go, brighter comes the light, as the town, the revolving roundabout, glides to a halt. He could be perched on a horse or astride a runaway train, his red tricycle rising and falling as the whirligig goes round. There is speed, he is moving but the town is still. Or is it the other way round? Is it he who must be still and the town which moves. Is it he who has always been still and the town which has always moved – leaving its inhabitants behind. Yes, that is it, it is the town that inhabits life, while we remain on our swings and our roundabouts and our red tricycles. It is the town, the wind running over it like water, the water running over it like wind, while it drains your face and washes you clean; this is where its spirit lies, and this is where he clings. He is here still, washed by the waters that removed him, a boy with electricity sparking in his hair and arcing out of his fingertips, hurtling down the moor, cold history whistling in his ears.

He rides the red tricycle through Flanders on Vimy Ridge. He hears their cries of Mary and charges with them. He rides his tricycle on the crest of century's flood, dead sheep and boulders rolling by, a virgin's arm of thwarted love beckoning him to a watery embrace. He rides his red tricycle across the ugly iron bridge, a pedalling red flag before the fuming train. He parks his red tricycle outside Dinsdale's and fills his boot with hand-rolled tobacco. When the refugees arrive he is waiting at the station, his red tricycle glowing through illuminated steam. He carries a peasant boy's belongings and lets him place his clumsy clogs upon the shining red frame; he is ambulance and fire engine. He sees flames take hold in the Middleton Hotel, sounds the shrill warning on his silver bell, and when the man stabs the schoolboy it is he who races ahead, he who hammers on the doctor's door. He is delivery boy and chauffeur. In his boot lodge Ilkley's dead, crowned with Ilkley's funeral flowers, Fletcher's fruit and Dinsdale's wine packed alongside them, delivering their songs as Professor Modley's son races past, telling jokes (so much Ilkley to contain).

He rides the red tricycle on the cobbled highway, bumping on memory's saddle, propelled by some giant's hand. He holds no one's now, age conspires against it, yet there are hands to be held, he sees them everywhere, by the river, on the bridge, over bed and breakfast tables. He thinks of the hands he has held, squeezed by darkened garden gates and midnight shrouded lanes, pulled across crowded dance floors, clasped in cars and Carole King roundabouts. All memory is loss.

He rides the red tricycle over Ilkley's graves, his wheels depressing fresh flowers into the wet earth. Below they hear him and smile in their finery, love him for his life as he loves them for theirs. He longs to take them with him, hitch a ride on his bright journey, to set them down to what they were and what they wanted to be. He parks his red tricycle by a young woman's grave, her family and friends love her still, bring her flowers and write her letters and lay them about where she lies. She is loved and always will be by those who have known.

He kicks the pedal and races on, his tricycle bumping against the grass of the regimented dead, their hair perfectly combed, the gravestones oblong and correct, but no worse for that (a father lying between his two sons, recalling Graham's cadence, He lost his sons! He lost his sons!). He pedals up the bumping steep to White Wells. He climbs the moor and weaves about the upright stones wishing Rombald might run with him for sport. He leaps upon the Calf, his signature his abrupt and precipitate halt.

He carries Trooper Ballardie as they race for safety to the kopje, his pedals splashed bright with the trooper's blood. He stands by its side in mourning for the old King. He stands on his saddle to welcome the new. He circles the bandstand, he turns on the tarn, he gathers flowers, crystals and juggles with snowballs along the frozen river. He races the moon's shadow along the bank and every night commands the silent streets. He is the daredevil of the open-air wedding cake, riding around its bubbling ledges. Spray rises from his wheels and cascades over those below while his mother and Michael look on. If he goes fast enough he will catch everything. If he goes fast enough he will catch the world and hold it in his grasp. If he goes fast enough he will catch Michael Airey and haul him from the water. If he goes fast enough he will never fall, never falter. There will be no bruises, no loss, the air will always be pure and the water fresh and clear of obstacles. If he goes fast enough.

And why did we come here, and why did we move? Was it unhappiness or father's job, or both (him away and my mother holding firm my hand as my brother's)? My father, my mother, how strange those words appear, how distant their resonance, how cold their meaning. They had names, they wrote their names, named me after them and their union, Leonard and Muriel, but their names are unfamiliar to me, their looks and actions too. For a time their world was here, they walked these paths, drove along these streets, climbed these steps, looked out on this bridge, laid together under this roof, worried over the household accounts, adding up the money they could not spend, planning the life they could not lead, while tramps marked their gates as I hid in the holly house with Nelson. Why here, what the pull, what the need for this Ilkley, for a mother and a father whose faces seem less familiar to me than this old pack bridge on which I stand (the hump of it sending me further away, nearer the river, unmasking my fragility, my loneliness at the hold of it all). What brought them here, to this unhappy solitude, where she could walk by the river and see the submerged mess of her life floating away.

She is not buried here, nor him, they lie separate as they should. I know where she lies but have never seen it since she first went there, though others walk it, and glance in her direction knowing nothing of her nor she of them, visitors unable to communicate anything except idle curiosity and pity. It has taken this long time for us to become equals, in the way that I know her not as she knows not me.

oh but she loved me

> (ironing in that high-ceilinged front room where I took the five-pound note in the silver box on the mantelpiece, cut it into small pieces, smaller than the fallen leaves on the Wharfe's water, smaller than the shreds of newspaper our rabbit tore, knowing the wickedness I was doing, loving its attention to naughty detail, my boldness cut in shapes and scattered on the floor,

My shapes are cut and scattered on the floor

My childhood cut and scattered on the floor

> (and what it took to put them together

I cut the pieces and scatter them on the floor

Ilkley cut and scattered on the floor
Its life broken and put together again, in a different way

oh but she loved me

> (and held my hand and walked me to the infant school; put her foot across the threshold before I would enter

oh but she loved me

>(and took me to the pool, thinking of the small maleness
inside of me, which she could never share

oh but she loved me

>(wanting so much for her boys, for that is what she called
us, her boys, and how it never worked, how uneven the
rate, and the injustice we felt at such usury

oh but she loved me

>(alone and us alone with her

oh but she loved me

>(and is gone, years away

oh but she loved me

>(and has gone many years, all the long years of me and
mine

oh but she loved me

>(yet could not make it true
and in her ignorance marked our cards, harboured the
fear of the world and her unhappiness at the hand it had
dealt her, as she bended the corners

oh but she loved me

>(too much love, so that it became of itself, love alone,
with no thought as to her dependence on it, what she
would do for love's fix

oh but she loved me

>(and I knew her not, and never will, except the height of
her and the span of her stride and the time I stole money
from her purse and placed my head upon her breast in
repentance, feeling my loss before I had realized my
childish title

oh but she loved me

> (and lies alone, unvisited, the bones of her all that is left memory whitened and without flesh. Oh she would not want this recollection, would weep to think that we thought of her so, that she had let us down so, and yet she did, and did not understand how or why, or the vast construction of her familial despair

oh but she loved me

will I lie like that

> (Will no one come one time and stand over me, say Oh how he loved me and how I loved him
> It would be enough to visit me one time – no matter when, warm me with the memory of love

ILKLEY (15)

It is time for him to leave Ilkley, as he did that day with his family in the old blue Daimler, leaving it for good he thought then, turning round and waving goodbye to all he knew, and in the leaving of it this time remembering those things that have left after him and not returned, the Moor Pavilion, the Bandstand, the hotels demolished. The Middleton, for instance, past which he walked every day, where his father drank to his sorrow, but that is nothing as compared with Ben Rhydding gone, pulled down in '55, the year after Michael Airey died. All that remains of its presence is the stone inscription bearing its founder's name, brought down to the safety of the Canker Gardens, and at Ben Rhydding itself the gatehouse and the old pillars to its baronial gates now mark the entrance to an enclosed and slightly paranoid housing estate. Requisitioned during the last war by the War Office, afterwards Ben Rhydding stood empty, its spacious drawing rooms and gymnasiums, its white airy bedrooms discarded, the only cries coming from Watson's principled ventilation system whispering through the long corridors. It had tried to move with the times between the wars, when the water cure had run its course, using its grounds and elevated history to transform itself into a golfing hotel, its coloured brochures claiming the sort of easy cosmopolitan sophistication that one might expect to find strolling down the promenade of a first-class liner or perched upon a bar stool in one of the better London hotels, with American cocktail bars and white-tailed orchestras, but Ben Rhydding was not built for idle wealth, and the Moor is no place for a parasol: the building and its clients simply did not know how to behave. Many in the town were not sorry to see it go, too big, too cumbersome, a hindrance to Ilkley's residential development, for on those slopes, under the shelter of the rock, there was room to build. Perhaps too it reminded the town of forgotten fable and a holding which had been lost, a place which for whatever reason had been seen as destination, as resort, and which, with the coming of the car and later the package holiday, would never return; a haunting they would rather do without. But it cannot be simply that, that they do not care for discarded ghosts looming up at them, for standing back, not fifty yards from the Grove, lies the extravagant ruin of the Charity Hospital, one time refuge to those homeless Belgians, and on whose lawns sat a succession of wooden-crutched and wheelchaired soldiers and thence a constant tide of peacetime invalids washed up on its green shores. Though its main entrance is half up a side road, when it was in use those who could walk could gain access via the small iron gateway on the Grove and path leading up. Now that it is deserted standing dark and abandoned in the heart of the town, its fairy-tale quality seems even more pronounced. There is no dried-up moat as there should be, and no sleeping beauty but thick tangles of blackberry bushes surround its precinct, and there are echoes in the the lofty magic of the inner courtyard where carriages would arrive, hoofs and boots sounding on the flagstone floor. What messages of hope, what gazes of aspirations would have been flung from these windows, what tentative footsteps guided upon the lawn? What unseeing eyes looked down upon the bustle below, what soft hand held another's in hope or love? Now, what steps taken falter from the cans and bottles thrown into the dank cellars while written on the huge boarded-up windows and the dark stone in between are Ilkley's most recent inscriptions, MIKE SUX DIC OLLY IS GAY DAVY JONES IS FUCKING FIT BIKE I LOVE STEPHEN BETH, DO YOU SLEEP ON YOUR BELLY? NO WELL CAN I? all confirming the Calf's old scripted observation. SINS, it would seem, find them out still. Its air is not simply of a building forgotten (and those who walk past on the wide pavement below refuse to look in its direction) but of a place waiting its time. There *is* a sleeping beauty here, the slumbering building itself, and somewhere hangs the hooded blade to cut the path, somewhere rests the hand to wield it.

Others have not been so lucky. The town's railway station, once the means and the measure of Ilkley's growth, was force fed

Beeching's powder, the line to Skipton closed. Now lost in these hollow passages that once echoed to Ilkley's early merchants on their way to Bradford and workers from that same city, spilling out from the packed excursion trains, to sup the air denied them for the rest of the year, lie incongruous stalls of fruit and vegetable and meat and a misconceived ticket office, with its air of embarrassed abandonment, all the while trying to maintain the illusion of the station as a *centre*. It is not. A hatched window and a face behind is all that is needed here, not these curves of glass looking out on a discarded past. Down the road on 10 July '66 they demolished the old railway bridge across Brook Street, took the track and the signal work out first, stripped it until all that was left were the iron girders picked bone-clean and those they left until the Sunday, five o'clock in the morning, when they set the oxyacetylene lamps to them and cut them up, slice by black slice, the sections laid out on the street below, like they do a whale, drawn up on the slaughtered slipway, the red life of its long years running down the gutters, to be shipped and melted down in a factory place, to become, what, wheels for tricycles, struts for outdoor swings. And though the hour chosen was designed to hide their vandalism as much as to alleviate the traffic, the town came anyway and parked their cars and stood in knots to see their giant felled, little bits of their life cut down to size and laid out on the pavement. It was ugly, the bridge, ungainly like a giant's foot, ugly with its black toenails and the dirt that would fall from it, but they feel it still, the stump where they cut it off, wishing that it was there to carry Ilkley's weight.

Yes, it is ordered now, Ilkley, mapped and laid, though future surprises lie somewhere within its leafy ways. It is in essence no different from any other town: new shopping centres, old shops renewed, the markings of their antiquity half obliterated; on Brook Street the arced whitewash on the wall proclaiming *Hampshire 1836, The Old Established Store, Game Fruit & Poultry* obscured by fresher brick; in the Grove the vine and tobacco plant carvings on Dinsdale's twin shop doors now glossed; a decoration without purpose, unless it is the wine-shop grapes now symbolise the charitable thirst of the Good Samaritan and the tobacco leaves the pressed and printed paper found on

Ilkley's handsome bookshop shelves. Up and down the inverted L of these two streets, along the Grove and down Brook Street, there is trade and commerce and places to eat and drink. There is bustle and throng still, more constant than in the past perhaps, less dependable on influx. No matter. Ilkley likes its trade, always has done, despite those burgeoning charity shops that are invading businesses' premises like unwanted cuckoos. Just another shoe and supermarket town, satchels, prams and broody Woolworth girls on their Monday morning way, lunchtime business pints, the paper read over a sausage sandwich and a shared joke, agents of estate and insurance, dealers in notes and nails from banks and hardware stores, spilling out at the evening's edges; wine and tapas bars and spaghetti houses with Italian waiters and garrulous northern chefs; an ordinary twenty-first-century town, then, though a northern one, its attachment to the municipal sees to that, that and Betty's with its cafe queue for teas and its relentless sale of cake (the young men and women who wait to take your order in their black and white uniforms an unconscious reminder of Ilkley's singular annual cricket game, when trade came out to play). A northern town then, but not like any other. It has an air to it hanging; it pervades. But it is not here at its centre that you find the peculiarity that is Ilkley, that has preserved this strangeness. For that you have to step out of Betty's, bag of buns in hand, turn left down the Grove, past the chocolate shop and W. H. Smith, past the empty hospital on the other side of the road, past the charity shop and the bookshop next door, until you come to Brook Street. Left again down Brook Street, past where the amputated iron bridge reaches across dark and invisible, like the phantom Bull Rock of the moor. Across the road down lower Brook Street where the smell of fish and chips reigns, down to where the new bridge crosses the water, opened in 1904. Here on this bridge can be seen that which has kept it apart. It is not the river which runs underneath it, and which is the receptacle of memory, nor is it the moor behind which follows its every move, its eternal shadowy soul. It is nothing at all but an elongated space, divided into two halves by the running of the river, a matter of a few hundred yards, a glancing throw from the town's centre, a liquorice-all-sorts of space in between the old pack bridge and this one. On one side there is parkland, allotments and graveyard, beds for municipal bulbs and infant swings, brambled scrubland skirting cabbage and gooseberry plots, a spur where the old and young lie in death, in fresh and forgotten graves; and on the other side the arena of activity, of sport, football stands and rugger pitches, white lines and goal posts, a cricket ground, a meadow for wild flowers and walks, and at the back, fenced off, heard but not seen, the open-air swimming pool. In March, as he stood feeding the ducks the disintegrating remnants of his fried fish, he saw four boys jumping off this fortress-like bridge into the river below, cursing with bravado as they rose out of the water's cold plume before hauling themselves out in their long and dripping shorts to climb the parapet and jump again. From the bridge they jumped and to the bridge they climbed and none gave a moment's thought to the spaces on either side. While it was not safe it was not seasonably dangerous. The river was idle as it can be in the coming of spring. A slightly foolish prank then; it is nothing much, to leap and shout, falling in the sharp air, brief freedom. Other boys jump in other rivers. But here it seemed a demonstration of the Ilkley's simplistic freedom, its strange capture of space, of turf and water. It is this space which has preserved Ilkley, this adherence to an emptiness almost at its very core. There are new houses built all around here, you can see them stealing down to the riverbank, planted in what had been other people's back gardens, you can see them climbing indecently up under the moor's very skirts to the first inkling of the damp heather of the hill. They have built where they can (and why not) but not here, in this long hollow, where commerce and domesticity could have settled so complacently. Instead they have kept the space complete, a reminder of what makes Ilkley great. Ilkley recognized space, the meaning of it, a long time ago. It was the greatest gift its forefathers gave the town, taught it this stern regard for space. Thanks to them they have it hanging high above them, overlooking the town, the troubled beauty of Rombalds Moor. Below them the Wharfe, above them the Moor, magnets in the town's compass. The Moor and the Wharfe. The Moor and the Wharfe. It is where Ilkley began, so it is where he will end. The Wharfe and the Moor. The Moor and the Wharfe.

In the summer he decides to spend his last night on the moor, not a camping night with a sleeping bag and a tent but an unadorned night, listening to Ilkley's murmurings, see the ghost of Ilkley's lights flickering, catch Job Senior stumbling back to his lair, or lend his ear to the path hearing the drum of Bradford men trudging home after a long day down by the river.

He will not tell anyone of his intent, not the guest house in which he is staying, not his family, he wants to be alone for this, without even the security of another's knowledge, nor will he prepare for it in any way save to buy some bars of bitter chocolate for the early morning hours. He stands outside a hardware shop for some time considering whether he should buy a cheap torch, but though nervous at the thought of being without light, not knowing how a moor might behave during such hours, he decides against it. He does not want light, except it be from a naked flame.

He is moderately apprehensive for another reason. Strange lights have been reported hovering over Rombalds of late, ethereal space visitations; apprehensive not that they might hover over him, hoover him up into their gleaming craft, but rather that he might come across some of those on the ground, who now set regular watch for these appearances and might have chosen to roam the moor this night too, who would question him as to his own purpose, furnish him with intrusive details of their own. He does not want this. He has his own itinerary planned. An early fish supper down by the river, then the slow climb to the Cow and Calf, where he intends to spend the first few hours, watching Ilkley grow dark, come out for its evening's play, see its shape change, its sounds muffle, follow the last patrol of the ducks, before setting off to the right, over the rise of the moor on to its high heathen surface, to the Twelve Apostles, where, Rombald willing, he will roam the rest of the night.

He spends the afternoon by the lido, knowing that it is to be his last day. He wanted to spend the time sitting by friendly water, watching other friends and families enjoying themselves, the democracy of mixed shapes, one rare beauty smiling at him as she caught him looking at her for a second time, her boyfriend haughty and imperious in his contempt, bathers sunbathing, reading books, smoking cigarettes, a gang of boys jumping in with their knees folded under their chest, eager fathers impatient to gainsay the appearance of their years, and all the while, the sloping shelf of the children's area, the dappled splash of blue, the happy squealing sounds, and at the back his fabled fountain, spouting its everlasting enjoyment. It is not easy to stay here without a heavy heart, to see his long-gone youth played before him, the child he was on the slide, the young man he was brushing beads of water from her ice-cream shoulder. He would have liked to have jumped in himself, floated himself into that hallowed shallow end, sat one last time on the magic fountain rim, let the water run over him: oh the soot bath, the iron swing, the red tricycle, the stone circles, this is what it is, movement, all swirling round and round, the summer house, the Strid, this fountain, Michael Airey tumbling away, this Ilkley.

Next to him the group of friends start a mock fight, jumping in the water to splash their sitting companions near the edge. He remembers the letter he read, concerning horseplay, how in its language he recognized the beginnings of his own adult time, the modern age jumping over the fence into this thirties water, how he wonders whether they remember it still, that silly prank, as he does his own young indiscretions, wishing that he had the will to behave just one more time with such freedom, knowing that he cannot, not only for fear of embarrassment, an older man's inability to join in, but cannot, cannot, his limbs no longer move like that any more. The noise grows louder, a young woman racing by him, the breath of her passing on his face, now wrestling freely in the water, an attendant stepping forward to warn them to calm down. He looks up at the moor. He feels like one of those mountaineers studying his adversary: how calm the rock looks, how warm, how placid, how very comforting, noticing too the darker shade it has taken on in the last half-hour. The night is slowly approaching. It is time to leave.

In the evening he buys his fish and chips and takes them down to the river, walking past the fenced children's area towards the old bridge. Opposite the modern public house, with its outside tables and its delineated cragginess, are the steps leading down to where Mr Dell the boatman plied his trade, fifteen steps to the long slabs of stone, fifteen steps with a stone sluice running amidships, to deposit more water at the lapping edges. Here along its cracked length stand the iron sentinels, some broken now, where his boats were moored, where Mr Dell stood, fixing ropes, drawing his charges to safety, or pushing them out, with a warning to the overconfident occupants when to return. From here he can see the old bridge, crossing the river so close to his old home. A few late-night people walk upon it; others, as he intends to do, lean on its parapet, watching the light play upon the water. It is humped, this old pack bridge, that is to say it reaches its apex quite clearly in the middle, an intended rise, and watching them move about he is struck by how unprotected the people seem to be. The walls on either side are very low, or rather the footpath laid between them is very high, so that it appears that they are walking on a mountain path, on some hillside or approaching the summit of a rocky ridge, exposed, and elevated, rather than standing on a bridge in the valley of a town.

He moves there quickly to see if it is true. He touches the iron bollard marking the bridge's entrance (remembering how he used to run it down from Stockeld Road, catch it in his hand and swing himself around, his own roundabout, his own summerhouse on wheels) before making his slight ascent, treading those squares of pavement his mother had trod, leaning against the parapet as she had, sharing her footsteps, the placing of her hands, spreading his feet and hands upon her imprints, obliterating her markings. How many times had she stood on this bridge alone, thought her lonely thoughts upon the water, looked to its lonely power, its solitary promise, thoughts of the jilted bride and all the others wanting Lister's old plot of land, that rusty concoction Paradise, wishing that by closing her eyes she could be transported there, along this magic water carpet, to a country of clarity, pure air, pure water, pure feelings.

It is true. He is high above the world on this bridge, as high as the rock on which he intends to spend the night, as high as the iron swing took him, Ilkley quiet in its modern lights and this old bridge ready to lift him to the stars. Moving to the left-hand side he looks up and seeing the water move towards him he feels as if all knowledge of the town, all knowledge of himself is moving towards him, ready to envelop him with its great peace. How purposefully it swims towards the bridge, how clear, how silent, how luxurious the swirls, how pleasurable it must be to touch, dangle a limb in its liquid heart, how soothing to feel its caress and its power running over you, how quiet, how very quiet it is, like the secrets it holds. He is intrigued by the silence of it, the way it glides underneath as if one piece. He moves to the other side, not four paces in between to where it emerges. How noisy, how insistent it comes, frothing and slicing through the dip of a manufactured fall, churning and wet with sucking noise: something has happened to it under this bridge, where men and women and children stand, thinking upon their lives as it rushes underneath, carrying their thoughts away as they watch it vanish round the bend, as if they are nothing but running water too.

Is this why his memory is so fickle, why it refuses to retain, why it is only general feelings, moods, images of flowing, darkness, light, curious hidden sounds as if coming from within deep recesses, caught in overhanging branches or lying in sediment of undisturbed pools, sodden logs half submerged in the still water, that he can remember? It is as though the river, this river, has drained him, taking away his past at that very moment of immersion, bleeding him, leaving him white and cool and fluid, almost embalmed, almost cleansed, with the detritus of his life (why, he imagined for a long time that he had pushed Michael Airey in himself – whether out of spite or a joke gone wrong – he could never quite work out, but push him in he did and watched him slide into the water and be carried away and with him his memory of it and who he was). It has been the same his life over, people he has known, quarrelled with, made love to, friends, all carried away, their echoes growing for ever fainter. Is this what the Wharfe has done, what Michael Airey did, take his present away from him, though he knew it not then, and does not fully understand it now? But it is here he remembers, standing on the humpbacked bridge, or sitting on the bank, eating his fish and chips, it is the river which stirs him, which curdles his memory into lumps once more, so that he might reach out and pull in from the eddies and ripples an old stick of it, and drag it out, swollen, misshapen, slippery, but recognizable all the same.

He stands there for a long time, three, four, five, hours or more. He knows he will not go to the moor now, the river has him. It was the river he lived by, the river that took his friend, the river that brought him back and now, the river by which he must spend his last few hours. There is nothing more for him to do, than let it roll underneath.

When dawn comes, the cold in his arms and his legs and his still body suddenly seizing him, he walks back up Stockeld towards Skipton Road. Halfway up he stops. He cannot hear the Wharfe any more, the Wharfe has held its breath, creeping past, careful not to wake the townsfolk, silent like a thief. It is almost as if the river is not there, only when he opens his eyes does it reappear. What would happen if they woke and found the Wharfe gone, woke and found themselves robbed of their dreams, their souls stolen, the river bed filled with the detritus of their past, the bones of lost dogs and drowned sheep, sunken boats and old gymshoes, and glittering out the mud, the shining handlebars of Michael Airey's stolen tricycle.

In the morning before he leaves he decides to climb the rock once more, to look for the marks of Michael he made in the beginning. The morning is clean and clear with no seeming signs of the mystery he felt running through the town the night before. It is shops and trains and cars finding free places to park; it is Betty's and banks, and restaurateurs writing the lunchtime menu on compulsory blackboards. The town at work.

Up on the moor the rocks are already at work, holding climbers in their gritstone grasp, but, mason that he is, he has no need for them now. It is an easy haul to the flat surface again, walking across other names, other muscle, to where he wrote the name, the date and the intent. He knows for sure where he stretched out, spanner in hand, how he scratched the dark white, the name, the date, the flourish above the town, but when he comes to the spot he cannot find it. His effort, his need, his mark seems to have disappeared, cancelled. He puts his hand out as if blind, hoping that the surface will reveal the letters, that his fingers might recognize the swirls and ladders he made, his hopeful connection to another age. He brushes the rock as he might a gravestone or a shoe, hoping that one might fit to make him walk, stroking the surface in wide sweeps, touching names and decades upon his palm, until, eventually, the rock relents, gives up its secrets. There, gripping on to the edge by its feeble fingertips, he sees the faint fashion of letters that he scratched those eighteen months ago, Michael Airey, but not firm, not cast in gritstone rock, but half slipped, still sliding, there to be washed and carried away by water.

Bibliography

All material on hydropathy taken from the following sources:

Life of Priessnitz by R. Metcalfe: Simpkin, Marshall & Co. 1889

The Rise and Progress of Hydropathy by R. Metcalfe: Simpkin, Marshall & Co. 1906

The Water Cure Journal 1847 edited by J. M. Gully and W. Macleod: T. Smethhurst

The Directory of Ben-Rhydding by William Macleod: London 1852

Ben Rhydding, its Amenities, Hygiene and Therapeutics by James Baird: A. G. Dennant 1877

Ben Rhydding. The Asclepia of England by R. Woodrow Thomas: Ilkley 1862

The Scenery of the Wharfe by Alice Mann: Leeds 1855

Ben Rhydding Ariel: Leeds 1852

Conversations with Women by A. Rabagliati MA, MD, FRCS, Ed: The author: Bradford 1910

The Church on the Moor. Sermons by William Danks, Preached in St Margaret's Church, Ilkley: John Dale & Co. 1886

A Night at Ben Rhydding by Baron Penaninski: Ben Rhydding, Published at the Office for the benefit of the hospital at Ilkley 1855

Letters of Charles Darwin volume 2

Ben Rhydding: The Principles of Hydropathy and the Compressed Air Bath by a Graduate of Edinburgh University: Hamilton, Adams & Co. and Webb, Millington & Co. 1858

Oneness with the Departed. Sermon preached on the occasion of William Macleod's Death in the Congregational Church on Sunday morning February 7th, 1875 by Samuel Hillman: London 1875